The Partitions of Poland 1772, 1793, 1795

JERZY LUKOWSKI

Longman
London and New York

Addison Wesley Longman Limited
Edinburgh Gate,
Harlow, Essex CM20 2JE, United Kingdom
and Associated Companies throughout the world.

Published in the United States of America by Addison Wesley Longman, New York.

First published 1999

ISBN 0–582–29275–1 CSD
ISBN 0–582–29274–3 PPR

British Library Cataloguing in Publication Data
A catalogue entry for this title is
available from the British Library

Library of Congress Cataloging-in-Publication Data
Lukowski, Jerzy.
The partitions of Poland : 1772, 1793, 1795 / Jerzy Lukowski.
p.   cm.
Includes bibliographical references and index.
ISBN 0–582–29275–1. — ISBN 0–582–29274–3 (pbk.)
1. Poland—History—Partition period, 1763–1796.   I. Title.
DK4329.L85   1998
943.8′02—dc21   98–8061
                                            CIP

Set by 35 in 10/12pt Baskerville
Produced by Addison Wesley Longman Singapore (Pte) Ltd.,
Printed in Singapore

Contents

List of maps

Foreword

It is impossible for any one individual to write anything approaching a complete, let alone 'definitive', history of the Polish Partitions – a subject which is as much concerned with the diplomatic history of late eighteenth-century Europe as a whole as the fate of an individual country. The existence of twentieth-century successor-states, not only of Poland and the partitioning powers, but also of the Holy Roman Empire and the Ottoman Porte, presents at least as many problems as opportunities to the historian. Even to attempt a 'definitive' history would demand research in the archives and libraries of Poland, Russia, Austria and Germany, just as a start. It would have to be complemented by a close trawl of the relevant holdings of France, England, Denmark, the Vatican, Italy, Turkey, Lithuania, the Ukraine, Byelorussia, Latvia and the Czech and Slovak Republics. Even this alarming list makes no claim to being complete. To secure the necessary funding, be it from public or private sources, would be a task as herculean as the enterprise itself (on the other hand, any very wealthy private patrons, with considerably more money than sense and with minimal expectations of an early return on their generosity, should contact the author).

Even allowing for this enormous *caveat*, perhaps now is the right time for a fresh, if necessarily incomplete, survey of the subject. It is certainly long overdue, not least in English. The Partitions, although they reshaped a massive area of central and eastern Europe, tend to be noted as a 'given', rather than explored in detail. Surprisingly little specific literature has been produced on them since the work of Adolf Beer and Alfred von Arneth in the 1860s and 1870s or Gustav Volz at the turn of the nineteenth and twentieth century. Robert H. Lord's *The Second Partition of Poland* (Cambridge, Mass., 1915) still remains the most up-to-date study of its subject, even for Polish historians. The most comprehensive survey of all three partitions in Polish, indeed, virtually the only such survey in that language, is a school textbook by Tadeusz Cegielski and Łukasz Kądziela, *Rozbiory Polski 1772–1793–1795* (Warsaw, 1990). Its nearest English equivalent, by baron Eversley, was published as long ago as 1915. Professor Herbert Kaplan's study of the First Partition, brought out in 1962, tells only a part of its story. Michael Müller's *Die Teilungen Polens* (Munich, 1984), for all its insights, remains an outline survey.

The dearth of work into a subject of such magnitude is, at first sight, puzzling. Polish historians have concentrated less on the diplomatic aspects, much more on analyses of the nature and problems of a society that was clearly in serious trouble. Principally, they have directed their attention to the Enlightenment, the reforming Four Years Sejm of 1788–92 and the Constitution of 3 May 1791, but at some cost to other aspects of the eighteenth century. And for all the work done by outstanding scholars such as Władysław Konopczyński, Emanuel Rostworowski, Bogusław Leśnodorski or Jerzy Michalski, to name but a few, their work cannot possibly embrace the totality of a vast subject. Critical areas remain unresolved. Such a basic question as the demography of the period is far from settled and attempts to revise old-accepted figures have raised more issues than they have resolved. Very little research has been done into the parliaments of 1773–75 and 1776, which were crucial in framing the constitutional settlement which accompanied the First Partition. Far too little is known about Polish diplomacy – or, let it be said, despite all that older generations of historians have written – about the diplomacy of Prussia, Austria and (least of all) Russia.

It is not too hard to find an explanation for this state of affairs. Even at the time the Partitions took place, those responsible for them were not without embarrassment at what they had perpetrated. Poland's sole 'crimes', if that is the word, were that it was weak and that those attempting to govern it would not do exactly as outside powers wished. At war with no one, its territories were lost because it was incapable of putting up effective resistance. Frederick the Great and Catherine the Great, among the most successful early practitioners of the arts of spin-doctoring, have always attracted something of a following among Europe's chattering classes, from Voltaire, Diderot and Grimm onwards. Their enlightenments seem so much more attractive than their *Realpolitik*, even to the extent of, in some eyes, justifying it. The whole problem of the Partitions has been further bedevilled by the subsequent history of all concerned – shot through with mutual anguish, suspicion, hostility, contempt or even guilt. Bismarck gave Heinrich von Sybel access to his government's hitherto closed archives on condition he produced publications 'im preussischem Sinne', 'of a Prussian inclination'. As for Polish historians in the same period, it has been pointed out by Norman Davies, that, uncertain of the future of a country which was not even in existence, they had great difficulty in making sense of its past. The broad-brush extermination policies visited by Hitler's Germany on Poland during the Second World War and the rather more selective ones practised by the Soviet Union in the same period and in its aftermath have not made life for historians, Polish, German or Russian, any easier. The last-named have made virtually no contribution to the study of the subject since Sergei Solov'ev's histories published in the 1860s – in the wake of the largest-scale Polish revolt against Russian rule before the First World War.

In practical terms, the greatest obstacle to a proper investigation of the Partitions has been that of access to the archives of Russia and the Soviet Union. Russia's was the dominant external influence in later eighteenth-century Poland. The relevant volumes of historical evidence published by the Imperial Russian Historical Society between 1867 and 1916, for all their irreplaceable value, were exercises in selective editing, subject to a more-or-less strict censorship (all praise to the editors for some of what they did manage to put into the public domain). Only two major scholars of the Partition era, Władysław Konopczyński and Robert Lord, were able to benefit from access to Russian archives in the brief period of liberalism before the First World War. As for the Soviet era, while limited access was given to Polish historians of approved periods and subjects, direct research into the Partitions remained firmly off limits. Only in 1994, when a young Polish historian, Łukasz Kądziela, went to Moscow almost on the off-chance, was he able to ascertain that *Perestroika* and *Glasnost'* had finally made possible access to the relevant archival sources. Łukasz's death from cancer in May 1997 was a tragic blow to his family, friends and profession, but his work is being continued by Dr Zofia Zielińska and her students, at the Historical Institute of the University of Warsaw. It will, however, inevitably take some years before their researches can inject themselves into the historiographic mainstream.

Research into the Partitions, then, stands on something of a cusp between the old and the new. Polish scholars find themselves able to look into a key area of their past, perhaps even the most important area, in a way they have long only been able to dream of doing. This may be all the more the appropriate time to present the labours of historians in preparation for what may yet come. The present work seeks to do this and to present the author's own contributions, mainly in the field of the Poles' own attitudes to the shocks that hit them in the later eighteenth century.

I owe many debts, first and foremost to Łukasz Kądziela and Zofia Zielińska, never stinting of their time and patience. Professor Jerzy Michalski has always been willing to share his immense erudition. Peter Jones reassured me that I had not gone wildly wrong in looking at the revolutionary era. Derek Beales read the 'final' version and provided many valuable suggestions, not all of which I have used as I should. All errors are my own.

The generosity of the British Academy enabled me to work in the Polish archives. I owe a particular debt to the Academy's Miss Elizabeth Ollard, whose delicate touch released grant monies from the labyrinthine toils of Birmingham University's financial mechanisms. My thanks to the (former) Faculty of Arts teaching relief fund which enabled me to eke out a few extra hours a week to complete the book; my thanks to Mr John Washbourne for providing that relief. On the moral front, my wife, Lesley, has been ever supportive, not least in enduring my jeremiads, while my children, Andrzej and Helena, have provided some perverse intellectual stimulation. Professor John Breuilly has given all the support one could expect of a Head of Department looking forward to the new millennium. I am immensely grateful to Grażyna, Jarek and Kasia Kocznur (and Olimp) for their hospitality, warmth and companionship. At Longmans, Andrew MacLennan provided enthusiasm and encouragement at a good time.

Birmingham, March 1998

Abbreviations

AGAD	Archiwum Główne Akt Dawnych (Central Historical Archive), Warsaw
AGS	*Arkhiv Gosudarstvennogo Soveta*, vol. I (St Petersburg, 1869)
Arneth, *GMT*	A. von Arneth, *Geschichte Maria Theresia's*, 10 vols (Vienna, 1863–79)
BPAN	Biblioteka Polskiej Akademii Nauk, Kraków
B.Cz.	Biblioteka Czartoryskich, Kraków
Chodźko	Chodźko, L.J.B. (pseud., comte D'Angeberg), ed., *Recueil des traités, conventions et actes diplomatiques concernant la Pologne 1762–1861*, I (Paris, 1862)
CTS	*Consolidated Treaty Series*, 231 vols, ed. C. Parry (Dobbs Ferry, New York, 1969–86)
HDP	*Historia Dyplomacji Polskiej*, tom II, 1572–1795, ed. Z. Wójcik (Warsaw, 1982)
PC	*Politische Correspondenz Friedrich's des Grossen*, 46 vols (Berlin, 1879–1939)
PRO/SP	Public Record Office (London), State Papers
PSB	*Polski Słownik Biograficzny*, ed. W. Konopczyński and others (Kraków, 1935–)
SIRIO	*Sbornik Imperatorskogo Russkogo Istoricheskogo Obshchestva* (St Petersburg, 148 vols in 141, 1867–1916)
Solov'ev, *IPP*	S.M. Solov'ev, *Istoriia Padeniia Pol'shi* (first published Moscow, 1863) in S.M. Solov'ev, *Sochineniia*, Bk XVI (Moscow, 1995)
Solov'ev, *IR*	S.M. Solov'ev, *Istoriia Rossii s' drevnikh vremen'* (29 vols, first published Moscow, 1864) in S.M. Solov'ev, *Sochineniia*, Bks I–XV (Moscow, 1988–95)
Testamente	G.B. Volz, ed., *Politische Correspondenz Friedrich's des Grossen. Ergänzungsband. Die Politischen Testamente Friedrichs des Grossen* (Berlin, 1920)
VL	*Volumina Legum*, 9 vols (St Petersburg–Kraków, 1859–89)
ZP	Zbiór Popielów (Popiel Collection) (in AGAD)

A note on Polish pronunciation

Anglo-Saxons seem to find Slavonic languages, not least Polish, something of a problem. The following is meant only as kind of idiot's guide to Polish pronunciation; it is not for philological or phonetic purists.

ą	vaguely similar to the French 'On', if crossed with the 'o' in 'home'
ę	vaguely similar to the French 'On', if crossed with the 'e' in 'help'
ó	u, as in 'hook'
y	i, as in 'hit'
ci	'chee', as in 'cheetah'
si	'she', as in 'sheet'
ć	'ch', as in 'church'
cz	as the above, but harsher
c	'ts' as in pencil, except in the combinations shown above
Ł, ł	'w' as in 'what'
ń	slightly softened 'n' – as in Spanish 'ñ'
ś	'sh' as in 'shut'
sz	as the above, but harsher
rz, ż	as the above, if said with a 'z' (zh as in 'Zhukov')
w	'v' as in vile
zi	pronounced as first two letters of French 'gîte'
ź	pronounced as first letter of French 'gîte'

A note on some Polish terms used in the text

It is impossible to be consistent with translations and renderings of Polish terminology. I have tried to take cognizance of the fact that there is a growing effort on the part of Anglo-Saxon commentators to grapple with Polish nomenclature, though it still has far to go. In the case of geographical terms, I have generally used the names employed by contemporary elites on the spot (thus, Danzig, rather than Gdańsk, Lwów rather than Lviv). The irredeemably politically correct and the die-hard nationalistic should consult the index for (some) alternative versions.

'Palatine' is the term used by contemporary Englishmen for 'wojewoda' (Latin, *palatinus*), who normally headed the most common major territorial-administrative unit, the *województwo* (hence 'palatinate').

The 'county' (*ziemia, terra*) was either a subdivision of the palatinate, or its equivalent, but without a palatine.

The 'district' (*powiat, districtus*) was the smallest administrative-cum-judicial unit.

The lesser territorial units were grouped into three great 'Provinces':

1. Wielkopolska, 'Great Poland', in the north and west (Wielkopolska was also often used in a narrower sense, referring to the palatinates of Poznań, Kalisz and (after 1768) Gniezno);
2. Małopolska, 'Little Poland', to the south and east;
3. Lithuania.

Sejm (plural Sejmy) – the Polish parliament; *sejmik* (plural *sejmiki*) – local assemblies of the nobility. Other terms are explained within the text.

In Memory of
Łukasz Kądziela,
30 October 1955–7 May 1997
A good friend and a good historian

CHAPTER ONE

Poland and Europe in the eighteenth century

Between 1772 and 1795, in the most drastic redrawing of European frontiers before the twentieth century, a state larger than France was removed from the political map. The Revolutionary and Napoleonic era witnessed the elimination of the Holy Roman Empire and the restructuring of the Italian polities, but something that contemporaries could call 'Germany' or 'Italy' survived. 'Poland' was excised altogether, even if its ghost never let European statesmen rest until its reincarnation in a very different body after the First World War. The First Partition sent shudders of novel alarm through the weaker states of Europe, even though many observers felt that the Poles had only themselves to blame; if not, indeed, that such enlightened rulers as Frederick the Great or Catherine the Great were doing them a service.

The nobility and the evolution of the Commonwealth

The 'Poland' that began to be dismembered in 1772 was, according to its official style, 'the Commonwealth of the Two Nations, the Polish and Lithuanian', the *Rzeczpospolita Obojga Narodów, Polskiego i Litewskiego*. A personal, dynastic union between the *Corona Regni Poloniae*, the 'Crown' of the Polish Realm, and the *Magnus Ducatus Lithuaniae*, the Grand Duchy of Lithuania, had existed since 1386. In 1569 this was converted into a constitutional union, in which the two huge 'Provinces' of the Crown and Lithuania enjoyed a common parliament and similar political institutions. The result, like Great Britain, defied easy categorisation: it was a kind of republic, run by its nobility, headed by an elected monarch. Native contemporaries talked of *Polska* and *Polacy*, 'Poland' and 'Poles', labels which bore meanings very different from twentieth-century usage. Partitions, wars and genocide have not only dramatically reduced and reshaped Poland's political cartography, they have stripped out a maddeningly complex cultural and ethnic diversity to leave a largely linguistically and religiously homogeneous residue. The Pole, *Polak*, of the 1750s or 1760s would not necessarily be regarded as such in the 1990s (not even by his descendants): for he might also be Lithuanian, Byelorussian, Ukrainian or German. He would most probably be a Roman Catholic; increasingly less, a Greek Catholic; perhaps a Lutheran or Calvinist; he might just be a Muslim – but he would not be a Jew, unless converted to Roman Catholicism. He would, however, be a nobleman – a *szlachcic*. The *Rzeczpospolita* formed the tangible embodiment of his rights, privileges, freedoms and liberties.

Who were the *szlachta*? 'Nobility' or 'gentry' can serve as only rough-and-ready generic approximations which obscure massive social, political and economic differentiation. The *szlachta* formed a hierarchy, topped by a score or so of families of princely wealth, based on the possession of huge estates composed of hundreds of villages and dozens of towns, scattered across every region of the state. At the bottom were hordes of landless beggars. In between the two extremes existed every possible variety of propertied and non-propertied individual with an acceptable claim to 'nobility', *szlachectwo*.

In 1772, the *szlachta* may have made up between 6 and 7 per cent, some 800,000 of Poland's 12,000,000-plus inhabitants, or, in meaningful political terms, about 120,000 adult male nobles. Barely one in twenty would have owned an entire village. What by Polish standards was an affluent noble might have to own several villages before he stood comparison with a well-to-do English tenant farmer, let alone an independent country gentleman.[1] Despite some ambivalent rhetoric, wholly landless nobles were treated as inferiors. The one-third or so of the *szlachta* who owned land were unusual in the comparative lack of *legal* differentiation. In law, though not, of course,

---

1. Early modern Polish demography teems with problems, even the history of the best documented, the *szlachta*. For the most sophisticated discussion and (admittedly, tentative) conclusions, as well as a review of the literature, see E. Rostworowski, 'Ilu było w Rzeczypospolitej szlachty', *Kwartalnik Historyczny* 94, no. 3 (1988), pp. 3–40. For wider comparisons, see H.M. Scott, ed., *The European nobilities in the seventeenth and eighteenth centuries*, 2 vols (London, 1995).

in fact, any such noble, no matter how minute his freehold, was the equal of the greatest magnate. True, the Polish parliament, the Sejm, contained a Senate, an 'upper chamber' which was above all the domain of the great lords, but unlike Britain's House of Lords, the Polish Senate was not hereditary: membership was determined by possession of a restricted range of non-hereditary offices and dignities. In theory at least (and practice did not wholly preclude it), any landowning noble could aspire to membership. In theory, too, the legislative function resided far more emphatically in the 'Chamber of Envoys' (*izba poselska*) than in Britain's House of Commons.

A distinct legal estate of higher nobles – a *Herrenstand* in the Austrian mould – had not developed in large measure because the monarchs of the fifteenth and sixteenth centuries had looked to the gentry for allies against aristocratic grandees. Poland's towns were neither powerful enough nor wealthy enough to furnish an alternative point of support. The *szlachta*'s price was privilege and a share in the political life of the state commensurate with that of the magnates, leaving no room for a separate estate of grandees. The process was far less advanced in the Grand Duchy of Lithuania, where lords – often kinsmen of the ruling House of Jagiellon – endowed with vast territorial holdings looked on the impoverished 'boyars' almost as their own chattels. In 1569, the gentry of the Ukrainian palatinates seceded from the Grand Duchy to join the Crown and the rest threatened to follow suit. The result was the Union of Lublin, setting up a genuinely constitutional merger of Poland and Lithuania.

Distasteful though magnates found the lack of hereditary distinction for their own kind, they came to appreciate the advantages of equality. In practice, they were its disproportionate beneficiaries. The list of noble 'freedoms' was imposing: no imprisonment without due process; no taxation without consent; no enactment of legislation without the consent of the Sejm; virtual exemption from customs duties; virtual monopoly of land ownership; full jurisdiction over peasants living on noble estates; a monopoly on the use of Poland's principal commercial artery, the river Vistula, for the shipment of bulk goods and commodities; a near-total monopoly on appointment to all senior ecclesiastical positions, from canonries upwards; the right to participate in the election of the monarch. And these were but the most important elements in a glittering portfolio secured even before the extinction of the Jagiellonian line in 1572 permitted the construction of a still more elaborate superstructure of rights and liberties.

The monarchy had been, in effect, elective since the death of the last Piast king in 1370; the fact that the kings were chosen first from the House of Anjou and then from the Lithuanian House of Gedymin-Jagiełło may have helped obscure the elective nature of the Polish throne to the outside world, but not to the *szlachta*. At his death in 1572, king Zygmunt August left no legitimate male heirs. In the ensuing interregnum the nobility seized their chance to ensure not only that they would continue to elect their kings but also that those kings would never be able to recover lost ground. The rule, first established in 1530, that the monarch could neither name nor secure the election of a successor *vivente rege*, during his own lifetime, was confirmed. A veritable Dutch auction for gentry support by squabbling magnate factions culminated in the resolution that all nobles were entitled to vote *viritim*, in person, for their future kings; no ruler would be allowed to take his place before confirming all the existing privileges of the nobility.

Monarchs increasingly came to be seen as a fount of rewards and concessions for supposed noble virtues and correspondingly less as effective legislators (they had been unable to proclaim law without parliamentary approval since 1505) or even executors of the law. Even their traditional role of judge was severely circumscribed between 1579 and 1581 when two separate, elective, courts of final appeal, the Tribunals (*Trybunały*), were set up in the Crown and in Lithuania, effectively transferring to the *szlachta* full control of their own civil and criminal judicature.[2] The powers that in the medieval past had belonged to the monarchy had largely been transferred to the nobility.

Central to the life of the *szlachta* were the *sejmiki*. These were the bodies of local self-government, meeting at different times of the year to elect officials and judges, manage local taxation and business. Among their most important tasks was the election of 'envoys' (*posłowie*) to the Sejm, which normally met (after 1572) only every two years for a statutory six-week session. The writ of the *sejmik* covered the geographic-administrative territory with which it was associated, usually the 'district' (*powiat, districtus*) or 'county' (*ziemia, terra*), occasionally the palatinate (*województwo, palatinatus*). Attendance might range from a handful to five or six thousand. Almost invariably the well-to-do were returned to elective office. For all the

---

2. Cases of treason and corruption and malversation among higher officials continued to be heard by special parliamentary courts. Royal courts continued to exercise ultimate jurisdiction over royal towns, fiefs, and peasants on royal domains. J. Bardach, ed., *Historia Państwa i Prawa Polski*, II (Warsaw, 1971), pp. 153–60.

differences of local or regional detail, the *sejmiki* formed a remarkably homogeneous institutional network across the Commonwealth, reiterating and articulating the communality of *szlachta* privilege.

One privilege overshadowed all others: the *liberum veto*, the right freely to forbid. To forbid what? The enactment of any law or measure deemed harmful to the Commonwealth. Every individual nobleman enjoyed this right, which emerged in all its destructive force in the second half of the seventeenth century. The veto developed with insidious slowness from king Alexander's law of 1505, *Nihil Novi . . .* : 'No new law is to be issued by Us or Our successors save by the common consent of Our counsellors and the envoys of the constituencies . . .'.[3] The veto, first used in 1652 to protest against the prolongation of the Sejm, was, by the 1680s, employed to wreck legislation and policy. Its application stopped the entire Sejm in its tracks and with it any and all enactments that might have already been agreed. It was applied in the same way in the *sejmiki*. Only the law courts, which decided by majority vote, were immune.

It is self-evident that the veto contributed towards the increasing political debility of the Commonwealth – but it did not cause it. *Nihil Novi* was able to evolve into a constitutional monstrosity because the Polish state and its kings were already on the defensive vis-à-vis the *szlachta*. The monarchy lacked the resources, patronage, strength and force to whip into line regions and localities, magnates and gentry demagogues. The personal credit and authority which any individual monarch might build up died with him, to be buried and reburied at every successive interregnum. The cumulative concession of privilege, the lack of an alternative political force to the *szlachta*, the ability of the magnates to manipulate the rhetoric of equality, liberty and social solidarity left the monarchy reeling against the ropes of constitutional and political conflict. Politics came to be seen not as a dynamic process but as a set of manoeuvres and restrictions designed to prevent any infraction of the dazzling array of privilege, of what the *szlachta* called their 'Golden Freedom', their *Złota Wolność, aurea libertas*.

Those who enjoyed 'Golden Freedom' were not merely noble, they were *the* noble nation, the *naród szlachecki*. Ultimately, nations and, for that matter, those genetically dubious entities, ethnic groups, make their own decisions on who belongs to them. There was only

---

3. *VL* I, p. 137. The formal title of the relevant legislation was 'De non faciendis constitutionibus sine consensu consiliariorum et nuntiorum terrestrium' but it was normally referred to as 'Nihil Novi'.

one nation in the Commonwealth of the Two – and, if ever there was a self-imagined nation, it was the *szlachta*. 'Poles' were conscious of being different from 'Lithuanians' or 'Ruthenes' or 'Prussians' but privilege welded them all into a single whole. Sixteenth-century humanism went a long way towards ironing out ethnic and regional tensions and contradictions by creating a supra-group myth: all true 'Poles' were noble; all nobles were Poles. Intermarriage, extensive colonisation and geographic mobility helped blur old divisions. Renaissance writers made the true ancestors of the Poles the Sarmatians, hardy tribesmen who, several centuries before Christ, had supposedly embarked on their own *Völkerwanderung* from around the lower Don and Volga, finally to settle in the Vistula basin.

As privilege and institutions spread geographically, so did polonisation. So long as they were nobles, they became Poles, even if they also happened to be Lithuanians/Ruthenes/Prussians – or others: Weyssenhoffs and Tyzenhauses (once Germans), Middletons (once Scots) and Butlers (once Irish), Rubinkowskis and Niewierowskis (once Jews). Sarmatism made Poles of them all – or even Sarmatians, for so they readily styled themselves.[4] The German-speaking nobles in Polish Prussia were becoming either linguistically assimilated or marginalised. By the mid-eighteenth century, in the Grand Duchy and in the Ukraine all *szlachta* of any significance used Polish as their mother-tongue. The Lithuanian and Ruthene vernaculars were for impoverished backwoodsmen and peasants. The same went for the Orthodox faith, once dominant in the Byelorussian and Ukrainian territories. Even Greek Catholicism was for peasants. Nobles practised the Latin rite.

In one respect the nobility of the Grand Duchy of Lithuania were more 'Polish' than the nobles of the Crown. Since 1697, the official language of the Lithuanian law courts had been Polish, whereas in the Crown it remained Latin.[5] Latin formed the staple fare of *szlachta* education throughout the Commonwealth, dispensed mainly through a network of Jesuit colleges (sixty-seven in 1760). An ossified Christian-humanist curriculum laid great stress on piety and devotion to the Catholic church. It glorified freedom, Poland's and ancient Rome's. The Roman republic was almost the only state

4. For an introduction to the Sarmatian myth, see S. Cynarski, 'The shape of Sarmatian ideology', *Acta Poloniae Historica* 19 (1968), pp. 5–17.

5. *VL* V, p. 418. Prior to 1697, the Lithuanian law courts used Byelorussian, at least occasionally. A written Lithuanian vernacular, apart from translations of the Bible, scarcely existed before the posthumous publication, in 1818, of Krystyn Donelaitis' (1714–80) epic poem of peasant life, *Metai* ('The Year'). J. Ochmański, *Historia Litwy* (Wrocław, 1990 edn), pp. 170–3.

the great majority of nobles were prepared to admire, staunchly believing that they had actually refined and improved its liberty, largely through the wise precaution of restricting it to themselves, without lavishing it indiscriminately on other social groupings.

Although the *naród szlachecki* spoke the language of racial exclusivity, in reality it was as porous as any continental nobility. Ennoblement came comparatively easily, even if it was, in theory, the exclusive prerogative of the Sejm. Knowing the right people, greasing the right palms, acceptance by the local courts or chanceries – that was sufficient to have one's hitherto unrecognised nobility confirmed. An affluent and preferably rural lifestyle helped, but was not essential. Porous this nation may have been, yet it was distinct: distinct from the peasantry, enserfed and bereft of rights, distinct too from the mainly impoverished townsmen, who maintained a sense of self-importance and civic pride mainly in the affluent towns of Royal Prussia, in particular Danzig (Gdańsk), Thorn (Toruń) and Elbing (Elblag), dominated by German-speaking, and mainly Lutheran, patriciates. The three 'great towns' of Royal Prussia had largely succeeded in maintaining intact their own privileges, consolidating their position as virtually autonomous city-states, in which the writ of *szlachta* law and privilege did not run. For that very reason, they valued the Commonwealth as much as the nobility did.

In 1760, the largest town in Poland-Lithuania outside Prussia was the capital, Warsaw, with a paltry 26,000 inhabitants. The nobility looked on townsmen and municipal 'patriciates' as little more than peasants. The wealthiest businessmen and merchants in Poland – certainly outside Warsaw and the Prussian towns – were mainly Jewish. There were probably as many Jews in the *Rzeczpospolita* as nobles. But they had their own culture, faith, dress, administration, often their own suburbs, quarters and townships, and were either barred from residence in the chartered municipalities proper, or forbidden from participating in regular municipal government. Jews were tolerated in Poland-Lithuania, quantitatively far more so than in any other European state – but they generally remained despised as deicidal outcasts, necessary for their (much exaggerated) commercial and financial skills.

Poland was thus a mix of many peoples and races, no matter how defined. In political terms, only one 'nation' counted: the *naród szlachecki*, densely settled in the west and centre, increasingly thinly spread towards the east, but always constituting a ruling veneer. The right to shape policy, to control administration – in short, to govern – belonged exclusively to the nobility. And when the Poles themselves discussed the 'nation', it was invariably the *szlachta* who talked and wrote of it with only themselves in mind. The idea that non-nobles might also be Poles or that they might receive rights, too, did not begin to take hold until after the First Partition.

The Commonwealth's politics

Privilege made the *szlachta* free and Poland ungovernable. Any form of government which might aspire to act in an effective manner would have no alternative but to restrict noble liberties and freedoms. The king was more the fount of honours and patronage than a meaningful ruler. Through the exercise of his 'distributory power', *ius distributivum*, he appointed to the great majority of offices, over two thousand in all, at central and local level.[6] He also disposed of a mass of so-called 'crown lands' (*królewszczyzny* or *starostwa*), which made up at least 15 per cent of Poland-Lithuania's territory and which he was bound by law to distribute to 'deserving' nobles.

Gaining access to and preferably control over royal patronage was what Polish politics was about, since the central offices and many of the crown estates were immensely lucrative or carried their own extensive reserves of patronage and influence. The monarch's power to put his *ius distributivum* to work in order to strengthen his own position was distinctly limited. The great offices at the centre – the chancellorships, court and grand marshalcies, treasurerships and the *hetman*ships (commands of the army) – virtually had to be given to great magnates, who, in turn, brokered the allocation of lesser offices among their own followings. All appointed offices and crown land tenures were held for life: only the Sejm, not the king, could dismiss from them.

The *szlachta* were chronically suspicious of anything that might smack of the use of royal patronage to strengthen the monarchy. Fear that the *ius distributivum* would be used to undermine and corrupt the integrity of the nobility pervades the political literature of the eighteenth century: England furnished the great object lesson of a monarchy which had corrupted its gentry and nobility to exercise supposedly authoritarian power. Yet although numerous proposals were floated to devolve the royal distributive powers to

6. On the difficult question of Polish 'administration', see J.T. Lukowski, *Liberty's Folly: the Polish–Lithuanian Commonwealth in the eighteenth century, 1697–1795* (London, 1991), pp. 101–9.

electoral bodies, nothing came of them: they would have required the approbation of the Sejm and therefore would have to leap the hurdle of the *liberum veto*. To place them at the disposal of local elective bodies would, in turn, have made such appointments vulnerable to the use of the veto. Those offices which were elective, mainly a range of judicial ones, were indeed all too liable not to be filled because appointment was subject to the veto. For all their suspicions of the distributive power, the *szlachta* preferred to let it remain with the monarch, for the almost certain alternative to patronage liable to abuse was no patronage at all.

What could the eighteenth-century Polish state achieve? Very little, which presumably explains why it features so little in the consciousness of non-Polish historians and readers. Noble privilege was so extensive that reform could come only by rolling it back; and that would mean the cutting back of many generations of supposed ancestral effort. The standard fare of *szlachta* histories emphasised that the way in which the nobility comported itself in the eighteenth century was the way in which their ancestors had done. Thus, Sejmy, *sejmiki* and even royal elections supposedly reached back to the mythological origins of the Polish state and its first ruling house, the 'Piasts', usually, if entirely spuriously, dated to the sixth century BC. The rights and privileges which the *szlachta* enjoyed had supposedly been earned by the readiness of virtuous forebears to die and suffer for their country, for their 'Fatherland', *Ojczyzna* or, as it was equally often invoked, 'the good mother, the Commonwealth'. To the end, the cry 'We will lay down our lives and fortunes for our Country!' served as a mawkishly heady slogan which substituted for any willingness to submit to fiscal or political discipline.

The strength of this emotional attachment should not be underestimated. That the sacrifices of the past were seen through the prism of a distorting mythology did not alter the fact that some at least of the nobility did show themselves ready to fight and die for their country, their values and their beliefs. The sincere if often misguided sacrifice of the few served to justify the hollow sloganeering of the many, while all remained bound by a stunted apparatus of state, incapable of focusing their energies on anything beyond preserving things as they were.

If the *szlachta* really wanted, they could suspend the veto. There existed, since the fourteenth century, the device of the Confederacy (*konfederacja*), a league set up for a specific set of goals: to preserve the peace, to demand arrears of pay, to resist invasion, to prevent harm to the Commonwealth from external or internal threats. The nobility would subscribe to a programme of objectives and entrust decision-making to a caucus of leaders and councillors, who agreed their policies by, in effect, majority vote. But always to preserve and safeguard the legacy of the past, never to alter it. Confederacies were usually set up during interregna, to try to maintain some kind of order. The majority of the Sejmy of the reign of Augustus II (1697–1733) which enacted legislation did so under the bond of a Confederacy; as did the Sejm of 1736, the sole parliament of the reign of Augustus III (1733–63) to pass legislation. To an outsider, Confederacies might have appeared useful. In Poland, they had a long history associated with disorder and rebellion; in the *szlachta*'s universe, they could only be dangerous. So much so that they were, technically, illegal: the Sejm of 1717 had banned them – but the prohibition had to be ignored, precisely in order to defend what the past had bequeathed.

Military and diplomatic weaknesses

The most striking symptom of Poland-Lithuania's debility was its army: it barely existed. Its size had been fixed in 1717 at a notional 24,000 'portions' of pay, meant to cover the costs of all ranks and arms. In reality, in 1764, immediately after the Seven Years War (in which Poland was not, and could not have been, an active participant), its army stood at barely half that number. Compare this with those of its neighbours and future partitioners: Russia had some 200,000 men (excluding almost half as many again irregulars) under arms; Prussia, around 150,000; and even battered Austria aimed at a peacetime establishment of 140,000. These were battle-hardened forces. Poland's were ill-disciplined and underpaid, incapable of protecting the country and serving mainly to provide their commanders-in-chief, the four *hetmani* of the Crown and Lithuania, with extra clout and patronage in their factional rivalries. Attempts to expand the Polish army in the 1740s and 1750s had come to nothing – and without the prior abolition of the veto (let alone a transformation in discipline, organisation and financing) such attempts were meaningless.

If the 'military revolution' of early modern Europe had passed Poland by, so too had the revolution in diplomatic practice, which by the early eighteenth century had equipped every self-respecting state with permanent representatives in every major capital. The Poles might at best send ad hoc diplomatic missions, often of a ceremonial nature, reminiscent of the practices of the Middle Ages. Since only the Sejm could confirm international agreements, foreign policy was supposedly its responsibility. Since the Sejm was ineffective, 'Polish' foreign policy inevitably became the private preserve of either the monarchs or individual magnates. King Jan Sobieski (reigned 1674–96) had managed to build up what might have been the basis of a small professional diplomatic corps – but even that was largely the monarch's, rather than the Commonwealth's, instrument.[7] The elected Wettin kings (in their own right, hereditary electors of Saxony), Augustus II and Augustus III, relied chiefly on their own Saxon diplomatic corps. If they made use of the services of individual Poles, it was only when political expediency demanded.

It was not so much 'diplomacy' that was practised in Poland, as homespun 'diplomacies'. What, indeed, could be more natural to those who regarded themselves as sovereign rulers on their own estates? In pursuit of their factional ambitions, they readily consulted and consorted with foreign agents, from whose largesse, influence and support they benefited – without appreciating that they, in their turn, were being exploited by Russia, or Prussia, or France, or even by their own Wettin kings. Almost without exception, those Polish magnates who cut fine figures at home found themselves adrift in a world of their own fantasies when they came to dealing with the calculating representatives and statesmen of the world beyond the Commonwealth's borders.[8]

The threat of partition

Poland had brushed with dismemberment in the mid-seventeenth century. On 6 December 1656, at Radnot, in Hungary, representatives of Sweden, Brandenburg, Transylvania, a rebellious Ukraine and Lithuanian separatists agreed to nothing less than the total dismemberment of the *Rzeczpospolita*.[9] Native resistance and the intervention of Denmark and the Habsburgs foiled this would-be Partition. But as Poland proved increasingly unable to stand up for its own interests, schemes for some kind of territorial rearrangements coursed around European chanceries. Amid the chaos of the Great

---

7. A.S. Kamiński, *Republic vs. Autocracy: Poland-Lithuania and Russia, 1686–1697* (Cambridge, Mass., 1993), esp. pp. 73–90, 146–75.

8. See J. Michalski, 'Polen und Preussen in der Epoche der Teilungen', *Jahrbuch für die Geschichte Mittel- und Ostdeutschlands* 30 (1981), pp. 38–9.

9. W. Konopczyński, *Dzieje Polski Nowożytnej*, 2 vols (Warsaw, 1986 edn), II, p. 23.

Northern War of 1700–21, into which the reluctant Commonwealth was dragged by the ambitious policies of its own Augustus II, Brandenburg-Prussia and Sweden had shown great interest in acquiring Polish territory. Augustus himself periodically offered to cede Polish territories in return for support for his plans to create a strong, dynastic monarchy which would match his rule in his hereditary electorate of Saxony. His offers were rejected, not because Peter the Great or Frederick William I were uninterested, but because they were not prepared to see the creation of a powerful Saxon-Polish state.

Peter the Great after 1717 looked on Poland as a dependency, to be kept intact in its 'liberty'; its territory was to be shared with no one, least of all an ambitious Prussia. Augustus II's rival, the Swedish-backed anti-king Stanisław Leszczyński, was not above offering slices of Poland to Russia or Prussia in return for their support, either during the Great Northern War or during the War of the Polish Succession of 1733–35.[10] If these offers were not always seriously meant, they were nevertheless eloquent testimony to the weaknesses of a state which had only its own territory with which to tempt potential allies.

Looking back at his country's history in 1789, the ideologue Hugon Kołłątaj insisted that the real process of Partition reached back to the seventeenth century. The prime mover was Russia. Kołłątaj claimed that it was Poland's final surrender in 1686 of Kiev and the extensive territories on the east bank of the Dnieper which had given Russia the resources to become a great power.[11] In fact, Moscow had disputed control of the vast Byelorussian and Ukrainian lands with the Grand Duchy of Lithuania since the fourteenth century; since the early sixteenth, Poland itself had become intimately involved in this struggle. By the later seventeenth century, Russia had clearly emerged the victor. The Commonwealth had won at least as many battles as it had lost, but nothing could compensate for its chaotic domestic politics, which wrecked all efforts to sustain coherence and continuity in its foreign, fiscal and military affairs.

10. For a summary of such proposals, see L.R. Lewitter, 'Zur Vorgeschichte der Teilungen Polens (1697–1721)', *Österreichische Osthefte* Jahrgang 32 (1990), pp. 333–57. J. Staszewski, 'Ostatni "Wielki Plan" Augusta Mocnego', *Rocznik Gdański* 46, no. 1 (1986), pp. 45–67 sounds a cautionary note against too readily taking the traditional view of Augustus II's willingness to dole out Polish territories. On Leszczyński, see J. Feldman, *Stanisław Leszczyński* (Warsaw, 1984 edn), pp. 192–6.

11. H. Kołłątaj, 'Uwagi nad wpływaniem do interesów Rzeczypospolitej dwóch mocarstw . . .', now edited by Z. Zielińska in *Kołłątaj i orientacja pruska u progu Sejmu Czteroletniego* (Warsaw, 1991). See esp. pp. 64–6. The treaty of Moscow of 1686 confirmed the territorial status quo of the truce of Andrussovo of 1667.

The savagery of Muscovite rule was not the least of factors behind the *szlachta*'s terror of *absolutum dominium*. The Poles could never truly reconcile themselves to the loss of the old eastern territories. Augustus II promised to recover them in 1697 and to restore the Commonwealth to 'the ancient fullness of its Sarmatian empire'.[12] His two successors reiterated that commitment (admittedly, in somewhat weaker form), Augustus III in 1736 and Stanisław August in 1764, notwithstanding the Russian military support which had placed them on the throne.[13] The Sejm did not formally ratify the Moscow treaty of 1686 until 1710. Perhaps the clearest and most tangible reminder to the Poles of their *avulsa*, the 'lands torn away', were the so-called *sejmiki exulantium*, the *sejmiki* of the exiles. Here assembled the descendants of nobles displaced from the palatinates of Czernichów and Smolensk, living constitutional fossils attesting to hurt feelings and Sarmatian irreality. They continued to meet even after the First Partition.[14]

The argument that Poland would survive despite its troubles, because its neighbours found its preservation to be in their own interests, was all the more dangerous in that it was not without its perverse merits. Russia, having taken away so much territory from the Commonwealth in the seventeenth century, was content to leave it as a kind of glacis, a passive outwork in a security cordon running down its western border – but only on condition that no reform was made in Poland that might usher in any kind of revival.[15] That did not mean that Russia was not concerned to acquire territory from Poland – quite the contrary, those areas which Russia was to annex under the terms of the First Partition were of growing interest to her politicians from at least the 1740s. The headwaters of the Dvina and the Dnieper rivers ran through lands comparatively rich in the valuable products of 'naval stores', timber, flax, potash, tar and, above all, hemp. Polish Byelorussia was part of the natural hinterland of the Russian port of Riga. There was growing pressure from Russian landowners around Pskov and Novgorod to push the frontier back to a clearly defined river boundary, which would make it much easier to stem the flow of serfs fleeing from their Russian masters to what were hopefully better conditions on the Polish

---

12. *VL* VI, p. 21.   13. *VL* VI, pp. 21, 303. Ibid. VII, p. 99.
14. H. Olszewski, *Sejm Rzeczypospolitej epoki oligarchii* (Poznań, 1966), pp. 60–6.
15. For a good summary of Russian policy see W. Mediger, 'Great Britain, Hanover and the rise of Prussia', in R. Hatton and M.S. Anderson, eds, *Studies in Diplomatic History* (London, 1970), pp. 206–10.

side of the border.[16] In 1744, the Russian chancellor, Alexei Bestuzhev-Riumin, formulated a plan whereby Austria and Russia would turn on Prussia, which would be obliged to cede the duchy of East Prussia to Poland. Poland, in turn, would cede its Byelorussian territories to Russia.

Another juicy picking in the eastern Baltic eyed by Russia was the duchy of Courland, covering much of the area of what is today southern Latvia. Since the sixteenth century, the duchy had been, in law, a Polish vassal: in practice, Russian influence had been uppermost since the reign of Peter the Great. The duchy, whose ruling Germanic nobility had often close family ties to their neighbours in Russian-ruled Livonia, was an invaluable source of educated diplomats and officials for St Petersburg. Between 1737 and 1741 it was a Russian choice, Ernst Johann von Bühren (Biron), himself a Courland noble, lover of the Empress Anna, who occupied the ducal seat. It was by grace and favour of the Empress Elizabeth that, in 1758, Augustus III's younger son, Charles, was made Courland's duke; and, in 1763, it was another empress, Catherine II, who decided that he should be deposed and Biron restored. In 1756, proposals involving the exchange of East Prussia for Byelorussia or Courland were floated, although by 1760 the Russians may have been planning to keep the duchy of East Prussia for themselves.[17]

Neighbouring rivalries and designs

The possibility of an East Prussian 'exchange' for Polish territories should serve as a reminder that relations between the three powers who finally came to partition Poland were rarely smooth and often bitterly hostile. That hardy perennial of continental diplomacy, rivalry between the Habsburgs and the Bourbons, maintained a

16. P. Dukes, *Catherine II and the Russian nobility* (Cambridge, 1967), pp. 116–17, 119; R.E. Jones, 'Runaway peasants and Russian motives for the Partitions of Poland', in H. Ragsdale, ed., *Imperial Russian Foreign Policy* (Cambridge, 1993), pp. 103–16.

17. W. Czapliński, 'Les territoires de l'ouest dans la politique de la Pologne de 1572 à 1764', *Acta Poloniae Historica* 9 (1964), pp. 26–7. W. Hubatsch, *Frederick the Great of Prussia: absolutism and administration* (London, 1975), pp. 118–19. T. Cegielski, *Das alte Reich und die Erste Teilung Polens 1768–1774* (Wiesbaden, 1988), pp. 58–9. Most recently, J.P. LeDonne, *The Russian empire and the world, 1700–1917. The geopolitics of expansion and containment* (New York, 1997), pp. 38–9 suggests that even at this early stage, Russia considered the annexation of extensive stretches of Poland's Ukraine.

vigorous existence until the Diplomatic Revolution of 1756. The Habsburgs had a natural community of interest with the Romanovs in their long-standing conflict with the Ottoman Porte, a community given expression in their alliance of 1726. Not least of the consequences of the 1756 reversal of alliances was to blunt Austria's hostility towards the Porte, which had long been a protégé of France; it did little, however, to efface Russian designs against the Turks.

The reign of Charles VI of Habsburg (1711–40) had brought the Hohenzollern of Prussia little but humiliation. The emperor had strung Frederick William I (1713–40) along over his claims to the Rhineland duchies of Jülich and Berg. He had misled him over Poland, which, for all its weaknesses, had the potential to be strong. A prolonged Polish–Saxon union was bound be a threat to the Hohenzollern state. In December 1732, Austrian and Russian diplomats promised Frederick William they would never allow the election of another Wettin monarch; one year later, their military intervention procured precisely that. The Poles' own candidate, Stanisław Leszczyński, was Louis XV of France's father-in-law and an old companion-in-arms to Charles XII of Sweden. Neither Austria nor Russia could contemplate such a candidature. Their empty assurances to Frederick William kept him out of the way while they disposed of Poland's throne to a perceived mediocrity who would remain dependent upon their support.

Frederick II's accession in Prussia changed everything with his audacious conquest of Silesia between 1740 and 1742. Prussia allied itself to France; and through France it gained uncomfortable links to Sweden. In 1743, Frederick II refused to marry off his sister, Ulrike, to the heir to the Russian throne, Duke Peter of Holstein (though he did arrange for his marriage to princess Sophie of Anhalt-Zerbst; he could be excused for not appreciating that this politically harmless fourteen-year-old would mature into Catherine the Great). Instead, in 1744, he married off Ulrike to Adolf Frederick, crown prince elect of Russia's unreconciled foe, Sweden. And Sweden, in 1743, encouraged by France, had just fought an unsuccessful war to recover the Baltic territories it had ceded to Russia in 1721. To Bestuzhev-Riumin and the new Russian empress, Elizabeth, Frederick's Prussia was a wild card which threatened to pave the way to a restoration of the old Swedish empire and weaken Russia's principal ally against Turkey. Peter the Great had set about establishing a huge security cordon along Russia's western borders out of the wreckage of once-strong Sweden and Poland, reducing them to near-vassal status. A rising Prussia threatened to carve out a rival influence in what Russia deemed its own Baltic preserve.[18] Set against this, Frederick II's commitment to the preservation of Polish anarchy was not enough. That was something which Russia could manage perfectly well on its own.

It may now seem less paradoxical that the state which had most to fear in terms of partition in 1756, when the Seven Years War erupted, was not weak Poland, but dynamic Prussia. The Seven Years War was the closest of close-run things. If Maria Theresa and Elizabeth and their diplomats had had their way, 'Prussia' would have ceased to exist: the Hohenzollern territories would have been cut back to a core based on Brandenburg and the rest shared out between Austria, Saxony, Sweden, France and minor German principalities.[19] The accession, in January 1762, of a besotted prussophile, Peter III, saved Frederick from what seemed assured destruction. In March Peter consigned years of suffering and effort by his armies to the dustbin when he concluded an armistice with Frederick. In June came an alliance.[20] In July, Peter was deposed and assassinated in a coup led by his wife Catherine – she who had once been the Sophie of Anhalt-Zerbst whose marriage Frederick II had brokered almost nineteen years before. Amid the exhaustion brought on by the Seven Years War, the Prusso-Russian peace held. Maria Theresa found it hard to forgive Russia's desertion. The old Austro-Russian alliance of 1726 was dead.

To look at the map is enough to appreciate the obvious interest which the Hohenzollern had in acquiring Polish territory, in order to join their duchy of East, or Ducal, Prussia, to their Brandenburg heartland. They had pursued that goal even before the treaties of Wehlau and Bromberg removed Polish suzerainty over East Prussia in 1657. Unable to acquire Polish (or Royal) Prussia in its entirety, the Hohenzollern settled for a long haul, perking up whenever promising opportunities appeared. Throughout the Great Northern War of 1700–21 Frederick I and his successor, Frederick William I, were constantly looking to Sweden, to Saxony, to Russia, even to the

18. Ibid., pp. 35–8, 236–8.

19. The complex partitioning provisions are to be found in the treaty of Versailles (France and Austria) of 1 May 1757, in *CTS* XLI, pp. 7–11 (articles 2–4) and in the Convention of St Petersburg (Russia and Austria) of 21 March 1760, ibid., pp. 394, 396–9 (article 5; separate article 1; secret and separate article [2] and secret Declaration).

20. C.S. Leonard, *Reform and regicide: the reign of Peter III of Russia* (Bloomington, 1993), pp. 125–37.

Poles themselves to secure, at the least, some form of land bridge between Ducal Prussia and the Neumark, in return for (possibly) military assistance or (preferably) benevolent neutrality or mediation.[21] Frederick I achieved a small, but tangible, gain, which spoke volumes for the Commonwealth's weakness. Since the Northern War of 1655–60, the town of Elbing had been in pawn to Brandenburg for the sum of 400,000 Thaler. Between 1698 and 1703, the Prussians were able to exploit the tensions and fighting in the Baltic to secure, not the town of Elbing, but the hinterland which belonged to it; the Poles were incapable of voting the monies to redeem these lands, even after Frederick I agreed to scale back the redemption sum to 300,000 Thaler; the lands of the Elbing district remained permanently under Prussian administration. To 1771, they yielded the Prussian treasury almost 2.4 million Thaler.[22]

It was the prospect of even such piecemeal acquisitions, 'a town here, a district there', which prompted Frederick the Great's observation that Poland should be eaten 'like an artichoke, leaf by leaf'.[23] But Frederick felt he could leave Poland almost to one side. The Commonwealth 'is a threat to no one', he observed in 1752. He was far more interested in the annexation of Saxony, head for head probably the most prosperous state in the Holy Roman Empire and an invaluable bulwark against Habsburg revanchism.[24] The international situation would mean he would have to settle for second best.

The Habsburgs showed virtually no interest in the acquisition of Polish territory. In the seventeenth century, if not earlier, Poland had been a battleground for influence between Austria and France. Richelieu and Mazarin had formulated the policy of a *Barrière de l'Est*, an elaborate linkage of states in the Habsburg rear. Brandenburg, Sweden, Poland and Turkey were to distract Austria while France pursued its expansionary aims in the west. If this *Barrière*

21. E. Hassinger, *Brandenburg-Preussen, Schweden und Russland 1700–1713* (Munich, 1953), *passim*.

22. Ibid., pp. 62, 102–3, 108–9, 121, 129, 131–3, 233–8, 243–5, 257–8, 260; W. Klesińska, 'Okupacja Elbląga przez Brandenburgię w latach 1698–1700', *Rocznik Elbląski* 4 (1969), pp. 85–121.

23. Frederick was consciously echoing the advice of Victor Amadeus II of Savoy to his son on the gradual acquisition of the Milanese from the Habsburgs: '*Mon fils, il faut manger le Milanais comme un artichaut, feuille par feuille.*' 'Testament Politique' of 1752, in *Testamente*, pp. 63–4. Frederick repeated the point in his 'Testament Politique' of 1768, ibid., p. 219.

24. 'Testament Politique' of 1752, ibid., p. 46. For Frederick's views on Saxony, ibid., pp. 61–3; and the 'Testament Politique' of 1768, ibid., pp. 215–16, 219.

existed more in the dreams of French politicians and diplomats than in international reality, the Habsburgs still had to keep an eye on what was happening in Poland. King Jan Sobieski may have decided at the last to come to the help of Vienna against the Turks in 1683, but for the first decade of his reign he was uncomfortably francophile; his successor, Augustus II, had dreamed of carving out even wider territories for himself at the expense of the Habsburgs, dreams which his son, Augustus III, shared, until his bitter experiences during the War of the Austrian Succession taught him that Frederick the Great was a more dangerous neighbour than Maria Theresa. For as long as there was scope for a pro-French monarchy in Poland, the Habsburgs preferred it to stay unreformed. In any case, they accepted that the price of their alliance with Russia was that Poland should remain a predominantly Romanov sphere of influence.[25]

The 'Diplomatic Revolution' of 1756, which saw the realignment of France from Austria's foe to her ally against Prussia, did little to alter Bourbon and Habsburg interests in Poland. Austria was too distracted by the Seven Years War to show much active interest in its northern neighbour. France retained its links with Poland, even though individual ministers like Choiseul had serious doubts about their value. Choiseul deeply mistrusted his ex-allies, the Russians. After 1762, he viewed them as a threat to both of France's friends in eastern Europe – Austria and the Porte. Worst of all, he regarded Russia as a potential ally of France's own enemy, Great Britain. He saw no point in pretending that the Poles could be transformed into an effective anti-Russian force – in that respect, the Ottoman Porte was a far better bet. Louis XV himself never quite gave up: after all, his own father-in-law was Polish; his son, the dauphin, was married to Augustus II's daughter, Maria-Josepha. Such dynastic links might produce any number of useful suits in the poker-game of European diplomacy. Louis XV maintained his own secret and ineffectual links to Poland, hidden even from his ministers, almost up to the First Partition.[26]

25. W. Konopczyński, 'Sejm grodzieński 1752 roku', *Mrok i Świt* (Warsaw, 1911), pp. 47–8, 58, 90–2, 105. Cf. D. Beales, *Joseph II* (Cambridge, 1987), I, pp. 275–6.

26. The complex diplomacy of Louis' *secret du roi* remains woefully unexplored. See D. Ozanam and M. Antoine, eds, *Correspondence secrète du comte de Broglie avec Louis XV (1756–1774)*, 2 vols (Paris, 1956). For the wider international perspective, see H.M. Scott, *British foreign policy in the age of the American Revolution* (Oxford, 1990), chs 3–6 and *idem*, 'Great Britain, Poland, and the Russian alliance, 1763–1767', *Historical Journal* 19, no. 1 (1976), pp. 53–74.

The erosion of Polish sovereignty

The interplay between the policies and interests of France and
Austria, Russia and Prussia, undoubtedly did help to preserve the
nominal independence of the Polish–Lithuanian *Rzeczpospolita.* But
at a price. In the course of the seventeenth and eighteenth centuries, sovereignty, the capacity of the Polish polity to conduct its own
affairs, had been dissolved and subsumed into the foreign policies
of others, who provided a kind of life-support system for the Commonwealth's institutionalised anarchy. Poland's own foreign agreements aided and abetted the process. Under the terms of the treaty
of Wehlau of 1657 with Brandenburg, Poland had finally surrendered its suzerainty over the duchy of East Prussia; but it had also
bound itself not to make any monetary, customs and tariff arrangements for its own Polish Prussian territories without consultation
with the elector of Brandenburg. Under the treaty of Oliva of 1660,
with Sweden, Brandenburg and the Empire, Poland promised to
leave the religious status quo in Polish Prussia intact. Under the
treaty of Moscow of 1686, the Poles promised not to alter the ecclesiastical and religious conditions of their Orthodox population, concentrated in Byelorussia and the Ukraine; they accorded them the
right of appeal to the tsar's subject, the Orthodox metropolitan of
Kiev.

All of these treaties were, sooner or later, ratified by the Sejm as
public law.[27] Poland's co-signatories – primarily Prussia and Russia
– were able to claim the right to intervene in Polish affairs both in
international law and under the heading of Poland's own domestic
legal arrangements. Inside the Commonwealth itself, those affected
or aggrieved by the non-observance of the letter of these enactments
felt themselves entitled to appeal to the foreign powers concerned.

Whoever was strong enough to do so could violate the territorial
integrity of the Commonwealth with impunity. The feeble Polish
army was unable even to protect the south-eastern borders against
the regular inroads of cossack marauders from the wild steppe
lands around the lower Dnieper. Poland's Ukraine lay astride the

---

27. Treaty of Wehlau, 19 September 1657, in *CTS* IV, pp. 437–52 and the supplementary treaty of Bromberg (Bydgoszcz), 6 November 1657, ibid., pp. 452–60. The
texts of these two treaties were not incorporated directly into the statutes of the
Sejm of 1658 but the Sejm gave its statutory approval to them, *VL* IV, p. 239. Treaty
of Oliva, 3 May 1660, *CTS* VI, pp. 11–36 and *VL* IV, pp. 344–57. Treaty of Moscow,
6 May 1686 in *CTS* XVII, pp. 493–501; approved and enacted into law by the Sejm
only in 1710, *VL* VI, pp. 73–82.

most convenient routes between Russia and the Balkans: in Russia's war of 1735–39 against the Ottoman Porte, Russian troops criss-crossed Polish territory to reach the main theatre of conflict, the Balkans, with scant regard for *szlachta* protests. During the Seven Years War, the *Rzeczpospolita*'s neutrality was regularly violated by Prussian, Russian and Austrian armies.

Prussia was by far the worst offender. In 1756, Frederick the Great seized the dies for Polish coins which were kept in the Dresden mint and helped his war finances by flooding the Commonwealth with debased and counterfeit currency.[28] As late as 1765, his forces were raiding western or 'great' Poland, Wielkopolska, for provisions, animals and settlers to assist in the Prussian post-war recovery pro-gramme.[29] Once Russian troops had entered Polish territory in 1758, they were not to leave for another thirty years. They were always there in greater or lesser numbers, either guarding stores and supplies, or enforcing the policies of St Petersburg. Most of the time, only comparatively small areas of the country were affected; it was in the interests of troops in transit to behave in a reasonably orderly manner; many landowners rushed to embrace the rare market opportunity which a well-disciplined army on the march furnished.[30] But this could only be a state which had lost control of its destiny.

Poland and its religions

In one crucial area, however, the Commonwealth manifested too much vigour for its own good: an aggressive, post-tridentine Cath-olicism was alive and well. The religious dynamic, unprotected and unrestrained by a strong state, was to play a key role in precipitating the catastrophe of the First Partition. Poland's religious affairs were of as much interest to outside powers as its politics. The archbishop-primate of Gniezno was the second-highest-ranking personage in the kingdom after the monarch. He was 'interrex', acting head of state,

---

28. Frederick practised similar operations against the lesser German states but it was Poland that bore the brunt. See J.K. Hoensch, 'Friedrichs II: Wahrungs-manipulationen im siebenjährigen Krieg und ihre Aufwirkung auf die polnische Münzreform von 1756/66', *Jahrbuch für Geschichte Mittel- und Ost-Deutschlands* 22 (1973), pp. 110–34.

29. W. Konopczyński, 'Precedens wywłaszczenia w Wielkopolsce', *Mrok i Świt* (Warsaw, 1911), pp. 233–72.

30. Stanisław August Poniatowski, *Mémoires du roi Stanislas-Auguste Poniatowski*, 2 vols (St Petersburg–Leningrad, 1914–24), I, pp. 511–12. Cf. J.T. Gieysztor to Adam Chmara, 6 Mar. 1767. Biblioteka Jagiellońska, Kraków, MS 6646II, t. 15.

when the throne fell vacant. By virtue of their membership of the Senate, the eighteen Latin Catholic bishops were as much politicians as ecclesiastics. Only about half of the population was Roman Catholic, but that half included the overwhelming majority of the *szlachta*.

The second most numerous religious grouping, approaching some 4,000,000 in 1770, was also Catholic – not Roman, but Greek Catholic, 'Uniate'. The Union of Brześć of 1596 had admitted into the Catholic church those Polish Orthodox prepared – or obliged – to acknowledge the authority of the Papacy. Liturgy, dogma and daily practice were little affected. Uniate secular clergy remained free to marry and have families. This lack of outward differentiation between Greek Catholic and Greek Orthodox churches made for great ease of conversion between the two – with the overwhelming bulk of this religious traffic flowing from Orthodoxy to Catholicism. The Orthodox diocesan structure had disappeared altogether with the Union of Brześć, although it was rebuilt between 1620 and 1632.

While the Sejmy of the seventeenth century accepted toleration for the Orthodox, they also legislated for the right of Uniates to maintain a parallel diocesan organisation. Bishops and parish clergy who converted from Orthodoxy insisted on taking their congregations with them. The overwhelmingly peasant Ukrainian and Byelorussian parishioners, even if they could appreciate the differences, had little choice, unless Orthodox replacements could be substituted, something unlikely to find favour with newly converted bishops or Catholic landowners. One by one, the Orthodox Polish bishops converted to the Greek Catholic union. In 1677, there were five Orthodox dioceses on the *Rzeczpospolita*'s territory: by 1702 there was only one, that of Mohylew in Byelorussia. Between the 1680s and the 1760s, some 150 Orthodox parish churches were taken over by the Uniates. That the Polish kings continued to recognise Orthodox bishops in Mohylew and confirm their appointments was due largely to Russian diplomatic pressure. Two eighteenth-century incumbents were neither nobles nor Poles: Arseniusz Berła (1729–32) and Iurii Konisski (1755–95) were Russian subjects, appointed at the behest of the Russian government.[31]

Russian and Polish communist historiography has viewed the Uniate church as little more than a cynical Catholic device to secure easy converts. Undoubtedly, there is some truth in this, but

31. L. Bieńkowski, 'Organizacja kościoła wschodniego w Polsce', in J. Kłoczowski, ed., *Kościół w Polsce*, II (Kraków, 1969), pp. 838–59; T. Śliwa, 'Kościół prawosławny w latach 1696–1764', in B. Kumor and Z. Obertyński, eds, *Historia Kościoła w Polsce*, I (Poznań, 1974), pp. 481–6. See also Solov'ev, *IPP*, p. 420.

the reality was far more complex. Orthodoxy was in no condition to
match Catholicism's systematic proselytising. There was no Polish
patriarchate. Spiritual jurisdiction over Poland's Orthodox resided
with the patriarch of Constantinople until 1676, when, amid Poland's
wars with the Turks, the Sejm decreed an end to such contacts.
The late seventeenth-century Russian church, boasting (sometimes
literally so) the most ignorant clergy in Europe, was riven by feuds
between Old and New Believers, and by the mutual suspicions of
xenophobic Muscovites and 'latinising' Ukrainians and Byelorussians.
It was incapable of offering spiritual leadership. Yet, in 1686, the
Polish diplomats who negotiated the treaty of Moscow reluctantly
conceded, under article IX, a tsarist protectorate over the Commonwealth's remaining Orthodox dioceses and monasteries; senior
Polish Orthodox clergy would be invested by the metropolitan of
Kiev – whose status as a Russian subject was confirmed by that very
treaty.[32]

Individual Polish, Catholic magnates continued to found new
Orthodox parishes but these were confined to the eastern extrem-
ities of the Polish Ukraine; the overwhelming tide of conversions,
voluntary, forced or indifferent, favoured the Uniates. Throughout
the eighteenth century, both sides accused each other of intimidation and abuse in their methods of conversion; and though the
truth of many of the detailed charges and counter-charges is impossible to establish, there is no question that, in Poland, it was
the Orthodox church which was on the defensive. Its clergy saw
realistic hopes of holding the line only in appeals to Russia, even
though its leaders appreciated that Moscow's interventions on their
behalf were motivated by political, rather than religious, considera-
tions.[33] On the eve of the First Partition, there were about half a
million Orthodox in Poland, compared with ten times as many
Uniates.

How many Lutherans and Calvinists – 'Dissidentes de Religione'
– lived in Poland before the First Partition can only be guessed at
– between 200,000 and 300,000 perhaps, chiefly to be found in

32. L.R. Lewitter, 'The Russo-Polish treaty of 1686 and its antecedents', *Polish Review* 9, nos. 3, 4 (1964), pp. 5–29, 21–37. Z. Wójcik, 'Rokowania polsko-rosyjskie o "Pokój Wieczysty" w Moskwie w roku 1686', in *Z dziejów polityki i dyplomacji polskiej* (Warsaw, 1994), pp. 38–55. On the condition of the Russian Orthodox church, see J. Cracraft, 'Feofan Prokopovich', in J.G. Garrard, ed., *The eighteenth century in Russia* (Oxford, 1973), pp. 75–90; M.J. Okenfuss, 'The Jesuit origins of Petrine education', ibid., pp. 106–30.
33. Z. Zielińska, *Walka 'Familii' o reformę Rzeczypospolitej 1743–1752* (Warsaw, 1983), pp. 240–1.

western Poland (Wielkopolska) and Polish Prussia. There could only have been a few hundred noble families among them – little more than a drop in the sea of the *szlachta* nation.[34] Though far less numerous than the Orthodox, they were to play a far more import-ant part in the crises of Polish politics in the 1760s. For unlike the Orthodox, the Protestants included self-respecting nobles, some of considerable wealth and genuine influence and usually much better educated than their Catholic counterparts.

In the late sixteenth century, Protestants and even Orthodox had been found at the very highest levels of the state, including senatorial offices; they had been noisily active in the Chamber of Envoys. But their 'rights' had never been defined in law: and, as the Counter-Reformation ran its course, their 'rights' came to be defined more clearly in their disfavour, until, between 1733 and 1736, they were definitively excluded from the Chamber of Envoys. They were not barred from the Senate in law, but in fact no Protestant was appointed to it after the end of the seventeenth century. Their religion marginalised them from the mainstream of political life, without excluding them completely. Yet the condition of Lutherans and Calvinists continued to compare favourably with that of reli-gious minorities in Britain or the Dutch Republic. The Protestant families of the Goltzes, the Unrugs, the Grabowskis retained a power-ful regional role in the politics of Polish Prussia. Protestants domin-ated the town councils of the three 'Great towns' of Royal Prussia, Danzig, Thorn and Elbing, where they worshipped openly. Protest-ants served in Poland's little army, up to and including the rank of general. Protestant favourites continued to receive lucrative crown land leases under Augustus III. Protestant nobles voted in the elec-tion of Stanisław Poniatowski in September 1764.

It is undeniable, however, that in Poland the majority of noble opinion was firmly on collision course with 'enlightened' European opinion. By the second half of the eighteenth century, while the trend among governing circles in most European countries was to extend toleration to religious minorities, even if only unofficially, the *szlachta* insisted that the momentum to squeeze the Protestants out of public office should be maintained: they could have tolera-tion, but little else. The *szlachta* were experiencing their own demo-graphic growth. The dissenters formed an 'out' group within the

34. The author of the most recent and most searching treatment of eighteenth-century Polish Protestantism concedes the near impossibility of putting a figure on their numbers. W. Kriegseisen, *Ewangelicy polscy i litewscy w epoce saskiej* (Warsaw, 1996), ch. 2.

nobility, a disproportionately small minority occupying offices and dignities which the Catholic majority wanted for themselves. The Orthodox looked to Russia for survival; a few among the Protestants were to look to it for advancement.[35]

Closed minds?

In 1732, the French ambassador to Poland, the marquis de Monti, tried to warn his acquaintances among the magnates of the potential threat from Russia, Austria and Prussia.

> They reply that Poland has always been governed this way; that the interest of Europe requires that Poland's present form of government should continue, lest any of the neighbouring princes annexes it.[36]

Was there, then, no way out? Why, how, could the *szlachta* put up with this state of affairs? There were, of course, critical voices. Criticism was voiced, however, at the level of men, not measures, not institutions. If things were bad, it was because of the corruption of the times and of individuals. Few were prepared to scrutinise the Commonwealth's failings more searchingly. Those that might have done so were constrained by the prejudices and politicking of the great majority. Poland was the only world the great mass of the gentry knew; behind it, in close support, came the universes of republican Rome and baroque religiosity, barely tainted by the new worlds of the Scientific Revolution and its child, the Enlightenment.

Yet the Commonwealth could not seal itself off from the outside world intellectually any more than it could politically. Poles did travel abroad, they did come into contact with foreigners, none more so than the clergy. The Catholic church could show itself concerned by the backwardness and complacency of some of its institutions in Poland. The Theatine Order sensed an opportunity to establish itself in Warsaw, where it set up a very small school in 1737, offering at least a smattering of a different sort of curriculum to the six or seven years' hard slog of Latin literature, grammar and philosophy

35. J.T. Lukowski, 'The Papacy, Poland, Russia and religious reform, 1764–8', *Journal of Ecclesiastical History* 39 (1988), pp. 66–94 and *idem*, 'Unhelpful and unnecessary: Voltaire's *Essai historique et critique sur les dissensions des Églises de Pologne* (1767)', in U. Kölving and C. Mervaud, eds, *Voltaire et ses combats*, 2 vols (Oxford, 1997), I, pp. 645–54.

36. Marquis de Monti to Louis XV, 11 Mar. 1732. Quoted in Michalski, 'Polen und Preussen', p. 37.

that was the staple fare of the Jesuit colleges. The Theatines offered modern languages, fencing, dancing, the new sciences and even the new literature, decorously purged of its anti-Christian overtones. In 1740, Father Stanisław Konarski of the Piarist Order set up a College of Nobles, the 'Collegium Nobilium', in the capital, teaching a much more systematic version of this modernised curriculum, similar to that offered by many Noble Academies throughout Europe. The teaching orders' own schools elsewhere in Europe, notably in France and Italy, kept abreast of new ideas. But, for some ten years or so, such ventures were only for individuals from elite circles, who were anxious to cut a European figure. The new boarding-schools charged fees, whereas the nobility expected their education to be provided free. They made little positive impact on the *szlachta* – indeed, their elite nature often aroused resentment. Konarski's reforms began to percolate through the wider network of Piarist schools only in the 1750s. In that decade, too, a similar programme began to be taken up by the Jesuits, as they came to appreciate that the new-fangled ideas had begun to find a lodgement even in Poland.

None of this made much difference. The new schools studiously avoided any direct criticism of the *szlachta*'s politics – ultimately, the nobility remained their patrons and paymasters. The best they could do was to graft new ideas and values onto the bedrock of the old, in the hope that their students would draw their own conclusions. For every Piarist or Jesuit who appreciated the need for change in Poland, there was at least another who clung to old certainties as grimly as any backwoods gentleman. The attachment of the nobility as a whole to its investment in centuries of accumulated privilege was intensified by an almost manichaean vision of the world. Whatever Poland's faults, its liberty made it infinitely preferable to the despotism of Prussia, Russia, Austria or France. The myth of a free Commonwealth was perfectly balanced by the black, unnuanced legend of absolutism. England was corrupt and its government, like Holland's, contaminated by commoners and merchants. If any contemporary state met Polish approval, it was Venice – for Venice, too, was ruled by its nobility; and Venice, too, never changed.

In any case, God and Europe would look after Poland. The Commonwealth had suffered so many disasters and so many invasions since the mid-seventeenth century that Divine Providence did indeed seem to account for its survival. Those noble ideologues who chose to peer beyond the sacred argued that Poland remained an essential component of the European balance. Poland's grain was supposedly

essential to other countries; while the states of Europe would ensure
Poland's survival because it was in their interest to prevent any
disruption of the balance of power which Poland-Lithuania's dismemberment would surely occasion.

Not everyone was so certain. In the *Epistolae Familiares sub tempus
Interregni*, 'Letters to Friends written during the Interregnum' published in 1733, Father Konarski warned his countrymen that their
freedom meant nothing unless it was exercised within a framework
of genuine independence and sovereignty. Poland had to rely primarily on itself, not on the supposedly amicable services of other
powers.[37] Such admonitions became a stock-in-trade of writers over
the next generation. Far from being heeded, they joined the ritual
incantations of a society which had become so accustomed to its
way of conducting itself that it could not slip into any other.

Such introspection involved the constant mythologisation both
of the past and the present. In the sixteenth and early seventeenth
centuries Polish grain had been important to Europe, but by the
eighteenth century Poland had long since ceased to be the 'granary
of Europe'. Poles either forgot that in 1667 and 1686 their Commonwealth had suffered massive territorial losses to Russia, or else they
continued to persuade themselves that these 'lands torn away' could
yet be regained. Poland's existence was nurtured by its neighbours
– but only on the explicit understanding that its anarchic constitution and the *liberum veto* would be preserved. By the treaty of
Stockholm of 1667, Sweden and Brandenburg had made the first
agreement pledging themselves to allow no reform in Poland. Similar agreements followed: between Sweden and Brandenburg again,
in 1686; Sweden and Russia, in 1724; Saxony and Russia, in 1733
and 1744; Saxony and Austria, in 1733; Turkey and Russia, in 1720;
and, most frequently of all, Russia and Prussia: in 1720, 1726, 1729,
1730 and 1743. The Poles were not party to these agreements,
largely because their Sejm would have been incapable of approving
them. A desperate rump of supporters of 'Polish liberty' did indeed
conclude such a treaty with France in September 1735 in return for
avowed French protection of their laws and freedoms, even as France
was negotiating over their heads with Austria to abandon them.[38]

37. 'Epistolae Familiares sub tempus interregni' (letter I) in S. Konarski, *Pisma
Wybrane*, 2 vols, J. Nowak-Dłużewski, ed. (Warsaw, 1955), I, pp. 87–101.
38. The treaty of Versailles, 18 September 1735. For these agreements see J.T.
Lukowski, 'Towards Partition: Polish magnates and Russian intervention in Poland
during the early reign of Stanisław August Poniatowski', *Historical Journal* 28 (1985),
pp. 559–63.

Opinion was naturally concerned by disorders and rampaging foreign armies. Political writers bewailed the possible loss of territories to more powerful neighbours, but most were more concerned by the chimeric spectre of monarchic despotism. The foreign threat was rarely dissected in detail. Konarski's *Epistolae Familiares* of 1733 offered little in the way of practical solutions. In 1763, he finally urged the unmentionable in the four volumes of his 'On the means to successful counsels': the abolition of the *liberum veto*.[39] He was much congratulated – but *szlachta* opinion remained divided. Even those who accepted his analysis of Poland's ills balked at his solutions. And for all of Konarski's readiness to tackle old shibboleths, he could not explain how the Commonwealth could realistically free itself of its over-mighty protectors.

One who did give quite exceptionally lengthy consideration to the dangers from outside was Szczepan Sienicki. Much of the first part (over three hundred and thirty pages) of his 'A new means for the conduct of public counsels . . .' of 1764 was given over to the territorial dangers from Poland's neighbours. He both deplored the disruption of the Sejmy and attacked Stanisław Konarski's advocacy of majority voting. He insisted that the preservation of the *liberum veto* was essential to true liberty and that true security came simply from adhering to ancient laws. The veto was being abused: Sienicki demanded its retention, but restricted its use to single items of legislation. He proposed subjecting its user to an astonishingly cumbersome process of parliamentary divisions, which would pronounce on the justice of his objections. If his grotesque, illogical, unreal and self-contradictory proposals had been adopted, parliamentary procedures would have ground to a halt within hours. The local *szlachta* were sufficiently impressed to urge that Sienicki should be rewarded for his work.[40] Sienicki was a local worthy, a minor judicial official and a quondam envoy to the Sejm. He lived close to the Prussian border and had ample experience of Russian transit marches and Prussian depredations. Yet he could not make the emotional wrench to break with the past. For him and for countless others, the veto was too much a part and parcel of liberty, too much a necessary safeguard against the bogey of *absolutum dominium*,

39. *O Skutecznym Rad Sposobie*, 4 vols (Warsaw, 1760–63).

40. Sz. Sienicki, *Sposób nowo-obmyślony konkludowania obrad publicznych, dla utwierdzenia praw kardynalnych wolności, libertatis sentiendi & juris vetandi . . .* ('A new means for concluding public counsels, for the affirmation of the cardinal laws of liberty, freedom of expression and the right to veto . . .'), 3 vols (Łowicz, 1764); instruction of the county of Nur to its envoys to the Sejm of 1766, Nur, 25 Aug. 1766, AGAD/Księgi grodzkie nurskie, relacje, oblaty no. 39, f. 88.

ever to be discarded. To survive, Poland had to mend its ways. It could only do that if its Sienickis were persuaded that an effective, working government did not have to be despotic; that the Commonwealth did not have to remain a litter of rights and privileges, but could become a truly sovereign state, capable of achieving something.[41]

The aftermath of the Seven Years War

As the Seven Years War drew to a close, many Poles congratulated themselves on escaping it, with an optimistic disregard for the repeated violation of their territories.[42] The international checks and balances which had indeed contributed to their preservation for so long were being altered. The Diplomatic Revolution of 1756 which aligned France with Austria greatly reduced the former's old interest in an anti-Habsburg *Barrière de l'Est* and in Poland's place in it. Peter III's alliance with Frederick the Great eliminated the Prussian threat, such as it was, to Russia's western borderlands.

Catherine II's coup of July 1762 caused Frederick some momentary anxiety; but she needed a breathing space to restore order to domestic and financial affairs. The treaty of St Petersburg of 11 April 1764 set up a new Russo-Prussian defensive alliance, to run for eight years in the first instance. A Russian guarantee of Prussian territorial possessions secured Frederick's Silesian booty. In return, Frederick agreed to follow Catherine's choice of candidate for the Polish throne, which had fallen vacant on the death of Augustus III on 5 October 1763. Both parties agreed that they would preserve the Polish constitution intact.[43]

The Wettins' hopes of retaining the Polish throne were blighted by disputes among their supporters and the untimely death of the new elector, Friedrich Christian I, in December 1763 (his successor, Friedrich August III, was only twelve years old). The election

41. There is a comparative dearth of up-to-date literature on eighteenth-century Poland in English. The most accessible account is Lukowski, *Liberty's Folly*. See also R. Frost, 'The nobility of Poland-Lithuania, 1569–1795', in Scott, ed., *The European nobilities*, II, pp. 183–222.

42. [W. Rzewuski], *Myśli o niezawodnym utrzymaniu Sejmów y Liberi Veto . . . 1764* [unpaginated]; S. Majchrowicz SJ, *Trwałość szczęśliwa królestw albo ich smutny upadek . . .* (Lwów, 1764), II, pp. 295–6.

43. W. Stribrny, *Die Russlandpolitik Friedrichs des Grossen 1764–1786* (Würzburg, 1966), pp. 9–15. Text of the treaty of St Petersburg of 11 April 1764 and the separate Convention of 24 April on the election of a Polish monarch in *CTS* XLIII, pp. 3–25.

by over 5,000 nobles of Catherine's preferred candidate, Stanisław Poniatowski, with some 14,000 Russian troops in the offing, duly followed on 6 September 1764.[44]

Rumours washed around Europe that Russia and Prussia intended to exploit the interregnum in order to acquire Polish territory. They were false. During the winter of 1763–64 both Catherine and Frederick could assure the Poles that no such plan existed. The gossip encouraged Maria Antonia Walpurgis, electress-dowager of Saxony, to suggest to Maria Theresa that Austria and Saxony, too, should be cut in on any such deal, which ought to provide for hereditary Wettin succession in what remained of Poland. Vienna showed no interest. It was reconciled to Poniatowski's election. Like Russia and Prussia, its priority lay in reconstruction after the Seven Years War.[45]

44. The best account of the interregnum remains S. Askenazy, *Die letzte polnische Königswahl* (Göttingen, 1894).

45. Declarations by Russia, 27 December 1763 and Prussia, 22 January 1764, delivered to the Polish primate, Władysław Łubieński, *Les partages de la Pologne et la lutte pour l'indépendance. Recueil des actes diplomatiques, traités et documents*, ed. K. Lutostański (Lausanne, 1918), pp. 4–6. Solov'ev, *IR* XXVIII, pp. 376–7.

CHAPTER TWO

The breakdown of reform

The new king and the new empress

After his election in May 1764, the new Polish king took the middle
name 'August' after that renovator of ancient Rome, the Emperor
Augustus. There, the resemblance largely ended. True, in September
1766, Antonio Visconti, the papal nuncio in Warsaw, observed that
the monarch

> possesses talent, ability and above all, an ardent desire to reform in
> one day (if only he could) the entire country and the whole nation,
> to raise it to the level of other, more cultivated nations.[1]

But Stanisław August was never master in his own house. His father,
also Stanisław, had had as distinguished a political career as Polish
conditions allowed, but he was closely tied to the much more powerful Czartoryski family: his brother-in-law, August, palatine of Ruś,
was one of the wealthiest landowners in Europe; another brother,
Michael, was Grand Chancellor of Lithuania. The younger Stanisław
Poniatowski was a member of a middling noble family whose aspirations would normally have not gone beyond senatorial office. His
uncles had only grudgingly reconciled themselves to their nephew's
royal candidature. August Czartoryski had hoped that he himself or
his own son, Adam Kazimierz, might stand. The Czartoryskis had
long envisaged major reforms – conditional on establishing their own
dominance over the *Rzeczpospolita*. These ambitions made the 'Familia',
as the Czartoryskis and their satellites were known, suspect to the

---

1. Visconti to cardinal Luigi Maria Torrigiani, secretary of state at the Vatican, 24
Sept. 1766, in A. Theiner, ed., *Vetera Monumenta Poloniae et Lithuaniae gentiumque
finitimarum historiam illustrantia* (Rome, 1864), IV, p. 96.

great majority of the *szlachta*. Aware that for all their wealth and resources, they were too weak to sweep aside their conservative opponents, the Czartoryskis had, early in the reign of Augustus III, accepted the need for an informal alliance with Russia. Their nephew, Stanisław Poniatowski, was not their choice for the Polish throne but the choice of Catherine the Great.

She knew him well, rather better than he knew her. In 1755 he had accompanied the British ambassador, Sir Charles Hanbury-Williams, to St Petersburg as his private secretary; he was back, from January 1757 to July 1758, for part of the time as the official representative of Augustus III. During his first stay, the Grand Duchess Catherine had taken him as a lover; after his second departure, she turned to the somewhat rougher charms of Grigorii Orlov. Although her old flame had not concealed from her his hopes of reviving Poland through the abolition of its veto under his hereditary kingship, Catherine did not doubt that Poniatowski was, for her purposes, 'un sujet . . . convenable'.[2]

Since the reign of Peter the Great, Russia's had been the dominant influence in Poland. The *Rzeczpospolita*'s anarchy did not make for easy management. Economy and expediency dictated a more orderly vassal – to make it useful, without its being a threat.[3] Catherine II was much drawn to the foreign policy ideas of her privy councillor, Nikita Panin, who actively pushed for the setting up of a 'Northern System', a net of alliances with Prussia, Denmark, Sweden and Great Britain under the Russian aegis. Although the ramifications of this unwieldy scheme have yet to be fully explored, it was in part designed to provide external security after the collapse of the Austrian alliance at the end of the Seven Years War, while simultaneously assuring Russia of hegemonic influence in north European affairs. Poland had its own, emphatically subordinate place in this scheme: a bridgehead and transit route which would allow Russia to extend its influence into the Holy Roman Empire; and a convenient passage into the Balkans in the inevitable future settling of scores with the Ottoman Porte.[4]

2. J. Fabre, *Stanislas-Auguste Poniatowski et l'Europe des Lumières* (Paris, 1952), pp. 213–24. Catherine II to Frederick II, 6/17 Oct. 1763, *SIRIO* XX, pp. 177–8.

3. Victor Solms von Sonnenwalde, Prussian ambassador in St Petersburg, to Frederick II, 9 Nov. 1764, *PC* XXIV, 15 329.

4. D.M. Griffiths, 'The rise and fall of the Northern System', *Canadian Slavic Studies* 4 (1970), pp. 547–69; R.E. Jones, 'Opposition to war and expansion in late eighteenth century Russia', *Jahrbücher für Geschichte Osteuropas* 32 (1984), pp. 37–42. On Poland's utility in a future conflict with Turkey, see Panin to Repnin, 29 Nov./ 9 Dec. 1767, *SIRIO* LXVII, pp. 516–17, 520.

Poland's weaknesses also held out the alluring prospect of cheap successes to compensate for the failures of the Seven Years War and bolster Catherine's own uncertain domestic position. The Election Sejm of 27 August–8 September 1764 recognised her as 'Empress of all Russia', 'Imperatrix totius Russiae' – a title which the Commonwealth had hitherto consistently withheld from the tsars, on the grounds that it could be construed to admit any claims they might advance to Polish–Lithuanian territories with Russian-speaking populations.[5] Naturally, Catherine sought more than diplomatic courtesies. She demanded better protection for Poland's Orthodox minority against religious harassment; she expected her Polish clients to seek a Russian guarantee of their form of government; and she wanted a territorial settlement. In November 1763, the acting president of the College of War, Zachar Chernyshev, urged 'a rounding off' of the border with Poland along the Dvina and upper Dnieper rivers, which, in sum, would have secured all the territories which Russia was to acquire in 1772; Catherine and her advisers modified Chernyshev's proposals to 'all Polish Livonia', by which they seem to have meant the territories north of the river Dvina, supposedly as compensation for her military support of Poniatowski. There was no suggestion of sharing Polish territory with anyone else.[6] The Coronation Sejm gratifyingly nominated the members of a commission to finalise a frontier demarcation, but the commission was never to be convened.[7]

For all her hopes of an early revision of the frontier, Catherine could not prevent her other objectives from getting in the way. If the Polish vassal state were to be useful, Catherine had little choice but to accept some political reforms. She and Panin acquiesced in the seemingly minor changes introduced by the first Sejm to meet immediately after Augustus's death, the Convocation Sejm of 7 May–23 June 1764. Their thrust was to improve administration at the centre: treasury commissions, taking all decisions by majority vote, were set up for the Crown and for Lithuania. Analogous commissions were created for the Crown and Lithuanian armies; their commanders, the *hetmani*, were reduced to little more than

5. *VL* VII, pp. 16–17, 96. The official Russian declarations on this matter carried assurances that no such claims were intended, ibid. The Poles likewise gave official recognition for the first time to Frederick the Great's title of 'King in Prussia', ibid., p. 17.

6. Instruction of 11/22 Nov. 1763 to the joint ambassadors to Poland, Hermann von Keyserling and Nicholas Repnin, *SIRIO* LI, pp. 92–101. For Chernyshev's proposal of 21 Nov. 1763, see Solov'ev, *IR* XXV, p. 241.

7. *VL* VII p. 158, cf. p. 285.

figurehead chairmen. In this way, an important first step was taken to introducing order into the Commonwealth's finances and accountable management into its armed forces. Such measures were only possible because the Czartoryski-headed reform grouping was able to act within the framework of a General Confederacy. That they passed the Convocation Sejm in the first place was probably due to the compliance of the ailing senior Russian ambassador, Hermann von Keyserling, who enjoyed a long-standing friendship with the Czartoryskis (Keyserling was to die in post on 30 September 1764) and the inexperience of his junior partner (and Panin's nephew), Nikolai Repnin.

Poniatowski and his uncles were fully aware of Russian objections to major reform. Where they deluded themselves was in the belief that they could somehow circumvent their Russian backers. For a time, they succeeded. It was to be another two years before Repnin (or for that matter, most observers) came to appreciate the significance of a tortuous and obscure formula inserted into the Convocation Sejm's legislation on the Crown treasury commission: the Sejm would decide all bills and other materials submitted by the commission, 'arising from whatever circumstances' '*figura iudiciaria*' – 'in the manner of the courts'.[8] And where courts had a panel of judges, they decided by majority vote. Thus did the reformers hope to embark on the surreptitious dismantling of the *liberum veto*. It was a formula that could remain hidden only for as long as it was not used.

Frederick the Great and Polish reform

The significance of the wording also escaped Frederick the Great – but the direction of the Poniatowski government's intentions did not. In Poland, Frederick was Catherine's uncomfortable junior partner. Her alliance had saved him from international isolation, but at a price: Catherine and Panin expected him to co-operate with the plans for their 'Northern System'. Frederick was adamantly opposed to any widening of a purely bilateral agreement, for additional alliance partners could only reduce his own influence on Russia. He was prepared to fall in with Russian ambitions in Poland – provided that no substantive political changes were introduced in the Commonwealth. His treaty of alliance with Russia of 11 April 1764 bound both powers to uphold the existing Polish constitution,

8. Ibid., p. 20.

to work together for a widening of the rights of Poland's Protestants and Orthodox and to follow Russia's lead in supporting the
election of Stanisław Poniatowski.[9] When he learned that Panin was
amenable to Polish arguments to restrict the *liberum veto* to single
bills, he was furious. This was no mere 'bagatelle' – it would be the
first step to the overthrow of the Commonwealth's constitution, in
time making it a danger to its neighbours, not least to Russia.
Poland's other neighbours, Turkey and Austria, would also object
on the same grounds. He heaved a sigh of relief when Catherine
declared herself convinced by his arguments.[10]

Frederick remained watchful. The Convocation Sejm had enacted
a general duty on all imports and exports, a measure which would
have boosted revenues sevenfold in comparison with existing customs and given the government a real measure of financial independence. That of course was why Frederick opposed it. Where the
river Vistula – the principal artery of Polish trade – touched the
East Prussian border at Marienwerder, he constructed in March
1765 a fortified customs house, manned by 200 soldiers with 10
cannon. They were to sink any vessels which would not submit to
payment of duties of between 10 and 33 per cent on the values of
their cargoes (by contrast, the Polish general duty was levied at
rates of between 2 and 12 per cent). He found an all too characteristic pretext in the treaty of Wehlau of 1657, which had specified
that all new customs duties in the Polish and East Prussian areas
were to be negotiated by common consent. The affair was submitted
to Catherine's mediation: her ruling of March 1766 was simple, but
crippling to Poland. Frederick was to stop his exactions and the
Poles were to abandon their general duty. There was no room for a
Rzeczpospolita which would decide its own policies within the Northern System.[11]

Protestants and Orthodox

It was the religious question which gave Russia and Prussia the
greatest cause for concern, though for rather different reasons.

9. Full text of the treaty of St Petersburg of 31 March/11 April 1764 in *CTS*
XLIII, pp. 3–25. The alliance was to run for eight years.
10. Solms to Frederick II, St Petersburg, 18 Sept., 9 Nov. 1764, *PC* XXIV, 15 267,
15 329. Frederick II to Solms, Potsdam, 6 Oct., 27 Nov., 6, 31 Dec. 1764, ibid., 15
267, 15 329, 15 341, 15 377.
11. J.K. Hoensch, 'Der Streit um den polnischen Generalzoll 1764–1766', *Jahrbücher
für Geschichte Osteuropas* NF 18 (1970), pp. 356–88.

Agitation on behalf of the overwhelmingly peasant Orthodox population was conducted almost single-handedly by bishop Iurii Konisski
of Mohylew. He was less interested in political rights and more
concerned with recovering ground lost over the previous hundred
years or so to the Polish Greek Catholic clergy. Konisski, as a com-
moner and a Russian subject, had no personal expectations of
office in Poland – non-Latin bishops had never been admitted into
the Senate. There were those among the Orthodox community
who actively encouraged the empress to think in terms of intervention by annexation of Polish territory. It is impossible to be sure if
Konisski was one of them, but he certainly spent sufficiently long
periods in St Petersburg to be regarded with grave suspicion in
Warsaw. Catherine expected him, as her loyal subject, to do as he
was told.[12] Given the hopelessly inferior social position of almost
all the Orthodox, the empress's efforts on behalf of the religious
minorities shifted inexorably towards the Protestants. They may have
been few in numbers, with perhaps half-a-dozen families at most
actively pressing to restore the rights they had enjoyed at the height
of the Reformation, but they enjoyed powerful connexions. The
Goltz family, in particular, had marital links to the Courland nobility, not least to the Keyserlings; and through the Courland nobility,
they had links to St Petersburg. Catherine was prepared to champion
them because Protestantism was a cause in which Frederick the
Great's interest and support could be aroused. More importantly,
she needed a resounding propaganda coup to convince enlightened
opinion abroad that she was something more than a murderous
usurper. She would be patient, up to a point. She was even prepared
to swallow not only the outright rejection of all religious concessions by the Sejmy of 1764, but even the additional restrictions
which they imposed. Her priority was, after all, to establish her
'sujet convenable' on the Polish throne. But she looked to significant progress on the dissenters' behalf from the 1766 Sejm.

Catherine brushed aside all attempts by the king and her ambassador to fudge the issue. In September 1766 she peremptorily demanded unfettered public freedom of worship for Protestants and
Orthodox; the election of dissenters to the Chamber of Envoys and
to the Tribunals; the opening of all other noble offices to them.
Her sole concession was to accept their continued exclusion from
the Senate and the *hetman*ships. Yet, as Repnin repeatedly warned
her, there was no prospect of the *szlachta* ever accepting such a

12. M.C. Łubieńska, *Sprawa dysydencka 1764–1766* (Kraków, 1911), pp. 6–17, 48–64.

settlement voluntarily. The great majority of the *sejmiki* of August 1766 rejected all suggestion of relaxation of dissenter laws – only a few assemblies where royal electoral influence was strong stood out against the trend. Bishop Kajetan Sołtyk of Kraków, an inveterate opponent of the new regime and a strong supporter of a Wettin restoration, led nationwide clerical agitation against all concessions. Yet despite the religious hysteria, the Sejm of October–December 1766 was to be a botched opportunity for Russia. Had Catherine been prepared to take what even her ally, Frederick, accepted as a reasonable attitude over the dissenters, she could have had a settlement.

Sołtyk was a politician, not a fanatic. He had happily worked with Protestant favourites under Augustus III, and even reproached the anti-Protestant zeal of his parish clergy. He was quite prepared to fish for Russian support. On 29 November, the very last day of the Sejm, it was at his behest that the Catholic bishops agreed to adopt a set of guidelines on relations between Catholics and dissenters which would have both formalised the existing status quo and could have been presented to the outside world as evidence of the efficacy of Catherine's 'enlightened' intervention. There were, it is true, weaknesses: the document was a code of practice for bishops and parish clergy and, though approved by the Sejm, it was not formally endorsed as law. Freedom of worship within the existing laws was reaffirmed; dissenters could repair and maintain, but not enlarge, existing churches, where these had been legally constructed; they could conduct their services discreetly in private houses; burials in Protestant churchyards and repairs to churches would require a licence from the Catholic bishop; Protestants (as opposed to Orthodox) were still expected to marry before Catholic clergy – but Protestants and Orthodox clergy could conduct their own christenings and burial services, provided that the fees charged on these occasions were paid to the local Catholic clergy (who were forbidden to demand higher fees than they would of their own parishioners). While this ostensibly gave the Catholic episcopate a strong controlling hand over Protestant life, theoretically at least it curbed the role of Catholic parish clergy, who were those most likely to get involved in disputes with the Protestants. Catholic clergy were not allowed to impose any fees on Protestants or Orthodox beyond those specified in the guidelines. The document endorsed the law of 1632 which reserved jurisdiction over Protestant clergy to the lay courts. Denmark's minister in Warsaw, Armand de Saint-Saphorin, who had seconded the Russian and Prussian demands, thought the bishops' articles accorded 'full toleration and protect[ed] them [Protestants] from abuses'. Frederick the Great, who heartily wished that Russia would drop the matter, argued that no one was actually disturbing the dissenters. Too favourable a settlement threatened to rob Frederick himself of immigrants at a time when he was desperately trying to reconstruct the Prussian economy.[13]

Political reaction, religious intervention

The dominating issue of the 1766 Sejm did not, however, prove to be the dissenters. For it was only during the course of this Sejm that Catherine and Panin came to realise how far their 'sujet convenable', Poniatowski, was pursuing his own ambitious reform agenda. There was strong concern in Poland at the continued activity of the General Confederacy of 1764. As a precautionary measure, the king and his uncles resolved on a clarification of the Convocation law which submitted all bills from the Treasury Commissions to decisions by majority vote. It was a mistake. Sołtyk's ally, Jerzy Mniszech, marshal of the Crown court, warned the Russian ambassador that the new bill would allow legislation on any issue to be passed by a simple majority, provided it came from the treasury commissions. A furious Repnin, seconded by the equally alarmed Prussian resident, Gedéon Benoît, warned the king that Russian forces would tear Warsaw down 'stone by stone' if the measure were passed. Everything, including the religious issue, was sacrificed to the priority of shoring up the *liberum veto*.

The king wanted to resist. When the Czartoryskis warned that it was pointless, he had to go along. Poland, after all, had no army worth the name and no allies. But the Russians went further. Mniszech's client, Michał Wielhorski, went on to propose the restoration, in full, of the *liberum veto*. The Chamber of Envoys agreed only under duress. Its members appreciated the destructive nature of the untrammelled veto, even if they may have been unclear about the alternatives. Repnin took the further precaution of ensuring that at the Sejm's last sitting – the same one to which the bishops submitted their guidelines on the dissenters – the now discredited

13. St Saphorin to Bernstorff, 10 Dec. 1766, Rigsarchivet, Copenhagen, MS TKUA Polen AIII45 (microfilm copy, AGAD). Frederick II to Solms, 28, 31 Dec. 1766, *PC* XXV, 16 418, 16 423; 19 Jan. 1767, ibid., XXVI, 16 454.

General Confederacy was dissolved. The military and treasury commissions remained the sole significant survivors of the 1764 reforms. Otherwise, Poland's constitution had, if anything, become even more anarchic. From Russia's point of view, Poland remained as unmanageable as ever.

The Russian response was to form a new series of confederacies. In March 1767, the Protestant nobility of Polish Prussia set up one such league in defence of their rights at Thorn; on the same day, the Protestants of Lithuania and the sole available Orthodox notable, bishop Konisski of Mohylew, formed a similar association at Słuck. Neither confederacy initially attracted more than three hundred signatories. The Protestant-dominated towns of Royal Prussia acceded only under threat of Russian military occupation. The confederacies caused outrage among the Catholic *szlachta*. In January 1767, the Czartoryskis had warned St Petersburg that it would be political suicide for them to co-operate with Russian policy.[14]

The Russians turned to the Family's opponents. By an imaginative combination of promises, bribery and intimidation, they were able to assemble an unwieldy coalition of disparate bigwigs, united largely by a loathing of Poniatowski and his uncles and a yearning for the supposedly fat, comfortable years of Augustus III. At Wilno, in Lithuania, on 2 June and at Radom, in the Crown, on 23 June, Repnin secured the Catholic confederacies without which no Sejm could pass legislation. The malcontent leaders hoped to generate enough momentum to carry the Russians on the dismantling of the new order. In fact, many *szlachta* subscribed to the Lithuanian and Crown confederacies under the impression that they would resist and punish the dissenters' demands. When the principal Crown Confederacy was set up at Radom on 23 June, the participants were brought to support the dissenters' demands only when Russian troops trained their artillery on them. In the meantime, Stanisław August secretly agreed to co-operate with Repnin, or at least not to oppose him, in return for the preservation of the remaining reforms enacted during the interregnum and the preservation of his own position. The malcontents persuaded themselves that the king had somehow suborned the ambassador and, if only they could get to Catherine in St Petersburg, they would be able to bring her round to their point of view.[15]

14. G.[J.]T. Lukowski, *The szlachta and the Confederacy of Radom, 1764–1767/68: a study of the Polish nobility* (= *Antemurale*, 21) (Rome, 1977), pp. 68–71.

15. Ibid., chs 3–7.

The Delegation Sejm: a flawed settlement

The explosive mixture of double-dealing and wishful thinking came to a head at the confederated Sejm of October 1767–March 1768. The Russians insisted that it should first regulate the question of the dissenters; it would then go on to deal with the form of government; and last, but not least, the Sejm would settle the question of the Polish–Russian border. In order to get this package of measures through, the Sejm was expected to agree to a constitutional novelty: it would bestow plenipotentiary powers on a 'Delegation', a core of some eighty senators and envoys drawn from across the political spectrum, whom the ambassador would bully or bribe into compliance. While the Delegation remained in session, the main body of the Sejm would be adjourned, reconvening only to rubber-stamp the Delegation's decisions. The measures approved would then be enshrined in a treaty between Russia and Poland, which Russia would underwrite with its solemn guarantee.[16] The transformation of the *Rzeczpospolita* into Russia's dependency would be complete.

Bishop Sołtyk resumed his agitation. Still resolutely hostile to Poniatowski, he was ready to co-operate with Russia if it would restore the Wettins, but, like so many Poles, he was genuinely alarmed at the implications of a Russian guarantee. He clung to the fiction that Repnin had in some way been suborned by the king into straying from the empress's instructions.[17] This belief received a brutal jolt on the night of 13 October. Russian troops arrested Sołtyk and three others prominent in their opposition to religious concessions: Andrzej Załuski, bishop of Kiev, Wacław Rzewuski, field-*hetman* of the Crown and his son, Seweryn. Within a few days, they were on their way under armed escort to Russia. They were to be released from their captivity in the town of Kaluga only in January 1773.[18]

The extraordinary Sejm had begun proceedings on 5 October. Despite the presence of 10,000 Russian troops around the capital, the great majority of envoys and senators were utterly hostile to the plenipotentiary Delegation. The arrests of 13 October broke opposition, but they were felt as a searing national humiliation. On 19 October the cowed Sejm agreed to set up the Delegation. Some of

16. Panin to Repnin, 14/25 Aug., 22 Aug./2 Sept., 21 Sept./2 Oct. 1767, *SIRIO* LXVII, pp. 417, 433, 462–3.
17. Panin to F.S. Potocki and J.Kl. Branicki, Moscow, 30 Sept./11 Oct. 1767, ibid., pp. 485–6, 488–9.
18. For an accessible account of the whole affair, see Lukowski, *The szlachta*, pp. 211–19.

its members were Russian stooges, others made genuine efforts to resist. Realistically, there was little they could do: Repnin pointed to the fate of Sołtyk and his companions whenever he encountered obstruction.

The bill detailing the concessions to the dissenters received the Delegates' signatures on 1 December. The primacy of Roman Catholicism as the state religion was acknowledged; non-Catholics were barred from the throne. Virtually all discriminatory legislation against dissenters and Orthodox was repealed: their nobility were declared 'competent to hold all offices of the Crown and the Grand Duchy of Lithuania', their townsmen were to enjoy 'full equality' with Roman Catholic townsmen. Persons 'of rural condition' would remain under the nobility's patrimonial jurisdiction, but were not to be harassed on religious grounds. Non-Catholics could restore and erect churches, schools and seminaries. They could maintain synodal or consistorial organisations. Mixed marriages could be conducted before clergy of any denomination; male children were to be brought up in the faith of the father, daughters in that of the mother. All trace of Catholic ecclesiastical jurisdiction over Protestants and Orthodox was removed. All disputes arising out of religious issues were to be heard by a *iudicium mixtum*, a 'mixed court' of Catholics and non-Catholics, under the *ex officio* presidency of the Orthodox bishop of Mohylew.

All in all, Poland received the most comprehensive, statutory enactment of religious toleration of any state in Europe. But Catherine and Panin accepted the need to keep any undesirable effects of such a policy in check. They remained alive to the supposed threat of Protestantism's creating an enlightened citizenry and to the incentives that Russian Orthodox serfs might receive to flee to Poland. Apostasy from Catholicism remained a crime, punishable by permanent banishment, to be judged not by the *iudicium mixtum*, but by the Crown and Lithuanian Tribunals.[19]

A new constitutional settlement was ready by 24 February 1768. Though Repnin was as brutally determined as ever to secure what the Russian court wanted, there is no doubt that in providing for a minimal degree of orderly, if emasculated, rule, the so-called 'Second Separate Act' met the aspirations of many Poles who wished to combine the preservation of the exuberant riot of *szlachta* prerogatives with the removal of the worst excesses of the old anarchy. Its

19. Text of the legislation (in Polish and Latin) in *VL* VII, pp. 256–76. Panin to Repnin, 14/25 Aug. 1767, *SIRIO* LXVII, pp. 409–10 articulates Russian reservations most explicitly.

principal architect was the primate, Gabriel Podoski. The concept of 'cardinal laws', reaching back at least to the 1650s, received formal codification for the first time. These were to be immutable – 'at no time, under any pretext, by anyone, not even by Confederacies or during interregna, nor by unanimity, may they be amended or changed'. The legislative power resided in the three estates of the Sejm – king, senators and 'knights'. Catholicism was reaffirmed as the ruling religion; and only a Catholic could be king. The old rules on royal elections were reaffirmed: they could not take place during the lifetime of a monarchic incumbent and were to be conducted by unanimity. Ordinary and extraordinary Sejmy were not to prolong their sessions beyond six and two weeks respectively, without the unanimous agreement of the participants. The key *szlachta* privilege of freedom from arrest without due process was reaffirmed. The nobility retained the right to withdraw obedience from the monarch if he attempted to infringe the cardinal laws or his *pacta conventa*. On the other hand, the 'cardinal laws' included some enlightened novelties: although noble jurisdiction over their serfs was restated, seigneurs lost their right to pass life and death sentences – such cases would now be heard in the local courts. Malicious killings of serfs by nobles were no longer to be 'punished' by fines but by death. The new religious settlement was incorporated into the cardinal laws.

Those laws also reaffirmed the *liberum veto* – but its application was limited to a specified range of issues known as 'materiae status' – matters of state. Taxes, tariffs, alliances, treaties, the size of the army, ennoblements, declarations of war and peace, creation of new offices, official exchange rates, the powers of the Senate and the Sejm's own standing orders – all remained subject to the veto. All business not falling within the cardinal laws or *materiae status* fell under the heading of 'economic matters' – *materye ekonomiczne*. In future, Sejmy were to settle these before moving on to any *materiae status*. Although the use of the *liberum veto* would bring an end to any further legislative discussion, the agreed 'economic matters' would remain in force.[20] The treaty of Warsaw, signed by the Delegation with Repnin on 24 February, contained a mutual guarantee of Poland's and Russia's European possessions and Russia's guarantee of the new Polish constitutional and religious arrangements, appended in two 'Separate Acts'.[21] On 5 March, the full Sejm ratified the Delegation's work almost without discussion. The Confederacy

20. Text of the Second Separate Act and the new standing orders, *VL* VII, pp. 276–85, 288–92.
21. Ibid., pp. 250–6.

of Radom and the dissenters' confederacies formally dissolved themselves on 6 March.

Of the 1764 reforms, only the army and treasury commissions
survived intact. The *materiae status*, Stanisław August complained, were
'so numerous and so important as to comprise everything essential
to the conduct of all government'. This left Poland scarcely more
'useful' to Russia than at the death of Augustus III. Such were the
fruits of a policy fraught with contradictions. Panin and Catherine
wanted a reliable Protestant agency within the Commonwealth – but
although the non-Catholic nobility now enjoyed theoretically equal
rights with Catholics, no machinery existed to ensure that they would
actually be appointed to office or returned to the Sejm. Panin and
Catherine did not want the Protestants to spearhead 'enlightenment'
in Poland – the Protestant leaders complained at the affirmation of
the apostasy laws. Panin and Catherine did not want to see any more
Russian Orthodox peasant runaways to Poland – Konisski complained
that nothing had been done to restore the Orthodox church's old
bishoprics and that St Petersburg seemed more interested in politics
than religion. Protestant artisans and traders complained that the
settlement only benefited nobles.[22]

Territorial changes seemed little closer. Catherine's overriding
priority was domestic: it lay in the quest for a reform platform, in
the complex shape of the great Legislative Commission which she
had called to Moscow in July 1767. Territorial negotiations with the
Poles could only prolong a fractious complication which distracted
her from more pressing business at home. Worse, they threatened
to bring about undesirable international repercussions.

Turkey's attitude gave grave cause for concern. The Porte had
looked askance at Russian activity in Poland since the interregnum,
when it feared that Russia would endorse innovations which would
turn Poland into an effective anti-Ottoman ally. Panin was anxious
to assuage all suspicions of any ulterior motives beyond helping the
religious minorities and settling the constitution: he ordered Repnin
to ensure that the Sejm did not drag on into the spring. In January,
the Russian minister in Constantinople, Alexei Obreskov, pressed
by the Turks, lost his nerve and gave assurances that Russian troops
would leave Poland as soon as the Sejm was over. Once again, the
frontier issue was shelved, although Catherine and Panin managed
to leave the door open to a future revision, notwithstanding their
guarantee of Poland's territorial integrity.

22. Lukowski, *The szlachta*, pp. 254–5.

The basis of that guarantee remained the 'perpetual' treaty of Moscow of 1686, including its provision for a future finalisation of the borders. And, at the Russian behest, the Delegation Sejm renewed the December 1764 statute setting up a frontier commission.[23] That the Russians had no intention of forgetting their territorial aspirations was demonstrated in July and early August 1767. For a period of some six weeks, detailed and extensive surveys were conducted by Russian officers and their cossack escorts of the Polish lands north of the river Dvina. Repnin appears to have had no prior knowledge of the surveys, which were authorised by Zachar Chernyshev's College of War. Panin and his ambassador tried to reassure the Poles that their officers were conducting standard military procedures associated with army supply, but the instructions to the surveyors went far beyond this. They were to draw up accurate summaries of landownership, property relations, agricultural and forestry resources, revenues, population and topography. Where local landowners would not co-operate, they were threatened with military reprisals. The Russian officers turned to Jews, peasants and the Orthodox clergy for information. The nobility of the palatinate of Połock sent panic-stricken pleas for reassurance to the king and the Confederacy of Radom. The surveys were halted in mid-August, perhaps so as not to cause even more alarm at the already touchy *sejmiki*. The growing indignation over Russian demands on the dissenters swamped the impact of the news of these surveys, but they must have furnished the Russians with valuable information about the lands they found so interesting.[24]

Panin himself tacitly acknowledged the shortcomings of the settlement. He urged Repnin to drag out the troop withdrawals for as long as possible, perhaps even long enough to ensure that there would still be troops in Poland in August 1768, when the elections to the next ordinary Sejm were due. If the Poles continued to prove difficult over returning dissenter envoys or over other matters, then a fresh Confederacy could be set up.[25] In other words, Russia would be back to square one.

23. On Turkish fears, see especially Panin to Repnin, 22 Dec. 1767/2 Jan. 1768, *SIRIO* LXVII, pp. 566–7; 29 Jan./9 Feb. 1768, ibid., pp. 20–1. On the frontier commission, Panin to Repnin, 22 Dec. 1767/2 Jan. 1768, ibid., p. 565 and *VL* VII, pp. 253, 285.
24. J.T. Lukowski, 'Guarantee or annexation: a note on Russian plans to acquire Polish territory prior to the First Partition of Poland', *Bulletin of the Institute of Historical Research* 56, no. 133 (1983), pp. 60–5.
25. Panin to Repnin, 29 Jan./9 Feb. 1768, *SIRIO* LXXXVII, pp. 20–2.

Repercussions: the Confederacy of Bar and war with Turkey

The reality proved worse. 'You cannot order a parliament around as though it were a regiment', Stanisław August once tried to convince the Russians.[26] From St Petersburg, Poland was an effete political entity which ought to be grateful for the exertions Russia was making to bring some order to its anarchy. For all the overbearing contact Russia had had with Poland since the reign of Peter the Great, it had never attempted to get as intimately involved with the Commonwealth's internal politics as it did after 1763. There was little understanding of the genuine depth of attachment among the *szlachta* to the rights and privileges which Catherine and Panin were trying to manipulate in the name of toleration and humanity. It is true that the king and the reformers were utterly naive in thinking that, once brought to power with Russian backing, they could somehow behave as if they could dispense with or hoodwink their uncomfortable patrons; but it was equally unrealistic of St Petersburg to refuse to accept that there were limits to how far the king and his uncles could give the lead to a fractious public noble opinion, especially in the religious sphere. 'Public opinion', on the Polish scale, was simply unknown in Russia. Repnin had tried to warn the empress and her minister, but had been ignored: soldier that he was, he got on with obeying orders.

The results of these parade ground methods in a state which revelled in its republican traditions were soon felt. On 6 March, the day after the Delegation Sejm closed, news reached Warsaw that on 29 February, at Bar, in the Polish Ukraine, a new Confederacy had been set up by disgruntled nobles determined to defend the Catholic faith and their ancient rights and liberties. Its founding father, insofar as it had one, Adam Krasiński, bishop of Kamieniec Podolski, envisaged the dethronement of Poniatowski, an elective monarchy within the Wettin dynasty, an increase in the army and, beyond that, only the vaguest programme of fiscal and constitutional reform. He looked to Turkish, French and Saxon backing for his enterprise. He even thought he could win over Frederick the Great. He was horrified when his associates set events in motion when he had

---

26. 'On ne commande pas une diète comme un régiment', Stanisław August to his envoy in St Petersburg, Franciszek Rzewuski, 17 Sept. 1766, ibid., LXVII, no. 1405, p. 125.

barely begun to put out exploratory feelers to his putative backers abroad.[27]

The Confederacy of Bar was a disaster for Poland, which was plunged into four years of guerrilla and near-civil war. Bar's leading circles, able to agree on little beyond the need to remove Poniatowski, were torn by mutual jealousies and given to exuberant self-delusion about the willingness of the outside world to support their cause. Although units of the little Polish army defected to it, it remained essentially an erratic, civilian rising of the *szlachta's levée-en-masse*, the *pospolite ruszenie*. It was badly led and incapable of meeting Russian troops on equal terms. It is unlikely that above 12,000 Poles fought on the Barist side at any one time.[28] On the other hand, this very lack of cohesion made it difficult to destroy. Russia had too few troops in Poland: perhaps 20,000 in March 1768, never more than 26,000 before 1772 and usually barely half that number, woefully few to maintain order in a hostile, resentful country larger than France.[29]

Between April 1768 and July 1769, Russian troops were diverted to help suppress a savage peasant uprising in the Polish Ukraine, in part brought about by unrealistic expectations of an end to exploitation by Polish landlords and Latin and Uniate clergy. St Petersburg's anxiety not to alarm the Porte led to a ban on Russian troops within fifteen miles of the Turkish border with Poland. This self-denial did not last: in June 1768, Russian cossacks subjected the Turkish frontier town of Balta to a four days' sack while supposedly in hot pursuit of their enemies.[30] Choiseul saw a golden opportunity to weaken Russian influence across eastern and northern Europe. He urged Turkey to go on to the offensive. When, on 6 October 1768, Obreskov in Constantinople was unable to give the furious Turks the assurances they demanded of an immediate Russian withdrawal from Poland, he was incarcerated in the castle of the Seven Towers. It was the Porte's way of declaring war.[31]

The conflict that Russia had been so anxious to avoid had now erupted, to be brought to an end only by the treaty of Kutchuk Kainardji on 21 July 1774. Russia's main military effort now focused on the Black Sea, the Balkans, even the Mediterranean. Only the

---

27. W. Konopczyński, *Konfederacja barska*, 2 vols (Warsaw, 1991 edn), I, pp. 32–42, 101; *Konfederacja barska: wybór tekstów*, ed. W. Konopczyński (Kraków, 1928), pp. 3–4, 23–4.
28. Konopczyński, *Konfederacja*, II, p. 842.   29. Ibid., I, pp. 46n., 49, 179–80.
30. Ibid., pp. 119–22.   31. Ibid., pp. 127–8.

poorest quality troops could be spared for Poland. Commanders and men alike viewed duty in Poland as an opportunity for plunder. Some units were so starved of resources that they took to petty trades to keep body and soul together; there were instances of their co-operating with Polish confederates to run local protection rackets.[32] The Confederacy itself claimed to represent the legal government of Poland and insisted on its 'right' to collect all state revenues. The creation of a formal governing body, the 'Generality' (*Generalność*), on 31 October 1769 did nothing to reduce the bickering and the tensions among the discontented magnates who laid claim to 'leadership' (open or clandestine) of the movement. Based in Habsburg territory, first at Biała in Austrian Silesia, from December 1769 at Eperyes in Hungarian Slovakia, and from September 1770 back in Silesia, at Teschen, the Generality enjoyed only as much authority in the lands of the Commonwealth as local confederates and notables thought fit to recognise. On the other hand, a web of official and semi-official agents, from Constantinople to Paris, from Vienna to Potsdam and Dresden, convinced the various Barist leaders that they were an international force to be taken seriously.

The king and his uncles found themselves in an almost impossible dilemma. In March 1768, they had asked for Russian assistance in putting down what seemed to be a localised escapade in political banditry. It rapidly dawned on them that the Barist movement represented a deep-rooted upsurge of feeling, which was by no means confined to opponents of Poniatowski and reform. Repnin and his two successors, prince Mikhail Volkonskii and Caspar von Saldern, took the line that the king and, more importantly, the Czartoryskis, should use their political influence and followings to align themselves wholeheartedly with Russia in the suppression of the Confederacy. Yet this would be to discredit themselves entirely in the eyes of the *szlachta* nation. At the same time, they sensed an opportunity to improve their domestic standing and to undo some of the constitutional damage wreaked by the Delegation Sejm. They repeatedly, and justifiably, warned that unless the Russians would agree to modify the religious settlement and surrender the constitutional guarantee of February 1768, their co-operation would achieve nothing.

These demands were quite unacceptable in St Petersburg. Russia's overriding priority was the successful prosecution of the Turkish war, but, to Catherine, this was no reason to soften her position in Poland.

---

32. See the complaints of the Russian ambassador, Caspar von Saldern, in May and June 1771, quoted in Solov'ev, *IPP*, pp. 479–81; *idem*, *IR* XXVIII, pp. 483–5.

She certainly wanted stable government there, but also malleable government, which would preserve the February 1768 settlement in full. Her plans to acquire the Livonian borderlands were once again necessarily set back, but she still expected the Poles to hand them over when circumstances permitted.[33]

Stanisław August's position was especially difficult. Relations with his uncles had never been easy – ever since his elevation, he had resented their treatment of him almost as an instrument of Czartoryski family ambition. In 1766, they had preferred to mend their fences with Russia rather than backing his (admittedly hopeless) resistance to the restoration of the *liberum veto*. But he needed them more than they needed him: they had the personal wealth and the clientele which he lacked. The Confederates of Bar took particular delight in plundering the extensive royal demesne lands in Lithuania, his chief source of income. Stanisław August had always been dependent on Catherine's financial support – during the years of Bar, even as he argued with Russian ambassadors, he was reduced to soliciting them for funds to keep his court and royal lifeguards in being. Given the men, money and effort which Russia had poured into Poland since 1763, not least in his support, Stanisław (like his uncles) was naive in thinking that Catherine could somehow be made to reverse her policies in Poland. Equally, the empress and Panin were no less unrealistic in their appraisal of what the king and his uncles might be expected to deliver. In this situation, the king and his uncles chose a policy of aloofness, to demonstrate to the *szlachta* that they were not standing shoulder-to-shoulder with Russia.

While the king and even the Czartoryskis were sufficiently impressed by the strength of noble feeling that Bar represented to contemplate the thought of some sort of rapprochement,[34] this attitude found little reflection on the Barist side. Such was the hatred of the king and his family, that confederate hardliners were able to convince themselves that occupation of the estates of Czartoryskis and their allies by Russian troops (aimed at securing their collaboration with Russian policies) was a cunning charade designed to mislead all right-thinking Poles.[35] On 9 April 1770, a group of confederates in Varna, on Turkish territory, issued a declaration of Poniatowski's dethronement, although it was not until 13 October that it was

33. See especially the instructions to ambassadors Mikhail Volkonskii, 31 March/ 11 April 1769, *SIRIO* LXVII, pp. 372–404; and Caspar von Saldern, 5/16 March 1771, *SIRIO* XCVII, pp. 216–28. I. de Madariaga, *Russia in the age of Catherine the Great* (London, 1981), p. 206.
34. Konopczyński, *Konfederacja*, I, p. 358.   35. Ibid., pp. 403–4.

formally endorsed by the Generality.[36] On the night of 3 November 1771, a band of confederates succeeded in kidnapping the king from Warsaw, in the hope of forcing his abdication. A royal servant was killed, another heavily wounded, the king himself cut by a sword blow. Unnerved by their own success, blundering about in the Warsaw fog, most of the assailants fled the scene. Stanisław August talked his way to safety. Astonishingly, confederate leaders continued to delude themselves that monarchic Europe would be sympathetic to their cause.[37]

After a shaky start for Russia in 1769, the Turkish war turned into an almost uninterrupted sequence of victories – in the steppes north of the Black Sea, in the Crimea, in the Balkans, even in the Mediterranean. The progress of Russian arms was hindered, but not stopped, by the plague which began to be carried along their supply-lines from the Balkans in late 1769. By the end of 1772, field marshal Petr Aleksandrovich Rumiantsev had driven the Turks back across the southern bank of the Danube.[38]

European statesmen gave the conflict their rapt attention. From Potsdam, Frederick II looked on the war as a potentially disastrous complication. Not only did he resent paying his heavy annual subsidy of 400,000 roubles (480,000 Thaler – or almost 3 per cent of the Prussian government's gross annual revenues), which he was bound to do under his treaty of alliance of April 1764, he feared the war would suck in France and Austria. He had concluded his Russian alliance not to engage in military adventurism but to preserve peace and allow his territories to recover from the Seven Years War.[39] The Russian onslaught threatened to destroy France's old helpmate, Turkey. In Austria, Maria Theresa, her emperor-son, Joseph II and chancellor Kaunitz feared for Habsburg influence and even for their long-term security in the Balkans.

Polish delusions

A sense of the potential consequences of Russian successes encouraged king and confederates alike in Micawberish hopes that the

36. Ibid., pp. 349–50, 414–18.

37. Ibid., II, pp. 576–9. W. Konopczyński, *Kazimierz Pułaski* (Kraków, 1931), chs 6, 9.

38. For an outline account of the war, see C. Duffy, *Russia's military way to the West: origins and nature of Russian military power 1700–1800* (London, 1981), pp. 168–78. For the plague, see J.T. Alexander, *Catherine the Great: life and legend* (Oxford, 1989), pp. 148–61.

39. W. Stribrny, *Die Russlandpolitik Friedrichs des Grossen 1764–1786* (Würzburg, 1966), pp. 28–31.

international scene was bound to turn up something to their advantage. In truth, the Barists, or at least a fair number of their leaders,
would themselves have come to an accommodation with Russia on
much the same terms as the king – throwing overboard the dissenters
and the guarantee; but at the further price of the king's removal,
and the rescindment of all the reforms surviving from 1764. This
would have set the Russians back even further than an accommodation acceptable to the Family. The Ottoman Porte, France and Austria
were the Barists' greatest hopes; broken little Saxony could offer
only discreet sympathy in the hope that something would happen
to change Russia's (and Prussia's) determination to keep Poniatowski
on the throne. The Turks, when not berating Barist incompetence
and unreliability, offered occasional subsidies and promises of military assistance.

The mere fact that ministers in Vienna or St Petersburg were
prepared to listen to their representations and made vaguely encouraging noises filled these Polish politicians, diplomatic *ingénus*
to a man, with the wildest expectations. Even in January 1772, the
doyen of Barist 'diplomats', Michał Wielhorski, could surmise that,
since Austria had not unequivocally condemned the proclamation
of the interregnum, it was 'at the very least not opposed to our
aims'; such 'indifference and even silence' surely rather betokened
'sincere support'.[40]

It was little better on the reformers' side. The king and his uncles
remained indomitably wedded to the ossified preconception that
an independent Poland was in the general European interest. Sooner
or later, they believed, France and Austria would recognise it to be
to their own advantage to prise off the Russian protectorate. The
near-total lack of a well-established diplomatic corps contributed
enormously to fostering such delusions. Poland had no permanent
representatives stationed in Paris or Vienna, who might have seen
through the non-committally encouraging noises emanating from
their policy-makers. Its representatives in St Petersburg, lacking ambassadorial status, had only limited access to high governing circles.

During the second half of 1769 Stanisław August put out unofficial feelers to Choiseul for French help in shaking off Russia's
protectorate, only for his correspondence to be intercepted by the
Russians. French responses to all such overtures were, at best, evasive. None of the Poles ever appear to have appreciated that France
wanted war, not peace. The duke of Choiseul, minister for foreign

40. Wielhorski to Jerzy Mniszech [Paris], 10 Jan. 1772, B.Cz. 3868, pp. 21–2.

affairs until his sudden dismissal in December 1770, valued Poland
only as a useful diversionary theatre to sap Russian strength and
blunt the edge of offensives against the Porte, and so keep Russia
from becoming a menace to France's ally Austria.[41] To keep Turkey
at war, Choiseul was ready to present it with the Ukrainian territories it had lost to Poland at the peace of Carlowitz in 1699.[42] With
the same end in view, Choiseul was also plotting to see a strong,
absolute monarchy restored in Sweden, not only to remove the
Scandinavian kingdom from the orbit of Russian influence in which
it had languished for years but to see it recover the Baltic territories
lost to Russia in 1721. In January 1770, he appointed captain Charles
François Dumouriez as instructor to the Barist forces, in order to
weld them into a more disciplined and effective fighting force. A
monthly subsidy of 100,000 livres was assigned to Bar. French officers
were encouraged to volunteer as freelances to fight alongside the
Poles. Without this help, the Confederacy might well have ground
to a halt. No wonder that Frederick called Choiseul 'the fire-raiser
of Europe'.[43]

Vienna, by contrast, felt its best interests would be served by
peace. Austrian policy was decided between a never fully unified
triumvirate of Maria Theresa, her son, the emperor Joseph II, and
the chancellor, Anton Wenzel von Kaunitz. Kaunitz and Maria Theresa
could never really reconcile themselves to the loss of Silesia; Joseph
was perhaps more open-minded on the matter. All three also felt
the loss of Russia's alliance all the more keenly because they feared
its military potential. In December 1768, months before Russia's
amazing sequence of victories over the Turks began, Kaunitz suggested another of his disconcerting diplomatic revolutions: Russia
would be checked by an alliance of Austria, Turkey and Prussia
(and, by implication, France). The Poles would be the new cement
between Austria and Prussia – for Poland would be made to relin-
quish Polish Prussia and the duchy of Courland to Frederick, who
would then restore to Austria upper Silesia and the strategically
important county of Glatz, uncomfortably wedged into Bohemia.

This impracticable scheme, dismissed by Joseph with flattering
sarcasm, was never put to Frederick. The emperor himself would
have preferred a restoration of the Russian alliance. Yes, Russia was
a dangerous power, even as a friend, but an intact Poland would

41. Konopczyński, *Konfederacja*, I, pp. 123, 132.   42. Ibid., p. 211.
43. Ibid., pp. 366–70. T. Cegielski and Ł. Kądziela, *Rozbiory Polski 1772–1793–
1795* (Warsaw, 1990), pp. 118–19.

keep it at a comfortable arm's length.[44] For as long as Russia had the upper hand over the Turks, Vienna's triumvirate adopted a wait-and-see policy of encouraging Stanisław August's hopes and those of his opponents of its support. The king's younger brother, Andrzej Poniatowski, a serving general in the Austrian army, proved a most useful, if unwitting, conduit for Austrian disinformation to the Polish court. The confederates, provided they behaved themselves, were allowed to cross into Austrian territory, even to the extent of the Generality's being permitted to establish its headquarters on Habsburg soil; occasional subsidies were paid out; the emperor Joseph II even deigned to pay a friendly visit to the Generality's base at Eperyes in June 1770. It was all an inexpensive way of sending signals to Russia of Austrian concern at its advances.[45] The international tensions and rivalries that had helped to preserve the Commonwealth for a good century past seemed to be bubbling along as vigorously as ever.

44. D.E.D. Beales, *Joseph II*, I: *In the shadow of Maria Theresa* (Cambridge, 1987), pp. 273–4, 279–82. For an excellent summary of Austrian policy in this period, see ch. 9.
45. Konopczyński, *Konfederacja*, I, pp. 244–6, 314–16, 397; II, pp. 594–5, 650–60. For 'diplomatic' relations between Poland and the European states in the Barist period, see J. Michalski, 'Dyplomacja polska w latach 1764–1795', in *HDP* II, pp. 513–27.

CHAPTER THREE

The First Partition

An uncomfortable alliance

In November 1768, penning his second 'Political Testament', Frederick the Great savoured anew his 'rêverie politique' of acquiring Polish Prussia. The Seven Years War had frustrated his territorial ambitions, just as it had those of Russia and Austria. Though all three had yet to recover from the damage of that conflict, each, in the prevailing atmosphere of international suspicion, was wary of anything that might bring new strength and resources to the others.[1] Frederick's 'rêverie' was a dream for a far-off future. Poland remained Russia's private bailiwick.[2] Frederick wanted to stay clear of its troubles. He stationed troops along his borders to keep stray confederates at bay, but, in that very month, he rejected a suggestion from Panin that he should send forces into the Commonwealth to cover for Russian troops diverted to the Balkans. He was not prepared to do anything which might encourage the escalation of what he regarded as a wholly unnecessary and dangerous conflict.[3] But he kept an eye on the main chance, ready to fly the occasional diplomatic kite.

There was a way of releasing the tensions that he foresaw would accumulate between Prussia and Russia on one side and Austria on the other. The three powers could sink their differences at the expense of Poland and help themselves to extensive slices of its

---

1. P.W. Schroeder, *The transformation of European politics 1763–1848* (Oxford, 1996 edn), pp. 5–11.

2. 'Testament Politique [1768]', in G.B. Volz, ed., *Politische Correspondenz Friedrichs des Grossen. Ergänzungsband. Die Politischen Testamente Friedrichs des Grossen* (Berlin, 1920), pp. 215–16, 219.

3. W. Stribrny, *Die Russlandpolitik Friedrichs des Grossen 1764–1786* (Würzburg, 1966), pp. 28–31.

territories. Prussia could take Polish Prussia; Austria could take the town of Lwów and the Polish enclave of Zips; and Russia could take 'whatever part of Poland it felt appropriate'. This was the plan he sent to his minister in St Petersburg, count Victor von Solms, in February 1769, claiming it had been put to him by a retired Danish diplomat, Rochus Lynar. It was almost certainly Frederick's own. Its prescient reasoning has his cynical intelligence stamped all over it.[4]

Panin claimed to be interested if Frederick would agree to Austria joining their alliance to 'to throw the Turks out of Europe and much of Asia' and set up a republic in Constantinople. Frederick had no truck with such crusading fantasies. The Lynar plan sank from sight.[5] Panin's proposal was as ridiculous as a suggestion which came from Choiseul, in March 1769, that Frederick could help himself to the principality of Warmia and Poland's fiefdom of Courland, albeit as an 'exchange' against Upper Silesia, which he would restore to Austria, break off his alliance with Russia and realign himself with the Habsburgs and the Bourbons.[6]

The idea of some kind of realignment was not entirely fanciful. Frederick had allied with Russia from necessity, not preference. But he feared his ally as capricious and unpredictable (not least because it was ruled by a woman), an overweening partner whose grandiose ambitions might drag him into war; indeed, he feared Russia as a potential, long-term threat to all Europe. 'Ces gens', 'these people', he disparagingly referred to the Russians. He was well aware, too, that they, at bottom, mistrusted his own ambitions.[7] Like Kaunitz in December 1768, Frederick toyed with the idea of a rapprochement with Austria in order to keep Russia in check, but he appreciated that the bone of contention that was Silesia made such a prospect exceedingly unlikely. No matter how badly the Austrians wanted Silesia back, he was even more determined not to let them have it.[8]

4. No draft of the 'Lynar plan' as such survives – its details derive only from Frederick's comments. Frederick to Solms, 2 Feb. 1769, *PC* XXVIII, 17 786.

5. Solms to Frederick II, 17 Feb. 1769 and Frederick to Solms, 5 Mar. 1769, ibid., 17 875. Solms to Frederick II, 3 Mar. 1769 and Frederick to Solms, 19 Mar. 1769, ibid., 17 917. Frederick to his brother, prince Henry of Prussia, 30 Nov. 1770, *PC* XXX, 19 484. On Russia's hostility to Prussia's acquisition of Polish territory, see Macartney to Stormont (from St Petersburg), 1 Dec. 1766, PRO/SP 91/77.

6. Bernhard Wilhelm von der Goltz, Prussian envoy in Paris, to Frederick II, 3 Mar. 1769, *PC* XXVIII, 17 899n.; Frederick to Solms, 13 Mar. 1769, ibid., 17 899.

7. e.g. Frederick to Henry of Prussia, 13 Apr. 1769, ibid., 18 003; 3 Jan. 1771, *PC* XXX, 19 568 and 19 570; 11 Jan. 1771, ibid., no. 19 591; Gottfried van Swieten, Austrian ambassador, to Kaunitz, 22 Jan. 1771, ibid., 19 608. See also Frederick's 'Testament Politique' of 1768, pp. 193, 196–7, 209–11, 214, 216, 221–2.

8. 'Testament Politique' of 1768, pp. 193, 195, 214, 215, 222–3.

Frederick knew that the Austrians were looking for 'compensation' for Silesia: in Germany, they had their eye on Bavaria, where the elector Karl Theodor was gratifyingly childless. They might even consider seizing ecclesiastical principalities in the Empire, or some useful territories in northern Italy. Frederick had no intention of allowing his old enemy to be strengthened, unless he himself obtained comparable advantages. He was not above using the threat of an agreement with Austria to manoeuvre a distracted Russia into supporting his own territorial ambitions: maybe not in Russia's preserve of Poland, but elsewhere. He intended to secure the reversion of the margravates of Bayreuth and Ansbach, held by a collateral Hohenzollern line, on the deaths of their childless rulers – not so much for their intrinsic value, but as territorial pawns which might be used in exchanges elsewhere in the Reich.[9]

There was much speculation in European chanceries when Frederick and Joseph II met at Neisse, in Silesia, between 25 and 28 August 1769. Sheer mutual curiosity was one reason behind the encounter, part serious, part charade. The two men wanted to sound each other out – particularly about keeping clear of the Russo-Turkish conflict. They also wished to send signals to Russia: Frederick, that he could not be taken for granted; Joseph, that Russia should consider renewing its alliance with the Habsburgs and ditching Prussia; the alternative, after all, might prove an Austro-Prussian axis, which could prove disastrous for Russia both in the Balkans and Poland. Frederick showed little compunction in complaining of the headaches that Russia caused him. Since he also made clear that he intended to renew the Russian alliance, Joseph did not take his complaints too seriously. They assured each other that they did not wish to see the war spread to the Empire, although, to Joseph's disappointment, Frederick refused to guarantee its neutrality. If Saxony made a bid for the Polish throne, he would intervene militarily against the Wettins. Joseph assured Frederick that Austria had given up all thought of the reconquest of Silesia, then spoiled the effect by recounting a rumour that Frederick would give Silesia back to Austria, if he could get his hands on Danzig. Frederick, taken aback, resolved an awkward situation by joking that he would as soon become king of Poland.[10]

Besides the hot air about their concern for humanity, Joseph and Frederick's encounter at Neisse had two results: one, an anodyne

9. T. Cegielski, *Das alte Reich und die erste Teilung Polens 1768–1774* (Stuttgart, 1988), pp. 40–1.

10. Joseph's account of the Neisse meeting is in *PC* XXIX, 18 351–3. See also D.E.D. Beales, *Joseph II*, I (Cambridge, 1987), pp. 284–5.

declaration that they would remain neutral in the conflict expected to arise between France, Spain and Britain – though since such a conflict was expected to arise as a result of disputes over the Falkland Isles, the chances of Prussia or Austria being sucked in were far less likely than the danger of involvement in an escalating Russo-Turkish war.[11] Secondly and more practically, Catherine was prodded into giving Frederick the additional security assurances he craved by an early renewal of their alliance, in October 1769, prolonging it to 1780. Catherine also guaranteed the reversion of Ansbach and Bayreuth to Prussia. Stanisław August was to be kept on the Polish throne, but the Russians continued to insist on the full extent of the concessions secured in 1768 for the dissenters.[12]

Frederick's priority remained peace between Russia and Turkey and peace in Poland. The two were inextricably linked: 'the war against the Turks will decide the affairs of Poland'.[13] The more spectacular Russia's successes against the Turks, the more tempted his ally was to seek a humiliating, victor's peace. The great naval victory at Chesmé in July 1770 threatened to turn the Black Sea into a Russian lake. By November, Russia had secured control of Moldavia and Bessarabia, springboards for an advance into Wallachia and territories that little more than thirty years previously had been Austrian.[14] The closer Rumiantsev's forces drew to their borders, the more the Habsburgs feared the subversive growth of Russian influence among their own Orthodox subjects.[15] The Confederacy of Bar added a further element of instability. Frederick urged the confederates to come to an accommodation with Stanisław August. Even as he warned the king to co-operate with Russia, he pressed it to soften its line on the dissenters. He even offered his own and Austrian services to mediate with the confederates.[16]

None of this meant that Frederick had abandoned the possibility of annexations from Poland or elsewhere. Everything would depend on circumstances. In December 1769, he told his brother Henry that Prussia could realistically expect substantial gains only on the

11. Frederick to Joseph, 27 Aug. 1769; Joseph to Frederick, 28 Aug., *PC* XXIX, 18 354.
12. Treaty of St Petersburg, 12/23 Oct. 1769, *CTS* XLIV, pp. 339–52; Political Testaments of 1752 and 1768, pp. 61, 213–14, 219–20.
13. Frederick II to Solms, 2 May 1770, *PC* XXIX, 18 971.
14. I. De Madariaga, *Russia in the age of Catherine the Great* (London, 1981), pp. 208–13.
15. Arneth, *GMT* VIII, p. 258; P.J. Adler, 'Habsburg school reform among the Orthodox minorities, 1770–1780', *Slavic Review*, 33 (1974), pp. 23–45.
16. Frederick to Benoît, 27 Dec. 1769, 31 Jan., 14 Mar. 1770, *PC* XXIX, 18 691, 18 769, 18 857; to Solms, 28 Mar., ibid., 18 890. Frederick to Catherine II, 14 Sept. 1770, *PC* XXX, 19 282.

death of the elector of Bavaria, 'who might live another forty years'.[17] Panin's reaction to the Lynar plan had taught caution. So long as dangerous constitutional changes and a restoration of the Wettins were ruled out in Poland, Frederick was content. His immediate worry was the spread of plague, which from early 1769 had been seeping into the *Rzeczpospolita* from Moldavia. Since the Poles themselves failed to set up a cordon sanitaire to check the northwards progress of the epidemic, Frederick began to send his troops into Poland to set up his own. By September 1770, Prussian troops had effectively cut most of Polish Prussia west of the Vistula off from the rest of the Commonwealth and were beginning to extend the cordon into western parts of Wielkopolska. Confederates unfortunate enough to encounter Frederick's troops were liable to be forcibly impressed into the Prussian army, with the result that during the course of 1770, Barist activity in Polish Prussia largely ceased.

Frederick's fears about the spread of plague were genuine (hardly surprising given the devastation which it had wreaked in East Prussia in the early eighteenth century), and yielded valuable economic bonuses. The inhabitants on Frederick's side of the cordon were encouraged, by persuasion or force, to migrate to Hohenzollern territory proper; the city of Danzig, which banned Prussian recruitment on its estates and which gave shelter to deserters, was blackmailed and bullied into paying reparations. Its booming prosperity was brutally interrupted by Frederick's exactions. The presence of the cordon sanitaire would, obviously, be conducive to any process of partition, but that was not its original purpose. The territories it encompassed were to be plundered, not annexed.[18]

An Austrian annexation

The cordoning of Polish territory was initiated not by Frederick, but by the Austrians. They, as a matter of course, had for years

17. Frederick II to Henry, 3 Dec. 1769, *PC* XXIX, 18 626.
18. On the plague, see e.g. Frederick to Rohd (Vienna), 25 July 1770. *PC* XXX, 19 166; to Benoît, 1, 30 Sept., ibid., 19 253, 19 323. On Prussian depredations, see J. Topolski, ed., *Dzieje Wielkopolski* (Poznań, 1969), I, pp. 866–7; G. Labuda, ed., *Historia Pomorza*, II (Poznań, 1984), p. 518. [John Lind], *Letters concerning the present state of Poland* (London, 1774 edn), pp. 113–14. Most recently, see H.-J. Bömelburg, *Zwischen polnischer Ständegesellschaft und preussischem Obrigkeitsstaat. Vom Königlichem Preussen zu Westpreussen 1756–1806* (Munich, 1995) and K. Friedrich, 'Facing both ways: new works on Prussia and Polish–Prussian relations', *German History* 15 (1997), pp. 256–67. I am grateful to Dr Friedrich for drawing my attention to Bömelburg's invaluable work.

maintained a cordon sanitaire against the spread of plague along their Balkan borders. When, as early as March 1768, it was clear that the Barists were closely involved with the Turks the Austrians extended their cordon along their border with Poland.[19] They took in behind it a small Polish enclave. Spisz (Zips to Germans, Spiš to the local Slovaks) was a rich copper-mining district, mortgaged to Poland by king Sigismund of Hungary in 1412. The loan had never been repaid, its exact size bedevilled by abstruse calculations of depreciation and interest. Maria Theresa and Kaunitz had been considering how to secure a peaceful revindication of this Polish enclave for over twenty years; the matter took on new urgency in the post-war reconstruction after 1763. When Zips was first taken in behind the cordon, the action was presented – and may well have been intended – as a police measure designed to check not only the plague but Barist raids across the frontier. In April 1769, the Austrians announced that the rights of the Polish crown would be fully preserved. Stanisław August at first even approved the Austrian cordon, as a means of protecting royal revenues from the confederates. Likewise, Frederick II, who was, after all, doing much the same with even greater gusto in Polish Prussia, saw nothing in what the Austrians were doing beyond a sensible security precaution. He remained unperturbed even when the Austrians began to levy taxes in Zips.[20] At Neisse, the matter was not even discussed.

The mountainous Carpathian border between Habsburg Hungary and Poland was poorly demarcated. In October 1769, an enthusiastic Hungarian bureaucrat, Joseph Török, began a detailed enquiry into the line of the frontier. Whether he was acting on superior orders, or whether he hoped to advance his own career with a display of bureaucratic zeal, or both, he concluded that Polish settlers had surreptitiously shifted the frontier during the fifteenth and sixteenth centuries. He sent his findings back to an unimpressed Kaunitz, who nonetheless appreciated Török's argument that the condition of Poland was such that Austria could peaceably enforce claims to its supposed former territories.

Joseph was much more enthusiastic. In July 1770, the Austrians began to push into Polish territory proper, cutting off the crown estates around Nowy Sącz and Nowy Targ. These were not deep

19. Much of what follows about Zips is based on H. Glassl, 'Der Rechtsstreit um die Zips vor ihrer Rückgliederung an Ungarn', *Ungarn-Jahrbuch* I (1969), pp. 23–50.

20. Arneth, *GMT* VIII, pp. 170–2. Frederick II to J.F. von Rohd, ambassador in Vienna, 15 Mar. 1769, *PC* XXVIII, 17 906; to Catherine II, 9 Apr. 1769, ibid., 17 985; to Solms, 30 Apr. 1769, ibid., 18 050.

thrusts – the Austrians penetrated by some twenty miles along a similar length of a tortuous border; they went no further for almost another eighteen months. By the end of July, however, these annexa-
'tions had been approved by Maria Theresa, Joseph and the *Staatsrat*. Kaunitz protested, presumably because he could demonstrate that his hands were clean, but he certainly did nothing material to oppose the annexations.

The Austrian decision seems to have been almost accidental. The occupied lands could, it was hoped, be plausibly represented as part of a general frontier adjustment in the Zips area, which was to be finalised in amicable fashion between Austria and Poland as soon as order was restored to the Commonwealth: this was the official response to the protest note which the Polish government sent on 28 July 1770. Even after the Austrians formally declared the reincorporation into Hungary of Zips and the adjacent zone on 20 November, Kaunitz continued to claim that this was a purely provisional and precautionary measure. He warned, however, that any further annexations would arouse the suspicions of Prussia and Russia.[21] The Austrians certainly tried to be discreet – it took Frederick's ambassador in Vienna, Jakob Friedrich von Rohd, another month to glean details of the annexation. Yet Frederick still believed, or affected to do so, that this was nothing more than a sensible set of measures by the Austrians to shorten the length of their cordon sanitaire, which he was confident that Austria would restore to Poland when peace finally came, both in Poland and between Russia and Turkey.[22]

It is hard to believe that, in a volatile international situation, Frederick was doing anything more than displaying the caution which he had acquired over many years. In March 1770, Austria had begun a modest, if significant, deployment of forces in Transylvania, along the Wallachian border, where stores for up to 40,000 troops began to be prepared. It was the beginning of a prolonged, but very dangerous game of bluff: to warn Russia not to push its successes too far and to persuade it to use Austrian medi-ation to arrange a peace settlement – the shape of which, of course, such mediation could influence. The Austrians were in no fit state

21. See Glassl, 'Rechtsstreit', esp. pp. 38–46. Glassl suggests that the original decision of annexation applied only to Zips and that it was Joseph who insisted on including the Polish crown lands. Maria Theresa to Stanisław August, 26 Jan. 1771, in A. Beer, ed., *Die Erste Theilung Polens*, 3 vols (Vienna, 1873), III, pp. 86–7.
22. Rohd to Frederick, 18 Aug., 22 Dec. 1770 and Frederick's replies of 23 Aug. and 30 Dec., *PC* XXX, 19 230, 19 555; Frederick to Benoît, 30 Dec., ibid., 19 556.

to undertake any large-scale military involvement, and they knew it, though no doubt reports from St Petersburg of intense war-weariness encouraged their posturing. Frederick warned that an escalation of the war might be inevitable.[23]

On 6 May 1770, the outgoing Austrian ambassador, Jakob Nugent, had his farewell audience with Frederick in the Sans Souci palace. It went rather beyond the usual courtesies. Ambassador and king alike tried to trip each other up into revealing themselves. Austria would surely like to acquire Bavaria, Frederick prompted. It was so inconvenient for widely dispersed territories not to be 'rounded off', to lack '*arrondissements*'. Perhaps Austria could expand its territories in northern Italy – 'something from Venice: that would be a most suitable *arrondissement*'. Frederick even jested that he could provide Austria with a plan for the reconquest of the former Habsburg territories of Alsace and Lorraine from its ally France. Nugent countered with his own banter: the best *arrondissement* for Frederick would be Polish Prussia with western Wielkopolska and its principal town of Posen (Poznań). To this, Frederick 'said nothing . . . but he became a little pensive and then said, smiling: it's all very well to talk like this, but . . .' and he changed the subject to deploring the Turkish war.[24]

Frederick's brother Henry took the exchanges rather more seriously. Confined to innocuous cultural pursuits in his palace at Rheinsberg, kept at arm's length from politics, despite, or perhaps because of, his signal services during the Seven Years War, he yearned for a more striking role. After the Neisse meeting, which he had attended, he had enthusiastically urged a close alliance with Austria, arguing that such an entente would dominate all Europe and keep Russia at bay. Frederick and Joseph could even partition the Empire between them. The king poured cold water on these enthusiasms – there was too much past bitterness between the two states for any such reconciliation in the foreseeable future.[25] In February 1770, Henry tried another tack: since Russia obviously

23. Memorandum prepared for Choiseul by Kaunitz, 26 Feb. 1770, Beer, *Die Erste Theilung*, III, pp. 7–11. Solms to Frederick, 20 Apr. 1770, *PC* XXIX, 18 980; Rohd to Frederick, 23 May 1770 and Frederick's reply, 30 May, ibid., 19 031; Frederick to Solms, 4 June 1770, ibid., 19 039. Von Seddeler, chargé d'affaires in St Petersburg, to Kaunitz, 18 Jan. 1771, *SIRIO* CIX, p. 428. See also Beales, *Joseph I*, pp. 286–7.

24. Nugent wrote a report on the audience to Kaunitz on 25 May 1770 after his return to Vienna. *PC* XXIX, 18 982.

25. Henry to Frederick, 22 Nov. 1769 and Frederick's response, 26 Nov., *PC* XXIX, 18 611.

valued his alliance, it should agree to his annexation of Polish Prussia. After Nugent's audience, Henry claimed that Frederick could become master of the Baltic. Once again, Frederick sounded a cautionary note: at bottom, he warned, neither Austria nor Russia favoured his territorial expansion.[26]

Early in September 1770, Frederick paid a return visit to Joseph at Neustadt in Habsburg Moravia. This time, Kaunitz was there, doing, according to an irritated Frederick, most of the talking. Again, the Turkish war dominated the discussions. Kaunitz warned that, unless Russia was prepared to accept a moderate peace settlement, Austria might well have no alternative but to go to war. Both sides took the issue so seriously that Frederick agreed he would endorse and co-operate with Austrian offers of mediation. Both men agreed that the sooner Poland was pacified and some form of stability restored, the better. The cordons sanitaires did not feature in the discussions. Kaunitz did, however, produce a working paper, what he called his 'Catéchisme Politique', which purported to lay down guidelines on Austro-Prussian relations. Much of it was waffle about the need for mutual trust and candour. In point 7, Kaunitz was presumably thinking of Austria's nibbles into Polish territory when he explained that 'when the matter in hand is not a substantial one and of no great importance' Austria and Prussia would not stand in each other's way, although when it came to major initiatives or 'substantial acquisitions', they would smooth the way by amicable, prior negotiations (point 8).[27]

On 14 September, Frederick wrote directly to Catherine with the suggestion of Austrian and Prussian mediation. As for Poland, he suggested that both he and the Austrians could bring pressure to bear on the confederates to conduct meaningful negotiations. It would help if the dissenters could be brought to reduce their demands. Although the empress was evasive on the Polish issue, she was sufficiently rattled by the Neustadt meeting to accept Prussia's and Austria's 'good offices' (a far more nebulous concept than mediation) in seeking peace.[28]

26. R. Koser, *Geschichte Friedrichs des Grossen*, 4 vols Darmstadt, 1974 edn, III, pp. 312–13; E. Rostworowski, *Popioły i korzenie* (Kraków, 1985), pp. 89–91.

27. Kaunitz's account of his meetings with Frederick on 3 and 4 September, contained in a report to Maria Theresa of 18 Sept. 1770, *PC* XXX, 19 257, 19 258; Frederick to Rohd, 5 Sept., ibid., 19 259.

28. Frederick II to Catherine II, 14 Sept. 1770, *PC* XXX, 19 282; Catherine II to Frederick, 28 Sept./9 Oct., ibid., 19 395. Her acceptance was conditional on the Turks' release of her minister, Obreskov.

Prince Henry in St Petersburg

In order to fathom how serious Catherine was about peace-making, prince Henry was sent to St Petersburg. He was originally to pay a supposedly private visit to his sister in Sweden, queen Ulrike, whom he had not seen in twenty-five years; the visit's real purpose followed from Frederick's renewal of his Russian alliance in October 1769. He had agreed then that, should his nephew, the francophile crown prince Gustav, try to restore absolute rule in Sweden and shake off Russian predominance, he would, at Russia's request, invade Swedish Pomerania. A new military complication was the last thing Frederick wanted. Henry was to warn his sister to restrain her son. Henry had also secretly contacted Catherine, asking her to write to Frederick to allow him to visit her in St Petersburg, which she did, soon after Henry had left for Sweden. He was far more optimistic than his elder brother about the prospect of Russia letting Prussia have some territory in Poland as compensation for the subsidies paid to Russia. And though Frederick remained sceptical, he did agree to Henry's visit as an unprecedented opportunity to sound out the empress and her ministers.[29]

Henry's visit to St Petersburg has often been seen as crucial in breaking through the elaborate game of nods, winks and diplomatic elbow-digs which had surrounded the whole issue of Polish territory. Frederick himself was later to congratulate his brother for bringing about the Partition. But this was a cheap compliment, tossed to Henry like a bone to a dog.[30] The main object of Henry's prolonged stay in St Petersburg, from 12 October 1770 to 31 January 1771, was not to angle for Polish territory (although that may well have been part of the prince's own plans) but to press the Russians over the question of peace with Turkey; as for Poland, Frederick instructed Henry to push for its pacification, not its partition.[31] The bulk of Henry's correspondence with Frederick deals with the Turkish war. His letters are cautious and hesitant, those of a younger sibling

29. Catherine to Frederick, 19/30 July 1770 and Frederick's reply, 12 Aug., *PC* XXX, 19 208; Frederick to Henry, 23 Aug., ibid., 19 229. G.B. Volz, 'Prinz Heinrich und die Vorgeschichte der Ersten Teilung Polens', *Forschungen zur Brandenburgischen und Preussischen Geschichte* 35 (1923), pp. 193–211.

30. Frederick to Henry, 31 Mar. 1771, *PC* XXXI, 19 795.

31. Frederick to Henry, 18 Sept., 8, 30 Oct. 1770, *PC* XXX, 19 298, 19 343, 19 404. Henry to Frederick, 18 Oct., ibid., 19 416; 27 and 30–31 Oct. and Frederick's responses of 11, 16 Nov., ibid., 19 437, 19 450. Cf. Panin to Volkonskii, 10/21 Nov., *SIRIO* LXXXVII, pp. 189–90.

who knew his place and knew better than to admit to any private initiatives.

Catherine and her ministers showed little readiness to take too seriously the 'good offices' of two powers which wished to restrict their prospective gains. On 18 November, Frederick wrote to his brother that if the empress persisted in her prevarications while pursuing a war which might well suck in France and Austria, then she could only count on his continued support in return for substantial territorial compensation: 'I do not intend to sacrifice the welfare and interests of a state with whose governance I am entrusted to the inflated notions of conquest of another power: that is the pill the Russians have to sweeten . . .'.[32] Yet whether even this was a serious bid for expansion by Frederick is by no means clear. It is at least as likely to have been a means of pressing the Russians into moderation. Neisse and Neustadt had done nothing to reduce Frederick's mistrust of Austria. Unless Catherine held back, then the war would indeed spin out of control. 'Peace, peace as soon as possible', he insisted at the end of November.[33]

Much to his concern, Panin kept reverting to his old suggestion of cajoling the Austrians into the 'Northern System'. Austria could even have a share in the Porte's Balkan territories. Panin appreciated that Prussia would also be entitled to territorial 'compensation' – in Germany, but not in Poland. At best, Polish Prussia might be used to compensate German princes that Frederick might dispossess. This was a brush-off, not at all what Frederick wanted. It could only lead to tighter links between Russia and Austria and Prussia's marginalisation.[34] Frederick's response was to renew his entreaties for peace and for a general pacification of the Commonwealth. He hoped Russia would soften its demands on the dissenters. But this was to be a genuine pacification – there was no hint of any carve-up. Panin himself had made clear to Henry he wished to keep Poland intact, though he was willing to see Russia's guarantee of the Polish constitution underwritten by Prussia and Austria. He insisted that all of Catherine's policies in Poland were 'indisputably based on the permanent interests of all the Republic's neighbours'.[35]

32. To Henry, 16 Nov. 1770, *PC* XXX, 19 453.

33. To Henry, 30 Nov. 1770, *PC* XXX, 19 484.

34. Henry to Frederick, 27 Nov., and Frederick's reply, 13 Dec. 1770, *PC* XXX, 19 515.

35. 'Précis des sentiments du comte de Panin . . . 22 octobre/2 novembre 1770' enclosed with Solms' despatch of 3 Nov. 1770. The concessions which the dissenters might agree to were a limit on the number of envoys they might elect to the Sejm and surrender of their right to hold senatorial and ministerial office. *PC* XXX, 19

Frederick reacted with a mixture of disbelief and curiosity to the reports which he began to receive in late December that Zips and the adjacent areas were indeed being looked on as *bona fide* Habsburg territory.[36] However, he showed far more concern at the official Russian peace proposals which he obtained from Henry on 3 January 1771. Catherine's demands, which included 'independence' from Turkish suzerainty for the Crimean Tatars and occupation of Moldavia and Wallachia for a term of twenty-five years as an indemnity for her exertions, infuriated him. This was simply an excuse for unprecedented Russian territorial annexation which would massively tip the balance of forces in south-east Europe not only against Turkey, but against Austria. He refused to pass these terms on to Vienna: the Habsburgs would see in them a virtual declaration of war. Moreover, if Russia did, as a result of its ambitions, find itself at war with Austria, he would not regard the *casus foederis* as applicable: he had made his alliance to protect Russia, not to allow it to aggrandise itself in the Balkans.[37] He repeated these views to the new Austrian ambassador, Gottfried Van Swieten, on 21 January, when he vented his spleen on 'ces gens-là'. He barely mentioned Poland.[38]

This is not wholly surprising. The despatches from Solms and Henry showed considerable divisions in St Petersburg. Few questioned that Turkey was Russia's principal foe. What was in dispute was whether the 'Northern System' was the appropriate mechanism to deal with the Porte. A supposedly malleable Poland had precipitated a debilitating war and a government put in place by Russian arms was doing nothing to ease Russia's problems. The powerful Orlov clan appreciated that if the Turks were to be expelled from the Balkans, it could only be in agreement with the Habsburgs, whom Panin's policies were threatening to bring into the war on Turkey's side. Partition would threaten to dilute Russia's influence

445. Frederick to Finckenstein, 15 Nov. 1770, ibid., 19 448 stresses the urgency of a positive response. Frederick to Rohd, in Vienna, 9, 16 Jan. 1771, ibid., 19 587, 19 599; Finckenstein to Frederick, 3 Feb. and Frederick's response, 4 Feb., ibid., 19 643.

36. Rohd to Frederick, 19, 22 Dec. 1770 and Frederick's reply of 30 Dec. *PC* XXX, 19 555; Frederick to Benoît, 30 Dec.

37. Henry to Frederick, 15 and 22 Dec. 1770; Frederick to Henry, 3 Jan. 1771, *PC* XXX, 19 568, 19 570; Frederick to Finckenstein [3 Jan.]; ibid., 19 572; Catherine II to Frederick, 9/20 Dec. 1770 and Frederick's reply of 4 Jan., ibid., 19 573. Frederick to Solms, 9 Jan., ibid., 19 589.

38. Van Swieten to Kaunitz, 22 Jan. 1771, *PC* XXX, 19 608. The Austrians were well aware of the extent of Russian demands and determined to resist them. Arneth, *GMT* VIII, pp. 244–6.

in Poland, but it might also offer opportunities for enrichment to Catherine's servants and ministers. Zachar Chernyshev was ready to cut a deal with Potsdam and Vienna, if that would procure Byelorussia. War-weariness was growing. Catherine had reaffirmed her support for Panin's Northern System in April 1770,[39] but balancing diverse viewpoints and factions was her way of ruling. There could be no certainty that she would endorse his line indefinitely.

Frederick was determined to hold back until he was absolutely sure of his ground. The catalyst was not Henry's mission to St Petersburg, but the ever more insistent reports in the New Year that Austria was indeed engaged in the outright annexation of Polish territory in the Carpathian foothills. Repnin had finished his tour of duty in May 1769 feeling a partition was inevitable; his equally disillusioned successor, prince Mikhail Volkonskii, was ready for a partition by March 1770.[40] Solms assured Frederick in January 1771 that there was growing support in St Petersburg for both Russia and Prussia to follow the Austrian lead.[41] The point was finally made at a soirée on 8 January by Catherine herself. 'Why shouldn't we all take something?' she said to Henry – although he could not be sure that she was serious. Frederick, he pointed out, had set up a cordon sanitaire, but, unlike the Austrians, he had not annexed any land.

> 'But', laughed the empress, 'why not take the land anyway?' A moment later count Chernyshev came up to me and talked on the same subject . . . 'Why not take the bishopric of Warmia? After all, everyone ought to have something.'[42]

Frederick, who received Henry's missive on 23 January, kept an iron self-control. Everything depended on the Austrians. Officially, they still maintained that their cordon was simply a security measure. The Turkish war still threatened: if Austria and France finally pitched in, everything would change with no certainty that Prussia would be able to profit from the situation. Warmia alone was not enough – acquiring it would not be worth the international rumpus

39. Catherine's rescript to prince Volkonskii of 3/14 April 1770, quoted in Solov'ev, *IPP*, pp. 473–4.

40. Repnin even felt that Turkey could be invited to share in a Partition. Konopczyński, *Konfederacja Barska*, I, pp. 154–5. On Volkonskii, see Benoît to Frederick II, 7 Mar. 1770; Frederick to Benoît, 14 Mar., *PC* XXIX, 18 857. Cf. Benoît to Frederick II, 12 Jan. 1771, *PC* XXX, 19 613. Cf. Caspar von Saldern to Panin, 15 July 1771, quoted in Solov'ev, *IR* XXVIII, p. 490.

41. Solms to Frederick II, 8 Jan. 1771, *PC* XXX, 19 615.

42. Henry to Frederick, 8 Jan. 1771, *PC* XXX, 19 616.

that might follow – 'but Polish Prussia, even without Danzig, that would be worth the trouble'.[43]

Frederick's push for Polish territory

Frederick would do nothing precipitate until Henry returned from St Petersburg on 18 February. What seems to have been crucial in persuading Frederick, as much as his brother's news that the opportunity to carve up Poland was now very real, was Rohd's despatch of 9 February, confirming that Vienna intended to hang on not only to Zips but also to the adjacent territories.[44] Frederick moved carefully. On 14 February, in an audience with Van Swieten, not only was Poland spoken of purely in the context of a plan of pacification, but Frederick even approved the Austrian manoeuvres in Transylvania as likely to inspire moderation in the Russians.[45] He did not wish to alarm the Austrians while he forged the sliver of land which they had occupied into a lever with which the territories of the *Rzeczpospolita* were to be prised apart.

Vienna's acquisitions, Frederick assured Rohd on 17 February, were 'little parcels' of no consequence, to be restored in a final peace settlement.[46] Next day, Henry briefed his brother on his Russian mission. Frederick stormed into action. On the 19th, he ordered Joachim Domhardt, head of the Königsberg War and Domains Chamber, to prepare, in the utmost secrecy, a conspectus of the revenues of Warmia.[47] The 'petites parcelles' became something very different when he wrote to Solms only three days after his interview with Van Swieten: Austria meant to keep territory covering 'several towns and as many as 97 villages'. He doubled the size of the annexed districts – inaugurating a systematic campaign of deliberate exaggeration of the Austrian share. To preserve the Republic's integrity, in view of the Austrian actions, was hopeless: what counted now was to 'stop this dismemberment from jeopardising the balance between the House of Austria and my own, the preservation of which is so important to me and of such direct concern to Russia'. He had little choice but to dust off 'ancient rights with which my archives will

43. Frederick to Solms, 23 Jan. 1771, *PC* XXX, 19 615; to Henry, 24, 31 Jan. 1771, *PC* XXX, 19 616, 19 635.

44. *PC* XXX, 16 675. For a view which attaches more weight to Henry's role, see C.V. Easum, *Prince Henry of Prussia* (Westport, 1971 edn), pp. 258–72.

45. Van Swieten to Kaunitz, 17 Feb. 1771, *PC* XXX, 19 670.   46. Ibid., 19 675.

47. M. Bär, *Westpreussen unter Friedrich dem Grossen*, 2 vols (Berlin, 1909), I, p. 19; Kabinettsorder to Domhardt, 19 Feb., II, p. 3.

furnish me . . . to some little province of Poland'. Solms was to do 'everything humanly possible to get me some part of Poland'.

A week later, Frederick sent Solms a copy of a passport, received from Benoît, made out to a Polish official living behind the Austrian cordon as 'a most faithful subject of Her Most Sacred, Imperial, Royal and Apostolic Majesty', Maria Theresa. Russia should find its territorial compensation for its war against Turkey from Poland (which had provoked the conflict in the first place) and Frederick, too, should secure some recompense for the subsidies he had paid to Russia.[48]

Frederick put his two closest collaborators, Kabinett-ministers Karl Wilhelm von Finckenstein and Ewald Friedrich von Hertzberg, to work to identify and justify which territories might be taken over. Legally, they pointed out, any Prussian claims were feeble. At this stage, neither they nor Frederick were prepared to stake a claim to all of Polish Prussia. 'The most useful' acquisition would be the territories west of the Vistula and north of the Netze (Noteć) river, which would furnish a substantial land link between East Prussia and the Brandenburg heartland. But Russia might well try to restrict Prussia's share to less valuable lands east of the Vistula. Catherine had to be handled carefully. Since, in view of her commitments to Poland, 'she affects to observe a kind of justice and moderation' she was likely to demand the same from her partners. In the meantime, the best policy to follow was that of the Austrians: occupy first, justify afterwards.[49] Frederick agreed that it was imperative to keep the Austrians on board the partition bandwagon on which they had clambered with such myopic opportunism. It was more important than ever to avert the danger of an Austro-Russian conflict. Van Swieten was to be told that his court was overreacting to Russia's successes; the Austrians were to be encouraged to extend their zone of occupation, 'which would entitle us to increase our own share'. On 6 and 10 March, Domhardt was ordered to extend his financial investigations to all of Polish Prussia.[50]

Frederick began to play both ends against the middle, in a diplomatic campaign as dazzling as anything on the battlefield and relying on much the same tactics: aggression, feint, deception. His role

48. Frederick to Solms, 20 Feb. (twice), 27 Feb., *PC* XXX, 19 687, 19 688, 19 710.
    49. Finckenstein and Hertzberg to Frederick, 27 Feb. 1771 and Frederick's undated reply, ibid., 19 716. The ministers to Frederick, 5 Mar., *PC* XXXI, 19 728. Frederick to Finckenstein, 25 Mar., ibid., 19 780.
    50. Instruction to Finckenstein, 10 Mar. 1771, ibid., 19 737. Kabinettsorders to Domhardt, 6, 10 Mar., Bär, *Westpreussen* II, pp. 3–4.

of go-between was strengthened by Turkey's release of the Russian ambassador, Obreskov, in April, in response to Prussian and Austrian efforts. Turkey was also ready to use his 'good offices' for peace. He could shuttle diplomatic initiatives freely between St Petersburg, Potsdam, Vienna and Constantinople.[51] He continued to play up the extent of the Austrian annexations, while playing down the value of his own prospective gains: he wanted only 'little parcels' of territory, 'a little province', land which was intrinsically of little value to Poland. He had to preserve an essential balance between his own and Austrian acquisitions. Russia, of course, could not possibly want the relative weakening of its faithful ally, Prussia.[52]

Austrian reticence

The Austrians were the great sticking-point. While they had been content to see Poland as a virtual Russian province before 1768, the possible extent of Russian territorial gains from the Porte gave them nightmares. The Russians were even talking of taking Constantinople. Joseph wanted to bluster the Russians into restraint: with his mother's reluctant assent, he intended to double the number of the 50,000 men already stationed in Hungary in February 1771.[53] It was bluff – Joseph and his principal military adviser, marshal Lacy, fully appreciated that they simply lacked the resources to fight Russia. On the other hand, Kaunitz enveloped himself in one of his periodic bouts of bellicosity and was willing to risk war; he even nursed hopes that Frederick might be cajoled into changing sides – after all, they had told each other at Neustadt that Russia was a menace to European civilisation.[54]

By late July 1771, the Austrians had confirmed that they found the Russian demands against Turkey unacceptable despite a Russian offer to hand Moldavia and Wallachia to Vienna.[55] Russia wanted a rapprochement, but for as long as the Russo-Prussian alliance also held, the Austrians were intensely sceptical.[56] To realign with

51. Frederick to Solms, 8, 12 May 1771, *PC* XXXI, 19 898, 19 905.

52. Frederick to Solms 17, 25 Mar. 1771, ibid., 19 757, 19 781.

53. Beales, *Joseph II*, I, pp. 286–90; K.A. Roider, *Austria's Eastern Question 1700–1790* (New Jersey, 1982), pp. 114–20.

54. Finckenstein to Frederick, reporting discussions with Van Swieten, 3 Feb. and 9 Mar. 1771, *PC* XXX, 19 643, 19 737. Van Swieten to Kaunitz, 17 Feb., ibid., 19 670. Beales, *Joseph II*, I, pp. 288–93.

55. Solov'ev, *IR* XXVIII, pp. 456–7; Arneth, *GMT* VIII, pp. 310–20.

56. Lobkowitz to Kaunitz, 26 Apr., 2 June 1771, *SIRIO* CIX, pp. 525, 547.

Russia against Turkey would certainly have meant the end of the
raison d'être of Kaunitz's career, the alliance with France (which,
inevitably, would have reverted to its old ties to Prussia). Maria
Theresa would not hear of it. She could not forget that during her
wars with Frederick the Turks had not availed themselves of the
opportunity to finish the Habsburgs off. She would not, in their
hour of need, stab them in the back. Not yet.

In the early months of 1771, while Frederick was bombarding
Solms with a hail of directives on wheedling Polish territory out of
the Russians, the Austrians began secret talks with the Turks in
order to encourage them to stay in the war. By holding out the
prospect (it was nothing more than this – Kaunitz had no intention
of getting himself into any kind of binding commitment) of their
intervention on the Porte's behalf, the Austrians hoped to extract a
generous subsidy towards their military build-up in Transylvania
and acquire yet more territory on the cheap: they hoped they could
coax the Turks into ceding the province of Lesser Wallachia, held
by Austria between 1718 and 1739. So desperate were the Turks
that they allowed themselves to be cajoled into signing such a treaty
on 6 July. They even paid a first instalment of the subsidy, although
they would hand over Lesser Wallachia only if Austria did indeed
succeed in engineering a peace based on the *status quo ante bellum.*
News of the treaty did not leak until early January 1772 (the Austrians
insisted on secrecy – they did not want to go so far as to provoke
the Russians), but its mere existence, which Frederick suspected
after only a few weeks, could only stoke up the fevered international
temperature.[57]

Frederick suspected the Austrian build-up to be a bluff – but he
could not be sure; and even bluff, he was well aware, could easily
spin out of control. Peace in Poland, he had hitherto reasoned,
would reduce the chances of a general conflagration. But with the
real prospect of major territorial gains, he was prepared to take risks.
He began to encourage the ferment in the Commonwealth, lest its
premature termination destroy the opportunity that beckoned. When
his namesake, Frederick II, Landgrave of Hesse-Cassel, approached
him in March 1771 for his support for a bid for the Polish throne,
offered him by the Barists, the Prussian king urged him to keep

---

57. The treaty was not an alliance. Kaunitz referred to it as a 'concert' – by which
he meant something akin to an understanding, but one which the Turks wholly
misunderstood. Roider, *Austria's Eastern Question*, pp. 117–29. See also Arneth, *GMT*
VIII, ch. 10. For Frederick's suspicions of a possible offensive alliance, see his letter
to Solms of 10 Aug. 1771, *PC* XXXI, 20 099.

confederate interest alive in the hope of a favourable twist of events. Having previously supported Russian schemes of pacification in Poland, he began to let it be known that they were doomed to failure.[58]

Frederick was able to use the threat of war both to browbeat the Russians into moderation and to extract territory for himself. It was entirely plausible that in any conflict the Austrians would be backed by the French and even by their client states in the Empire. Prussia, obliged to come to its ally's aid, would have to fend off Habsburg, Bourbon and Imperial forces, in a situation almost as bad as that it had faced during the Seven Years War.[59] Generous recompense was essential. At the same time, in order to avert a general war, Russia should be persuaded to abandon Moldavia and Wallachia. Yet it need not be the loser thereby: for what it sacrificed in the Balkans, it could make up in Poland. As far as Frederick was concerned, Russia could have *carte blanche* to take what it wished. But it was essential to preserve the balance of power: so Prussia and Austria would have to take their 'part au gâteau', their 'share of the cake'. And if Austria would not play along, then Prussia and Russia could proceed without her.[60] To cover himself, Frederick began to angle for a military convention with Russia, over and above existing agreements, which would be aimed directly against any Austrian aggression; and indirectly against France and the states of the Empire, should they back Austria.

By late April, Frederick was sufficiently encouraged by signals from St Petersburg to tackle Van Swieten directly on the Austrian position. The ambassador was decidedly cool. Austria's occupation of the border zone was only temporary – most of the territories would be returned to Poland once it was pacified. She had real claims only to Zips. Lobkowitz, the Habsburg ambassador in St Petersburg, was pushing the same line. Frederick would not be discountenanced. He advised the Austrians to ferret out more old claims in their archives. That was what he and the Russians were doing. And these, he said, were surely the sorts of acquisitions to which Kaunitz had felt they could help themselves in his 'Catéchisme Politique' – 'The district I'm after is poor country'. The whole arrangement would help secure peace. There was even a solution to

58. Frederick II of Hesse-Cassel to Frederick the Great and the latter's reply, 28 Feb., 4 Mar. 1771, *PC* XXX, 19 723. Frederick to Benoît, 27 Feb., 6 Mar., 1 May, ibid., 19 709, *PC* XXXI, 19 730, 19 882.

59. Frederick to Solms, 27 Mar., 3, 7 Apr. 1771, ibid., 19 787, 19 800, 19 814.

60. Frederick to Rohd, 20 Mar. 1771, ibid., 19 763; to Solms, 2 June, ibid., 19 946.

the vexed question of Moldavia and Wallachia – Russia was prepared to compensate Poland with them.[61]

Frederick's despatches to Solms, however, once again portrayed something else entirely: that Van Swieten had assured him that Austria had every intention of keeping not only Zips, but all the Polish lands it had occupied. If only Catherine would drop Moldavia and Wallachia, Poland could be made to serve as surrogate compensation and a means of soothing the tensions building up with Austria.[62] Thus was the spirit of the Lynar plan revived. In mid-May, after further instructions from Kaunitz, Van Swieten was even more discouraging to Finckenstein: Vienna could not approve the proposed 'démembrement' – unless Silesia was restored. Not only did Austria not intend to annex the border zone, but it was ready to pull out of it altogether as soon as Prussia and Russia withdrew their troops.[63] Indeed, at the beginning of August, with the plague abating, the Austrians, although they did not withdraw from the occupied border zone, wound up their military patrols. Frederick kept his nerve: he reduced his own cordon, even rejecting a Russian request to send in more troops in order to help out against the Barists.[64]

Frederick could still not be sure of St Petersburg. Panin might be on the defensive, but he remained wedded to a territorially whole Poland. A meeting of Catherine's advisory Council in mid-February reiterated the wish to acquire Polish Livonia, but was extremely reluctant to see why Austria and Prussia should be allowed in, when all the real military burdens were being shouldered by Russia.[65] Even as Henry looked for straws in the wind in St Petersburg, Panin was preparing to send one of his closest collaborators, Caspar von Saldern, to replace the burnt-out Volkonskii in a final effort to retrieve the situation, pacify the Commonwealth and, with that, salvage not only his Northern System but his own standing in the empress's eyes. It was to be Saldern's task to win Polish confidence by the restoration of the almost non-existent discipline among the Russian soldiery. Partition was not part of his brief.[66]

61. Van Swieten to Kaunitz, 27 Apr., ibid., 19 868.
62. Solms to Frederick, 9 Apr. and Frederick's reply, 24 Apr., ibid., 19 862; Frederick to Rohd, 24 Apr., ibid., 19 863. Frederick to Solms, 28 Apr., 8 May, ibid., 19 869, 19 898; to Finckenstein, 14 May, ibid., 19 911.
63. Frederick even instructed Finckenstein to tell Van Swieten that the whole business was Russia's idea. That way, the Austrians might be less likely to argue. Finckenstein to Frederick, and Frederick's reply 13, 15 May 1771, ibid., 19 911, 19 917. Arneth, *GMT* VIII, pp. 306–8.
64. Frederick to Solms, 25 Aug. 1771, *PC* XXXI, 20 131.
65. Solov'ev, *IR* XXVIII, pp. 449–50.
66. Henry to Frederick, 25 Jan. 1771, *PC* XXX, 19 659; Saldern's instruction, 5/16 Mar. 1771, *SIRIO* LXXXXVII, pp. 216–28.

Panin's last stand

But it may as well have been. Saldern's instructions envisaged no substantial concessions. They even enjoined on him the peculiarly contorted task of 'assuring the Poles of their independence while maintaining our [constitutional] guarantee'. It was this kind of impossible policy which had led first Repnin, then Volkonskii to move from argument and persuasion to force and from wishing to keep the Commonwealth as Russia's exclusive backyard to letting in the neighbours. Saldern was on a well-worn path.

Panin also tried to alert Stanisław August. The Czartoryskis insisted that it was possible to reach an agreement with the confederates. Stanisław August, who had hitherto gone along with this, felt, after Bar's proclamation of an interregnum in October 1770, that he had no choice but to look afresh to Russia. From mid-January to mid-March 1771, his confidant Ksawery Branicki was in St Petersburg. Panin warned him of what was afoot. Branicki used his raffish charms and braggadocio to persuade Catherine that there was still time to reassert Russia's influence over a Commonwealth that would remain its exclusive preserve.[67] Panin's nephew, ex-ambassador Repnin, passing through Warsaw in March, warned the king what to expect.[68] Yet the king's uncles refused to take the threats seriously. To them, the succession of ambassadors and their pleas for co-operation were a sign of weakness: Russia was surely exhausted by war, Moscow was in the grip of plague, Austria was at loggerheads with Russia, it required only that elusive Turkish victory to transform everything. Poland had perhaps one competent, professional diplomat in post, where it should have mattered most – Jakub Psarski in the Russian capital. He, too, was getting wind of what was going on, but his warnings were also ignored. The Czartoryskis insisted that the Russians were desperate and that Panin was simply trying to manipulate them into co-operating with his plans. The king should not listen.[69]

Stanisław August was in two minds: on the one hand, he recognised the possibility of partition, on the other, at least until April 1772, he was getting reassurances from Vienna that Austria would

67. W. Konopczyński's entry on Branicki in *PSB*, II, pp. 398–401; J. Michalski, 'Dyplomacja polska w latach 1654–1795', in *HDP* II, pp. 526, 540–1. Catherine to Stanisław August, 5/16 Mar., *SIRIO* LXXXXVII, p. 216.
68. Two letters from Panin to Stanisław August, 10/21 Mar. 1771, ibid., pp. 239–40, 240–1.
69. Psarski to Jacek Ogrodzki (Stanisław August's Cabinet secretary), 3 Dec. 1771, 10 Mar., 12 June 1772. AGAD/ZP 84, pp. 880, 915, 946–7. Michalski, 'Dyplomacja polska', pp. 526, 540–1.

oppose any such eventuality.[70] But he was sufficiently alarmed to strive for much closer co-operation with Saldern. In May 1771, for the first time, he ordered loyal cavalry units, stiffened by Russian troops under Ksawery Branicki's nominal command, to take the field against the confederates.[71] It was too little, too late. Not only did royal troops make little difference to operations, but the gesture further damaged Poniatowski's standing in the eyes of the Poles. It also infuriated the Czartoryskis, who did not take kindly to their nephew's bid for emancipation from their tutelage. They never forgave him.

Unable to make headway in Poland, faced with Austrian stone-walling over Zips and their build-up in Transylvania, harassed by Solms and Frederick, undermined by Chernyshev and the Orlovs, Panin threw in the towel. On 27 May he admitted to the Council that Austrian intransigence threatened war. It could be avoided by agreement at the expense of Poland: Austria had annexed Polish lands, Frederick felt compelled to do likewise, Russia had little choice but to follow suit. Panin was very much under the impression that Austria would simply stick with the lands it already occupied. At this stage, too, it was still not certain how much the Prussians were claiming. He proposed that the Commonwealth, too, should be compensated. The idea of giving it territory in the Balkans, in return for falling in with Russian policy, had been mooted in the autumn of 1769. The Council now agreed it should receive Moldavia and Wallachia, in a territorial reshuffle which would also bring significant numbers of high-ranking Orthodox nobles in to the *Rzeczpospolita* (and its Sejm). They would naturally look to Russian protection. Such a move was also meant presumably to reassure Vienna. As for the Russians themselves, they would take the lands originally proposed by Chernyshev in November 1763 – territory much more extensive than anything Frederick laid claim to and immeasurably greater than Austria's zone.[72]

In discussions with Solms on 29 and 31 May, Panin did what he could to clamp down on Prussian claims, which he wished to confine to the wedges of Polish territory east of the Vistula. This was almost the opposite of what Frederick wanted: the quadrilateral of land bounded by East Prussia and the Neumark, the Vistula and the Netze, to include Danzig. Frederick's proposals would lead to

---

70. Benoît to Frederick, 10 Aug. 1771, *PC* XXXI, 20 129; Konopczyński, *Konfederacja barska*, II, pp. 588–9, 594–5, 650–3; Michalski, 'Dyplomacja polska', pp. 526–7, 548–50.
71. Konopczyński, *Konfederacja*, II, pp. 504–5.
72. *AGS*, cols 82–4. Solov'ev, *IPP*, p. 469 and *IR* XXVIII, p. 457.

the full joining up of East Prussia with Brandenburg; Panin's would merely permit the 'rounding-off' of East Prussia, which would remain separated from the Hohenzollern core lands. Panin feared that the loss of Danzig, Poland's principal port, would deal a crippling economic blow to the Commonwealth with adverse repercussions for Russia's own trade. If Frederick had to make do without Danzig, he wanted all the Vistula–Netze quadrilateral, plus the East Prussian *arrondissements*. Solms had also submitted claims to further Polish territories, running the entire length of Poland's Silesian border, taking in Poznań, the chief town of western Poland. These 'rights' could be 'exchanged' for the Vistula–Netze lands, less Danzig, which would, in turn, be 'traded' for the territories between the Vistula and East Prussia.

Frederick had, of course, urged the Austrians to take more territory, if they wished. Should they not be satisfied with what they held in Poland, they could seize Venetian territory around Trieste.[73] On the other hand, if the Austrians were not prepared to co-operate, then they should get nothing beyond what they already occupied. Finckenstein had a draft territorial convention ready by 14 June. Frederick pushed his luck as far as he dared: he plumped for all of Polish Prussia, except Danzig; Russia would take Polish Livonia and other convenient lands; secrecy was to be preserved, although Austria would be invited to participate; and formal Polish consent would be secured in order to legitimise the whole operation. Frederick sent the draft to Solms, who was to tell Panin that if Moldavia and Wallachia did go to the Poles, they would have nothing to complain about – on the contrary, they would really do rather well out of the whole business.[74]

The niggling matter of the Russian guarantee of Poland's territorial integrity of February 1768 was easily solved. The Polish government itself had repeatedly sought the rescinding of the guarantee; it had refused to co-operate against the Barists or with Catherine's unstinting efforts to bring peace to its country. Worse, it was the Poles who had got Russia involved in the Turkish war in the first place. The state of the country was such that unless its neighbours restored order, they might be sucked into further conflicts among

73. Frederick to Solms, 24 Mar., *PC* XXXI, 19 772; Solms to Frederick, 31 May and 1 June; Frederick's reply of 14 June, ibid., 19 969. Solms to Frederick, 5 July and Frederick's reply, 21 July, ibid., 20 052.
74. Finckenstein to Frederick, 14 June, enclosing his 'Projet d'une convention secrète ...'; Frederick's reply, 14 (15?) June; to Solms, 19 June, 3 July, ibid., 19 970, 19 981, 20 010.

themselves. The Poles had only themselves to blame that Russia's guarantees no longer applied.[75]

War with Austria?

For as long as Russia insisted on holding on to the Danubian principalities war with Austria could not be ruled out, whatever agreements Frederick and Catherine reached over Poland. Vienna found even the suggestion of transferring the principalities to a third party unacceptable – it would still constitute an unacceptable debilitation of Turkey and threatened to leave Russia in effective, if indirect, control. The only sensible course, Frederick reiterated, was to give up the Balkans and look to Poland.[76] Panin was sufficiently alarmed by the possibility of war with Austria to welcome, even encourage, a fresh military agreement with Frederick.[77] Frederick felt sufficiently sure of himself to put in a bid for Danzig. He was much encouraged by a report from his representative in Paris, Daniel Alfons von Sandoz Rollin, who was informed directly by Choiseul's successor, the duke of Aiguillon, that France would not support any aggressive move by Austria against Russia: French treaty obligations were purely defensive. Even better, France would not support Austria even if Frederick were to 'take possession of various districts in Poland and of the town of Danzig' and Austria attacked him. D'Aiguillon was frank: France needed peace and financial reform.[78]

Far from reassuring St Petersburg, Frederick continued his scaremongering. The more he put the wind up the Russians, the more he would get. War, he told Solms, was a continuing possibility; 240,000 Austrian, French and Imperial troops would bear down on his 130,000.[79] At the same time, a despatch was on its way from Solms. Panin was making a final bid to salvage Poland: surely there was a real danger that Russia's and Prussia's proposed annexations in Poland would bring about war with Austria. Did Frederick still feel the two allies should proceed? Would he support Russia against

75. Frederick to Solms, 25 Mar. 1771, ibid., 19 781; Panin to Saldern 11/22 June 1771, *SIRIO* LXXXXVII, p. 336.

76. Solms to Frederick, 28 July; Frederick to Solms, 10 Aug., *PC* XXXI, 20 099. Van Swieten to Kaunitz, 14 Aug. (on an audience the previous day with Frederick), ibid., 20 112.

77. Solms to Frederick II, 28 July 1771, ibid., 20 099.

78. Sandoz Rollin to Frederick, 25 Aug. 1771 and Frederick's reply of 7 Sept., ibid., 20 157.

79. Frederick to Solms, 11 Sept. 1770, ibid., 20 169.

an Austrian attack? The response piled on the pressure. Of course partition should go ahead, but Frederick remained coy on the question of military support. He had no obligations to the Russians over the Balkans and, in any case, Austria was more likely to attack him in Silesia than the Russians from Transylvania.[80] If only the Russians would not insist on Moldavia and Wallachia . . . As for compensating the Commonwealth with the principalities, he now agreed with the Austrians. The Poles deserved nothing. The partition was, after all, all about the enforcement of 'ancient rights' and it was the Poles themselves who were the cause of all the troubles Russia faced.[81]

Increasingly confident, though never entirely certain, that war with Austria would not take place, Frederick began to prepare all the more energetically for just this eventuality, on paper. The gout that wracked him through these months did nothing to reduce his clarity of purpose. At the end of September he instructed Solms to speed up the talks on the military convention with Russia. He let Van Swieten know that, much as it pained him, he would come to Russia's aid against any Austrian attack.[82] With impeccable timing, Polish insurgents had launched a fresh rising in the Grand Duchy of Lithuania in mid-August. The defeat of a small Russian detachment on 7 September caused Saldern to panic. He feared that his forces were so overstretched that the entire Russian position would crumble. False alarm it may have been – general Suvorov routed the Lithuanian confederates beyond all hope of recovery on 19 September, but Russia was shown to be as far away as ever from solving the Polish problem.[83]

The threat of Austrian intervention persuaded the Russians to commit themselves to raising a completely fresh army of 50,000 men to operate in southern Poland against Austria. In fact, Russian resources were so stretched that they could barely raise 30,000.[84] In mid-October, they again approached Frederick to relieve the pressure on their forces in Poland by occupying Poznań. This time, he agreed. Prussian troops crossed into Wielkopolska with a vengeance – looting, requisitioning, 'paying' with counterfeit and

80. Solms to Frederick, 3 Sept., Frederick's response of 18 Sept., ibid., 20 190.
81. Frederick to Solms, 18 Sept; to Finckenstein, 20 Sept., ibid., 20 190, 20 199.
82. Van Swieten to Kaunitz, 18 Sept., on an audience held the previous day, ibid., 20 188; Frederick to Solms, 25 Sept., ibid., 20 212. Frederick to Solms, 30 Sept., with proposals for a military convention, ibid., 20 224. Cf. Frederick to Rohd, 20 Oct., ibid., 20 286.
83. Konopczyński, *Konfederacja*, II, pp. 543–57. Solov'ev, *IR* XXVIII, pp. 494–7.
84. *AGS* (sessions of 22 Aug./2 Sept., 25 Aug./5 Sept.), cols 104–7; Solms to Frederick II, 10 Sept. 1771, *PC* XXXI, 20 212. Solov'ev, *IR* XXVIII, pp. 467, 475.

debased coin.[85] The perception, so artfully nourished by Frederick, that war with Austria was a real possibility, achieved its object. On 4 November the Russians resigned themselves, in a sulk, to pull out of the principalities in the final peace.[86]

News of this decision was to reach Vienna only in the New Year.[87] In the meantime, the strain was telling on Maria Theresa. On 5 September she admitted to Rohd that she was desperate to avoid war. She would accept the Russians' swallowing Crimea but she drew the line at Moldavia and Wallachia. She begged Frederick to moderate the Russians and to urge the Turks to come to terms (having only two months previously given the Porte every indication of her military support against Russia, she could hardly take the initiative in reining the Turks in).[88] Kaunitz complained bitterly to the empress that she had blown three years of bluff, undermining his stance so much that he now had little alternative but to go along with a partition which would, above all, strengthen Prussia. The empress protested that her pacific inclinations had been exaggerated. The chancellor's complaint had little real basis. Frederick and Catherine were prepared to fight, whereas Maria Theresa and, in the final analysis, Joseph were not. Austria lost the game of international poker because it had a weak hand, not because of Maria Theresa's anguished gushings.[89]

Kaunitz approached Rohd on 2 October. Even if Russia were to give way over the principalities, the war would end to its great advantage, and the interests of the balance of power required that Austria and Prussia should also get something. A guilty Maria Theresa confessed that she had furnished the pretext for others in Poland, by occupying Zips and the border zone. All that followed was 'an unfortunate misunderstanding'. The Austrians wished to keep Zips, rightfully belonging to Hungary, and would redeem the original debt. Once Poland was pacified, the border could be properly demarcated. She wished to go no further. If, on the other hand, Russia and Prussia did intend 'to lay claim to several Polish provinces . . . then she could not permit herself to be forgotten' – but she would prefer if it did not come to such a pass.[90]

85. Frederick II to Finckenstein, 20, 22 Oct. *PC* XXXI, 20 288, 20 294. Konopczyński, *Konfederacja*, II, pp. 607–9, 642.

86. Solms to Frederick, 27 Sept. 1771, *PC* XXXI, 20 260; *AGS*, sessions of 24 Oct./ 4 Nov., 22 Nov./3 Dec., cols 115–16, 126.

87. Lobkowitz to Kaunitz, 13 Dec., *SIRIO* CIX, p. 611.

88. Rohd to Frederick, 7 Sept., *PC* XXXI, 20 179.

89. Arneth, *GMT* VIII, pp. 322–7. Beales, *Joseph II*, I, p. 295.

90. Rohd to Frederick, 2 Oct. 1771, *PC* XXXI, 20 253.

On 24 October, Kaunitz raised the subject of prospective partition for the first time with the Russian minister in Vienna, Dimitrii Golitsyn: if the principalities were restored to Turkey, Austria would go along as a last resort. It would be preferable, however, for everyone to pull back from the Commonwealth (except, of course, Zips).[91] For his part, Frederick continued to press Domhardt for more information on Royal Prussia (in September, it was population data) and to warn Panin, almost to the last moment, that war with Austria might still break out.[92] Peace, naturally, was preferable. So, on 1 November, he tackled Van Swieten: Russia, he was sure, would give way on the principalities, but it would seek compensation in Poland. Van Swieten would not be drawn.[93] Frederick reacted to such reticence by urging the Russians to present Austria with a signed and sealed *fait accompli*, to which it could adhere if it wished.[94]

Austrian agreement

This was, in effect, what happened. On 17 January 1772, Solms reported that the Russians were ready to commit themselves to paper.[95] He signed the convention on 17 February. It largely followed Finckenstein's draft of the previous June. The respective occupations would take place in mid-June. Austria would be invited to join, but a series of secret, separate articles laid down detailed provisions for collaboration between a corps of 50,000 Russians and 20,000 Prussians should Vienna oppose their intentions. Just as preparations for the signature were being completed, news arrived from Golitsyn in Vienna that, since Russia no longer insisted on removing Wallachia and Moldavia from Turkey, the Austrians conceded the principle of partition.[96] Solms and his co-signatories, Panin and vice-chancellor Golitsyn, agreed it would be more tactful, in view of the anti-Austrian content, to antedate the treaty to 4 January. The provisions for military collaboration against Austria would not, of course, be revealed. Frederick did not quibble. He was miffed

---

91. Arneth, *GMT* VIII, pp. 330–2.
92. Frederick to Rohd, 15 Sept. 1771, *PC* XXXI, 20 179. Rohd to Frederick, 14, 21 Sept., ibid., 20 202, 20 221. Frederick to Solms, 20, 30 Oct., 6 Nov., 13, 4 Dec. 1771, ibid., 20 285, 20 315, 20 341, 20 367, 20 426. Kabinettsorder to Domhardt, 17 Sept., Bär, *Westpreussen* II, pp. 4–5.
93. Frederick to Solms, 30 Oct. 1771, *PC* XXXI, 20 315; Van Swieten to Kaunitz, 4 Nov., on his audience on 1 Nov., ibid., 20 324.
94. Frederick to Solms, 29 Dec. 1771, ibid., 20 492.   95. Ibid., 20 584.
96. *AGS*, cols 145–6 (session of 1/12 February).

that Danzig had eluded him, but, even so, 'the signature of the convention has given me infinite pleasure'.[97] A stream of directives poured out to Domhardt and other officials to put everything in place for annexation.[98] Frederick and Catherine congratulated each other on the benefits which their 'prudence . . . good faith and firmness' had brought them.[99]

Frederick could cash in his chips. By threatening Russia with Austria, he had manoeuvred it into letting him into the most economically valuable part of its Polish backyard. By supporting his ally Russia, he had forced Austria to latch on to the partition which its cheap annexations in southern Poland had set in motion. Kaunitz knew it meant not the expansion of Austria, but 'the aggrandisement of our strongest and our natural enemy'.[100] He tried one last time to prevent the inevitable. He had always been ready to present Polish territory to Frederick, provided Silesia was restored to Austria. With almost insane optimism, on 17 January, he laid out seven different foreign policy options. The first three involved taking territories from the unfortunate Turks, still under the impression that Austria was their friend: Maria Theresa would have none of this. She approved Kaunitz's fourth variant: take as much territory as possible from Poland. Frederick could then be persuaded to exchange Breslau, Upper Silesia and Glatz for Austria's share.[101]

It was on this basis that Van Swieten approached Frederick on 4 February, charged with recovering on his own, in one afternoon, what the military machines of Austria, Russia, France, Sweden and the Empire had failed to regain in seven years of fighting.

> What? what? shouted the king . . . Oh, no, Sir! . . . This cannot be. I ask for and want nothing more than Polish Prussia. Take your share wherever suits you best, but not at my expense . . . I've got gout in my feet . . . not in my head![102]

97. Text of the Convention in *CTS* XLIV, pp. 467–81 bears the date of 4 January. Frederick to Solms, 4 Jan. 1772, *PC* XXXI, 20 511; Solms to Frederick, 18 Feb. and Frederick's reply of 1 Mar., ibid., 20 686; Solms to Frederick, 25 Feb., *PC* XXXII 20 702.

98. See the documents in Bär, *Westpreussen* II, pp. 8–75.

99. Catherine to Frederick, 8/19 Feb. 1772; Frederick to Catherine, 2 Mar., *PC* XXXI, 20 689.

100. From prince Khevenhüller's diary – entry for 23 Aug. 1772, quoted in Beales, *Joseph II*, I, p. 298 and see pp. 294–8; Arneth, *GMT* VIII, pp. 247–8.

101. Rostworowski, *Popioły*, pp. 96–7. For the Kaunitz variations, see G.B. Volz, 'Die Massinischen Vorschläge', *Historische Vierteljahrschrift* 10 (1907), pp. 355–81.

102. Van Swieten to Kaunitz, 5 Feb. 1772, *PC* XXXI, 20 591. The crack about gout does not appear in Van Swieten's account, but in Frederick's, to Solms, 5 Feb., ibid., 20 592. Staircase wit, perhaps? But then, staid Austrian ambassadors did not expect crowned heads to say such things.

Short of not participating in the Partition, the only alternative, Kaunitz pointed out, was to reduce what Austria would take from Poland, but balance this by territory from the Porte. Given the complications this would provoke, it is hard to see the suggestion as anything more than a device to coax along Maria Theresa's tortured conscience. On 19 February, instructions were sent to Van Swieten to reassure Frederick that Austria had no designs against Silesia, but would participate fully in the partition.[103] On 28 February, the ambassador handed over to Frederick the formal Declaration, assuring him of his court's full co-operation. Lobkowitz delivered the same Declaration in St Petersburg on 8 March. The document insisted that all acquisitions from Poland should 'be perfectly equal; the share of any one power should not exceed that of any other . . .'. All three courts agreed to abide by this principle.[104] The necessary niceties would be negotiated in St Petersburg.

Vienna's ideas on what constituted 'perfect equality' were rather different from those of Frederick and the Russians. So long as he had Polish Prussia, Frederick did not care much for what the Russians took. Yet he was the real winner: in terms of its strategic and economic value, Polish Prussia, welding together the bulk of the scattered Hohenzollern dominions, far outweighed anything Austria or Russia might acquire.[105] When, in mid-April, Van Swieten and Lobkowitz presented the full extent of Austrian pretensions at their respective courts, they tried to argue that 'complete equality' could not just mean geographic extent but fertility, population and 'political value'. They demanded a massive wedge of territory between Silesia and Moldavia, thrusting to some sixty miles south of Warsaw. 'Heavens, Gentlemen, you don't suffer from indigestion. You do have a good appetite' was the reaction from Frederick. Joseph would have liked to have gone further, acquiring a strip along the north bank of the Vistula, which would have given Austria Kraków and Sandomierz. He also hoped to get the frontier fortress of Kamieniec Podolski.[106]

103. Arneth, *GMT* VIII, pp. 336–68; Beales, *Joseph II*, I, pp. 292–7.

104. Text of Declaration in *CTS* XLIV, p. 493; and with Van Swieten's account (5 March) of his audience of 28 February, *PC* XXXI, 20 680. Frederick to Solms, 29 Feb., ibid., 20 681. Panin to Golitsyn in Vienna, 9/20 Mar., *SIRIO* CXVIII, pp. 29–30.

105. Panin to D.M. Golitsyn, 16/27 May, ibid., no. 2205, p. 117.

106. Van Swieten to Kaunitz, 21 Apr. 1772, *PC* XXXII, 20 865. Cf. Frederick to Solms, 29 Feb. 1772, *PC* XXXI, 20 681; to Finckenstein, 13 June, *PC* XXXII, 21 017. H. Glassl, *Das österreichische Einrichtungswerk in Galizien (1772–1790)* (Wiesbaden, 1975), p. 77. Frederick was well aware of the real value of his own 'morsel'. To prince Henry, 18 June, *PC* XXXII, 21 033.

The Austrian demands took in the rich salt-mines of Bochnia and Wieliczka, a major source of revenue for Stanisław August, as well as Poland's principal southern commercial centre, the town of Lwów. Taking into account Frederick's share, the *Rzeczpospolita* would be economically prostrated. Acquisitions on this scale would also, it was feared, give Austria undue influence in Poland in the future. Panin and the Council wanted to reduce the Austrian share by well over half to a broad stretch of land running parallel to the Polish–Hungarian border, south of Lwów and the salt-mines.[107]

The Austrians knew how to create facts. In mid-April, 20,000 troops under general Hadik began crossing into Polish territory. By the end of June, they had secured Lwów and the salt-mines. There were even minor clashes between them and Russian troops stationed in the south. The original mid-June schedule for formal annexation came and went.[108] It was the Austrians, too, who broke the news of the three powers' intentions to a disbelieving session of the Generality of Bar at Eperyes on 15 April.[109] Frederick could afford to wait. The Austrian moves allowed him to try to pin the blame for the whole business on them.[110] It would do no harm if the Russian arguments with the Austrians prevented them from getting too cosy with each other. In the name of 'la plus parfaite égalité' Frederick proposed he should take Thorn and extend his border further south.[111]

Panin and Catherine complained that this territorial leapfrogging would lead only to chaos, confusion and, instead of mutual friendship, enmity. The Austrians, who all along had pitched their demands high in the expectation of reducing them later, agreed, in early July, to pull back their new border further south, so as to restore the palatinate of Lublin and the county of Chełm to Poland.[112] It was enough to appease Frederick, who congratulated himself

107. Panin to Saldern, 5/16 May 1772, *SIRIO* CXVIII, pp. 112–13; to Golitsyn, 16/27 May, ibid., pp. 117–18, with the enclosed 'Observations fondées sur l'amitié et la bonne foi . . .', ibid., pp. 118–22. Solov'ev, *IR* XXVIII, pp. 538–40.

108. Panin to Saldern, 1/12 Dec. 1771, *SIRIO* LXXXXVII, pp. 495–8; Frederick to Finckenstein, 8 Mar., 5 Apr. 1772, *PC* XXXII, 20 712, 20 809.

109. Konopczyński, *Konfederacja*, II, p. 655.

110. Frederick to Benoît, 14 June, *PC* XXXII, 21 021; to colonel Goltz in Paris, 15 June, ibid., 21 025.

111. To Solms, 7, 14, 17 June, *PC* XXXII, 20 989, 21 019, 21 030; to Finckenstein, 13 June, ibid., 21 017; to Solms, 8 July, ibid., 21 093.

112. Panin to D.M. Golitsyn, 16/27 May, with enclosed 'Observations fondées sur l'amitié et la bonne foi . . .', *SIRIO* CXVIII, pp. 117–22; Van Swieten to Kaunitz, 14 July (on an audience of 12 July), *PC* XXXII, 21 101; Solms to Frederick, 26 June, ibid., 21 102.

on his public-spiritedness in accepting a raw deal. Catherine found the Austrian 'concessions' enough.[113] As a gesture of goodwill, the Austrians revealed the terms of their agreement with Turkey of July 1771, a move which only succeeded in confirming Frederick's suspicions that they still hankered after Balkan territory: if that were to happen, he and Russia would have to press Austria to disgorge even more of what it had grabbed from the Poles.[114] But there was enough common ground to allow the requisite conventions to be signed in the Russian capital on 5 August.

To avoid sticky questions of protocol (who should take precedence over whom), the Partition 'treaty' took the shape of three separate conventions, between Russia and Prussia, Russia and Austria, Austria and Prussia. They were largely identical in wording, save for the outlining of the respective shares. In justification of the dismemberment, the preambles cited not only the anarchy which had caused Poland's neighbours so much grief, but also the three powers' 'ancient and legitimate rights'. Article IV of each convention pointed to the link with the Turkish war: Catherine would not annex Moldavia or Wallachia, while Maria Theresa undertook to help broker peace between Russia and the Porte.[115] The Prussians announced the incorporation of their share to their new subjects on 13 September, the Russians three days later, the Austrians on 14 October. It remained to secure the Commonwealth's formal assent.

---

113. Frederick to von Edelsheim in Vienna, 19 July, *PC* XXXII, 21 124; Van Swieten to Kaunitz (on an audience of 31 July), 3 Aug., ibid., 21 161. Solms to Frederick, 24, 28 July, ibid., 21 186, 21 199; Frederick to Solms, 5, 9 Aug., ibid., 21 176, 21 186.
114. Solms to Frederick, 31 July 1772; Frederick to Solms, 21 Aug., ibid., 21 215.
115. Text of the three conventions, *CTS* XLV, pp. 57–79.

CHAPTER FOUR

Consent and settlement

First reactions

The *Rzeczpospolita* was helpless. Its demoralised, minuscule army
could not possibly take on the forces of the three powers: 20,000
Austrians in the south, 30,000 Russians in Lithuania and the centre,
over 10,000 Prussians in the west and north. The tiny garrison in
Elbing pulled out after token resistance. Only in the summer of
1774 did regimentary Kraszewski stand up to Prussian border forays
into Wielkopolska by pulling up the new frontier markers and even
attacking Prussian troops – but this was virtually the only action of
its kind.[1] Contingents of Barists maintained sporadic activity into
the autumn, but, as news of the three-power agreement spread,
most simply went home. There was a brief buzz of excitement in
September after Gustav III, much assisted by the Russians' diver-
sion in Poland, sprang his monarchic coup in Stockholm, but it was
insanely unrealistic to imagine it could be emulated in Warsaw.[2]
No one could seriously contemplate resistance, or even criticism.
The printers dared not publish. 'Our Father, who art in Vienna,
Berlin and Petersburg, hallowed be thy name in those countries,
secure your kingdom in our Poland, thy will be done in Austria,
Brandenburg, as it is in Moscow . . .' Such bitter squibs could only
be repeated by word of mouth or circulated on scraps of paper.[3]

1. Stanisław August to general Monet, 22 Sept. 1772, in E. Mottaz, ed., *Stanislas
Poniatowski et Maurice Glayre. Correspondence relative aux partages de la Pologne* (Paris,
1897), pp. 41–2; Frederick II to Henry, 26 Sept., *PC* XXXII, 21 332; to Solms, 3 July
1774, *PC* XXXV 23 143. J. Topolski, 'The Polish–Prussian frontier during the period
of the First Partition (1772–1777)', *Polish Western Affairs* 10 (1969), pp. 95–6.
2. Ignacy Twardowski to Jerzy Mniszech, 3, 10 Sept. 1772, B.Cz. 3868, pp. 511,
514.
3. B.Cz. 320, ff. 305, 343–4.

The long-predicted event took many European politicians aback. Not that they were prepared to do anything about it. Stanisław August's protesting missives to European courts elicited no more than sympathetic evasions. The British government tut-tutted at 'this curious transaction' but saw no reason to get involved. To Edmund Burke's question, 'Poland was but a breakfast . . . Where will they dine?' the answer seemed to be that no one, among the major powers, was much bothered.[4] On the other hand, news of the event almost certainly precipitated the royalist coup in Stockholm, where Gustav III feared that Sweden would be the next course. The Turks shared their fears and resolved to soldier on: their armistice negotiations with Russia at Fokshany and Bucharest came to nothing.[5] The French were vexed at being hoodwinked by the Austrians, fearful of the consequences for their old protégé, Turkey, but they were in no position to do anything. D'Aiguillon's overtures to Lord North's ministry to work together to restrain Russia fell on deaf ears. When the French engraver, Noël Le Mire, produced his allegory of the Partition, 'Le gâteau des Rois', 'the cake of kings', in February 1773, his government immediately ordered all the plates to be destroyed. Austria was its ally and in Louis XV's France crowned heads were not a fit object of public criticism.[6] Among enlightened absolutism's philosophe fan-club, reactions ranged from raptures of sycophancy to a sense of distaste. Voltaire told Frederick he was certain he was the driving force since the deed bore the hallmark of genius. The king modestly disclaimed the credit, but congratulated himself on an acquisition 'without bloodshed'.[7]

Securing a Sejm

The Poles were on their own. A new Russian ambassador, Otto Magnus von Stackelberg, urbane, smooth-talking and patient, took

4. H.M. Scott, *British foreign policy in the age of the American Revolution* (Oxford, 1990), pp. 177–81. Burke to A.H. von Borcke, 8 Jan. 1774, in L.S. Sutherland, ed., *The correspondence of Edmund Burke* (Cambridge, 1960), II, p. 514. Polish ministerial protests and the exchanges between Stanisław August and Louis XV and George III, in Chodźko, pp. 109–19.

5. J.P. LeDonne, *The Russian empire and the world, 1700–1917. The geopolitics of expansion and containment* (New York, 1997), pp. 50–2, 105.

6. H. Widacka, '*Kołacz Królewski*, czyli alegoria rozbioru Polski w grafice XVIII i XIX wieku', *Kronika Zamkowa* 1/33 (1996), pp. 8–22.

7. Frederick II to Voltaire, 1 Nov., 6 Dec. 1772; Voltaire to Frederick, 18 Nov., in T. Bestermann, ed., *The Complete Works of Voltaire*, CXXIII (= *Correspondence*, XXXIX), D 17992, D 18066; D 18019. J. Fabre, *Stanislas-Auguste Poniatowski et l'Europe des Lumières* (Paris, 1952), pp. 355–60.

over. On 18 September, he and Benoît delivered identically worded notifications of the partition to the Crown and Lithuanian chancellors. The Austrian ambassador, Carl von Reviczky, arrived four days later and submitted his notification on the 26th. Its text matched that of the others.[8] Throughout the proceedings, the Austrians generally participated fully in maintaining harmonious appearances with their partners, but always managed to seem just slightly out of step. The declarations demanded a Sejm to ratify the cessions and legalize them in Polish and international law.

In the hope that their frantic appeals to non-involved monarchs would yield something, Stanisław August and his ministers tried to spin out proceedings for as long as they dared. Only on 8 February 1773 did the king issue writs for an extraordinary Sejm to meet on 19 April. But it was to be a 'free' Sejm, exposed to disruption by the *liberum veto*. The king hoped to create procedural irregularities which might, at some future time, enable the legality of the decisions which they knew they would be forced to take to be questioned. From the king's cabinet, Felix Łoyko produced systematic refutations of the three powers' claims. They had to be printed anonymously in London.[9] The more the king argued and obfuscated, the more he hoped to clear his own reputation in the eyes of a public opinion which believed that 'king Poniatowski' was colluding in the dismemberment of his own country in order to establish his *absolutum dominium*. This diplomatic kicking and screaming only led the irritated diplomats to threaten military reprisals, more annexations, even outright war.[10]

Frederick may have been the driving force behind the carve-up of Poland, but he was well aware that the Russians continued to view the truncated Commonwealth as their preserve. Provided the fundamentals of the Polish constitution were left unaltered, he was as content as ever to leave the complexities of settling its internal affairs to Russia. The Austrians took the same line: if Poland were to be a Russian vassal then it should remain a weak

8. Ignacy Twardowski to Jerzy Mniszech, 24 Sept. 1772, B.Cz. 3868, p. 551; Frederick II to Benoît, 30 Sept., *PC* XXXII, 21 345.

9. [F. Łoyko], *Les droits des trois puissances sur plusieurs provinces de la République de Pologne . . .* , 2 vols (London, 1774). Z. Libiszowska, *Życie polskie w Londynie w XVIII wieku* (Warsaw, 1972), pp. 72–3. See also H. Madurowicz-Urbańska, 'Łoyko, Feliks Franciszek', *PSB* XVIII, pp. 447–51.

10. Russian declaration of 14/25 Dec. 1772 and the Austrian declaration of 20 Jan. 1773 in *CTS* XLV, pp. 119–21, 122–6. The following is heavily indebted to J. Michalski, 'Rejtan i dylematy Polaków w dobie pierwszego rozbioru', *Kwartalnik Historyczny* 93 (1987 for 1986), pp. 969–1013.

one.[11] To pilot the requisite legislation through the Sejm, Panin and Catherine opted for a much-indebted gamester, Adam Poniński. He was in St Petersburg for prolonged consultations during the winter of 1772–73, as a result of which Panin expressed his appreciation that 'a man of his merits should be found in his country's present circumstances'.[12] The general amnesty to which the ministers agreed, which excepted only the small-fry 'regicides' who had bungled the abduction of Stanisław August, was as much a device to permit them to co-operate with the king's old enemies as it was a means of restoring calm to Poland.[13]

The ministers co-operated to secure the return of compliant envoys at the *sejmiki* which met in March 1773. A common corruption fund was set up – Frederick characteristically warned Benoît not to resort to it except when absolutely necessary. All three powers stationed armed detachments at the *sejmik* venues. Contributions and billeting were imposed on likely troublemakers.[14] Additional pressure was mounted on magnates with estates or crown properties in the annexed areas with the threat of sequesters. The Czartoryskis were singled out as an example: August Czartoryski's estate of Szklów in Byelorussia, one of his most lucrative properties, was confiscated. Those Polish nobles who were allowed to retain ownership of their lands behind the new frontier cordons had to take an oath of fealty to their new rulers for them.[15]

The task of securing amenable *sejmiki* in late March and early April was made simpler by the three powers' refusal to allow them to be held in their new territories and the ban on the participation of senators whose titles derived from them.[16] The non-annexed lands were divided into zones of military occupation. Russia, Prussia and Austria each sent a senior general to Warsaw to co-ordinate

11. Frederick to Solms, 17 June 1772, *PC* XXXII, 21 030; to Benoît, 21 Apr. 1773, *PC* XXXIII, 22 015; Panin to D.M. Golitsyn, 15/26 Feb. 1773, *SIRIO* CXVIII, p. 332. 'Projet d'un plan pour la conduite des trois ministres . . .' sent by Panin to Stackelberg on 24 Feb./7 Mar., ibid., pp. 338–58.
12. Panin to Antoni Ostrowski, bishop of Brześć Kujawski, 23 Feb./6 Mar. 1773, ibid., pp. 335–6.
13. Michalski, 'Rejtan', pp. 988–9.
14. Frederick to Solms, 10 Nov. 1772, *PC* XXXIII, 21 482; to Benoît, 10 Mar. 1773, ibid., 21 874; to Solms, 11 Mar., ibid., 21 879; to Benoît, 7 Apr., ibid., 21 965. Panin to Stackelberg, 24 Feb./7 Mar. 1773, *SIRIO* CXVIII, pp. 337–8 and the attached 'Projet d'un plan . . .', esp. pp. 340–1.
15. Z. Chernyshev's 'Plakat' of 5/16 Sept. 1772, B.Cz. 3868, pp. 562–3. W.I. Mieleszko, 'Formy i struktura feudalnej własności ziemskiej we wschodniej Białorusi w drugiej połowie XVII i w XVIII wieku', *Roczniki Dziejów Społecznych i Gospodarczych* 33 (1972), pp. 33–59.
16. Frederick to Benoît, 8 Nov. 1772, *PC* XXXIII, 21 472.

their troop activities.[17] Sixty-eight *sejmiki* in the old Commonwealth
had returned around 230 envoys. Of the fifty-two assemblies entitled to return envoys, at least a dozen folded without doing so. By
a curious anomaly, the *sejmiki*-in-exile of Czernichów, Smolensk and
Starodub, representing the descendants of *szlachta* who had fled
territories ceded to Russia in 1667, survived, since they met at venues
which remained attached to Poland (though only the last-named
actually returned envoys in 1773). At Liw, the Russian troops made
the disrupted *sejmik* reassemble, in order to return Poniński as envoy.

Overall, there seems to have been little outright violence.[18] Attendance was generally very poor: the *szlachta* electorate was numbed,
intimidated or saw no way out, save going through the motions.
The instructions issued were unusually laconic. There was much
hand-wringing over the attempted 'regicide'. Only two *sejmiki*, at
Nowogródek, in Lithuania, and Łęczyca, in western Poland, dared
to urge outright rejection of any territorial cessions. The lands of
those envoys and senators who did attend the Sejm were, at least to
begin with, exempted from military billets and contributions.[19] Most
of the corruption funds available to the three powers' ministers
seem to have been spent in Warsaw itself, on a never-ending round
of parties, balls, receptions and fêtes, weaving the dismemberment
of the Polish–Lithuanian Commonwealth into a bizarre *danse macabre*.
To soften the Poles up and to introduce a further distraction, in
February, Catherine authorised the return to Poland of bishops
Sołtyk and Załuski and the two Rzewuskis, arrested and deported by
Repnin in October 1767.

The Partition Sejm begins

The Sejm had to be confederated – a 'free' Sejm, as called for in
the royal writs, was out of the question. The veto could not be
allowed to operate. It was also decided that, as in 1767–68, the Sejm
would entrust all negotiation to a plenipotentiary delegation.[20] On

17. Solms to Frederick, 1, 11 Dec. 1772; Frederick to Solms, 15 Dec., ibid., 21 603,
21 643; to Solms, 16 Jan. 1773, ibid., 21 693; Edelsheim to Frederick, 16 Jan. 1773,
ibid., 21 715. Frederick to Benoît, 24 Mar., ibid., 21 920.
18. Panin to Stackelberg, 28 May/8 June 1773, *SIRIO* CXVIII, p. 403. Michalski,
'Rejtan', pp. 992–4.
19. Benoît to Frederick II, 10 Apr. 1773 and Frederick's reply, 18 Apr., *PC* XXXIII,
22 000.
20. Stackelberg's ambassadorial instruction, 11/22 Aug. 1772, *SIRIO* CXVIII, p. 186;
Panin's 'Projet d'un plan pour la conduite des trois ministres . . .', sent to Stackelberg

16 April, a Confederacy was formally inaugurated by a group of nine senators and sixty-three envoys. Since neither a confederated Sejm had been announced in the royal proclamations, nor had local confederacies been formed at constituency level, the whole procedure was highly irregular. It was on these technical grounds that Tadeusz Rejtan, envoy for Nowogródek, made the protest which has acquired near-mythological status in Polish folk memory. For four days, from 19 to 22 April, relying on his parliamentary immunity and the support of around thirty envoys, he refused Poniński access to the Chamber of Envoys in the royal palace; in effect, he threatened to conduct his own 'free' Sejm.

Despite suspicions that he was being put up by the king and the Czartoryskis to protest, Rejtan's action was almost certainly an independent one. He knew full well that he would have to give way. He was also well aware that his actions could lead to military reprisals and even an extension of the Partition. He was determined, however, to underline the illegality of the inevitable cessions and the mendacity of the proceedings: if the three ministers were prepared to admit that the Sejm would be acting under duress, he would withdraw immediately. The Prussian general Lentulus wanted him arrested. Stackelberg used other means. A confederated kangaroo court condemned Rejtan as 'a disturber of the public peace and a rebel against his country', sentencing him to confiscation of his property and reserving the right to impose further, unspecified penalties. During the course of 22 April, the king and most of the remaining senators and envoys acceded to the Confederacy. Stackelberg had warned them that he would otherwise order the devastation of the countryside around Warsaw. By 10 o'clock in the evening, down to two supporters, without food for thirty-six hours, Rejtan caved in. The three ministers promised him full immunity, and the judgements against him were reversed. Rejtan promised to apologise to Poniński (who had to be given a bodyguard of Prussian troops for his own safety),[21] but never seems to have got round to it.

It took almost another month to secure satisfactory terms for the Plenipotentiary Delegation. Again, Stanisław August tried to prevaricate, to restrict its terms of reference, to involve other powers. The response was always the same: he was only making matters worse. Squadrons of Prussian, Austrian and Russian cavalry ostentatiously

---

on 24 Feb./7 Mar. 1773, ibid., pp. 338, 341–2, 344. Frederick to Solms, 11 May 1773, *PC* XXXIII, 22 076.
    21. General Lentulus to Frederick II, 21 Apr. 1773, *PC* XXXIII, 22 032.

patrolled the Warsaw streets. Objectors were warned that troops
would be billeted on their town houses. The king was threatened
with deposition.[22] On 13 May, Poniński's bill for a Delegation which
had full powers of decision, without reference to the Sejm, was
passed by fifty-eight votes to fifty-two, a majority small enough to
demonstrate the strength of feeling but perfectly adequate to secure
what the three powers wanted.

Ninety-seven senators and envoys were appointed to the Delegation,
an unwieldy number, but, as in 1767–68, the aim was to involve as
wide a cross-section of the nobility as possible. In any case, only a
minority were to attend on a regular basis. To be valid, decisions of
the Delegation required only thirty signatures.[23] Many, if not most,
of the regular participants were on retainers from the three courts.
On 18 May, the full Sejm was adjourned until 15 September, when
it would reconvene in order to give formal ratification of the Delegation's binding decisions on the territorial cessions. Only then
would the Delegation move to the constitutional settlement.[24]

Stackelberg, though always ready to threaten all sorts of dire
consequences to get his way, was nevertheless anxious to avoid the
strong-arm tactics Repnin had employed. His softly-softly approach
reduced the pace of proceedings. So too, did external events. From
7 June to 28 August, the trial of the regicides furnished a distraction. The small fry put up to do the dirty work went to the scaffold,
despite Stanisław August's pleas for clemency.[25] The chief inspirer of
the attempt on the king's life, Teodor Wessel, the notoriously venal
grand Crown treasurer, sat on the Delegation. Then there was the
problem of the Jesuit Order, abolished by pope Clement XIV under
pressure from the Bourbon powers in July 1773. Given the importance of the Jesuits as educators, the extent of their properties and
endowments, and the genuine regard in which they were held in
the Commonwealth, the Delegation had no choice but to discuss
the consequences of their abolition, whatever its other priorities.

Disagreements among the three ministers and courts over their
respective shares did nothing to accelerate the proceedings. Frederick
resented both the size of the Austrian share and the difficulties

22. Solov'ev, *IR* XXIX, pp. 40–1.   23. *VL* VIII, pp. 5–6.
24. There is still no full account of the workings of the Delegation Sejm of 1773–
75. The following is based mainly on Michalski, 'Rejtan' and M. Drozdowski, 'Przyjęcie
traktatów rozbiorowych przez Delegację i sejm polski w 1773r.', *Roczniki Historyczne*
46 (1975), pp. 81–124.
25. Two men were beheaded on 10 Sept. Another two were sentenced to death *in
absentia*. Walenty Łukawski's wife, made to watch his execution, died of shock two
days later. W. Szczygielski, 'Łukawski, Walenty', in *PSB* XVIII, pp. 554–5.

which Russia was putting in the way of his acquisition of Danzig. He compensated himself by a very liberal interpretation of the terms of the conventions of February and August 1772. Those had assigned, as his new southern frontier, a tributary of the Oder, the river Noteć (German Netze), 'in such a way . . . that this river belongs to [the king of Prussia] in its entirety'. When the conventions were first drafted, Panin had worried about how this might be interpreted. Frederick had pooh-poohed his objections: he wanted to make sure he had both banks of the river, so as to avoid the 'chicanes désagréables' which were all that could be expected from the Poles.[26] Franz von Brenckenhoff, in charge of establishing the Prussian border, was pushing it as far south as he could towards the sources of the Noteć. The Russian and Austrian ambassadors conceded that a literal interpretation permitted this, but it did not conform to what they understood by the sense of the conventions. Frederick and Benoît stoutly maintained otherwise.[27]

In Vienna, Kaunitz warned that the Prussian view that ownership of both banks of the river entitled them to extend their territory for half a German mile (or about four English miles) south of the Noteć was certainly not intended by the conventions. Frederick was suitably indignant: there were precedents in international law to regard the flood plain as part of a river; and, anyway, he knew perfectly well that the Austrians were surreptitiously extending their borders.[28] It was true. On Giovanni Zannoni's map of Poland, published in January 1772 and used to mark out the Partition, the eastern boundary of the Austrian share was to run along the river Podgórze. But the map was wrong: there was no such river. The only alternatives were the Seret, or the Zbrucz, about twenty miles further to the east. Joseph, inspecting his new prize in August 1773, was much taken by the fertility of the area: the Zbrucz it would be. Frederick argued that he was only doing what the Austrians were, and he was quite content for the Russians to do likewise. While

26. Convention of St Petersburg (Russia and Prussia), 4 Jan. (sc. 18 Feb.) 1772, *CTS* XLIV, p. 471; repeated in the Prusso-Austrian and Prusso-Austrian conventions of 5 Aug. 1772, *CTS* XLV, pp. 70, 77–8. Cf. Solms to Frederick, 17 Jan. 1772 and Frederick's reply, 2 Feb., *PC* XXXI, 20 584.

27. Finckenstein and Hertzberg to Frederick, 19 Apr. 1773, *PC* XXXIII, 22 012; Benoît to Frederick, 1, 5 May and Frederick's replies, 9, 12 May, ibid., 22 068, 22 078; Frederick to Finckenstein and Hertzberg, 9 May, ibid., 22 069. Frederick to Solms and Edelsheim, 11 May, ibid., 22 076. See especially the exchanges between Solms, Panin and Frederick, 15 and 29 June, ibid., 22 193.

28. Frederick to Solms, 11 May, ibid., 22 076; Edelsheim to Frederick, 22 May, and Frederick's reply, 30 May, ibid., 22 126.

complaining to the Russians about the Austrian extensions, he discreetly encouraged the latter to carry on.[29]

The territorial settlement

For all the genuine irritation which such infractions caused Catherine and Panin, their prime concern remained to steam-roller all treaties through: as far as possible, they would conform to the wording of the original conventions, while the fine and not so fine details of the frontier could be entrusted to commissions of demarcation. In the interests of diplomatic protocol, the Poles would work out their treaty first with Reviczky, as the representative of the Holy Roman Emperor, then with Stackelberg, then with Benoît. The Delegation sought preconditions in concessions and privileges for the *szlachta* in the lost territories, it sought to reserve reversionary rights for the Commonwealth, it tried to argue over the new frontier lines – to no avail. The chairman of the Delegation, bishop Antoni Ostrowski of Brześć Kujawski and the marshals of the Confederacy, Adam Poniński and Michał Radziwiłł, signed the treaty of cession with Reviczky on 21 August, to take effect at the same time as the Russian and Prussian treaties. The delighted ambassador took off to convey the news in person to Joseph II, at Zamość, just across his new Polish–Austrian border.[30]

Stackelberg and Benoît were no less insistent than Reviczky in demanding an unconditional agreement to their treaties of territorial cession. They had no time for the Delegation's efforts to raise other issues, such as the position of the Catholic church or despairing complaints at Russian and Prussian military exactions or commercial abuses. Stackelberg threatened to sack Warsaw before Ostrowski and the two marshals would put their signatures to the Polish–Russian treaty on 1 September. More threats were required before the treaty with Prussia was signed on 11 September. The thirty signatures required to validate the three treaties were obtained on 18 September. Under the Delegation's terms of reference, the full, reassembled Sejm should have given its ratification automatically. The treaties were submitted to it on the 21st, to encounter a barrage of criticism. On 27 September, the three ministers warned that failure

29. Solms to Frederick II, 14 May and Frederick's reply, 30 May, ibid., 22 127. Benoît to Frederick, 9 June and Frederick's reply, 16 June, ibid., 22 161. Frederick to Edelsheim, 30 May, ibid., 22 126. Arneth, *GMT* VIII, pp. 423–5.
30. Arneth, *GMT* VIII, pp. 411–13.

to ratify 'will call forth a declaration of war'. The treaties were confirmed the next day. The Sejm adjourned on 30 September to 22 January 1774.[31]

The wording of article II of each of the three treaties of territorial cession matched that of the conventions of St Petersburg of 4 January and 5 August, in the Austrian case even to the extent of including the now known to be non-existent river Podgórze. The treaties went on to state, in identical terms, that the final, precise demarcation of the new borders would be entrusted to commissioners appointed by Poland and the three powers. In case of disagreement between the Poles and the members of any other commission, the dispute would be referred to the arbitration of the other two partitioning powers; such mixed commissions would also resolve any future border disagreements. Article XII of the Prussian treaty also referred the settlement of disagreements over Danzig to a separate commission of Polish, Prussian and Russian representatives.

Poland and the powers assured each other of 'inviolable peace, sincere union and perfect friendship'. Poland formally renounced all claims to all the territories it had ceded, as well as any other territories to which it might have any claims. In turn, Austria, Russia and Prussia renounced all further claims on Polish territories. The Polish–Prussian treaty was slightly more complex than the other two in this respect, for it carried a formal renunciation by Poland of all reversionary rights to the duchy of East Prussia and other, lesser fiefs, to which it had been entitled by the treaties of Wehlau and Bydgoszcz of 1657. On paper at least, all claims and feudal connexions were neatly severed. Under article VI of each treaty, the partitioning powers 'formally and in the strongest manner guarantee to His Majesty the king of Poland and his successors and to the Republic of Poland, all their present possessions'. The Austrians promised to conserve their new Orthodox and Protestant subjects in their existing religious rights, with similar promises being made to Catholics, Uniates included, by Russia and Prussia.

This was only the start. The new frontier lines had to be demarcated on the ground. The status of those owning property on both sides of the new borders had to be regulated; outstanding business transactions and lawsuits remained to be settled. The economic unity of the old Commonwealth was ripped apart by the partition; some form of settlement of commercial relationships with each of the three powers was essential. The treaties of cession specified that

31. B.Cz. 825, pp. 598–695.

such contingent matters would be worked out later by the Delegation, and would be largely regulated in 'Separate Acts' which would be considered part of the treaties themselves. Diocesan and ecclesiastical structures needed reshaping and renegotiation. The fate of the ex-Jesuit estate had to be settled. Stability and some form of acceptable government had to be restored. The awkward matter of the dissenters still remained to be resolved. There were those in the Delegation, not least marshal Poniński, who were anxious not to bring matters to a speedy conclusion because they were on generous pensions and backhanders from the three powers, which would come to an end as soon as their task was done. It is not therefore surprising that seven separate adjournments were necessary before the Sejm reassembled for its final run of plenary sittings between 20 March and 11 April 1775. It reconvened periodically to ratify the legislation coming up from the Delegation.

The demarcation of the border was painfully slow. In no case was it brought to a conclusion before the end of the Sejm. All three powers resorted to varying mixtures of threats and bribes to persuade the Polish commissioners to accept interpretations or alterations of the borders favourable to the partitioners. The Austrians pushed their borders to the Zbrucz. Frederick was much exercised by the Austrian annexation of the town of Brody, the biggest Jewish commercial centre in Europe.[32] He took his resentment out on the Poles, in the end filching about five times as much additional land as the Austrians, over and above the shares laid down in the St Petersburg conventions; Frederick also gained an extra 120,000 subjects. Poland's agreement with Russia was concluded only on 18 July 1775; with Austria on 9 February 1776; and with Prussia, as late as 17 July 1777.[33]

The commercial settlement

Frederick also pursued an unremitting campaign of economic and territorial harassment against Thorn and Danzig, which he planned to put under such pressure that they would beg to be taken under his protection. Danzig was hardest hit. Hertzberg and his officials combed old archives and documents with a zeal that any French *feudiste* would have admired. Frederick took over Danzig's main

---

32. Frederick II to Solms, 26 Dec. 1772, *PC* XXXIII, 21 643.
33. Arneth, *GMT* VIII, pp. 492–533; Topolski, 'The Polish–Prussian frontier', pp. 81–110.

port, on the grounds that it was built on land held on long-term lease from the abbot of Oliva – who, under the Partition, had become a Prussian subject. Frederick let the town use the port facilities, but insisted on levying customs duties equal to Danzig's own. Since the boundaries of neither 'Danzig' nor 'Thorn' were defined in the partition conventions, Frederick took over suburbs and villages long regarded as part of the two towns, if they were not specified as such in their founding medieval charters. He imposed restrictions on trade, set up rival markets and fairs, used the pretext of recovering deserters to demand financial compensation or even to send search parties into the towns. The result was constant appeals from Danzig and Thorn to Warsaw and, more importantly, to St Petersburg, where Frederick's conduct caused growing annoyance. This was of little comfort to Danzig, which, surrounded on land by Prussian territory, found itself in steep economic decline under the impact of Frederick's remorseless vendetta.[34]

Commercial negotiations continued on and off throughout the Sejm. The Poles' demand for free trade, not only with their former possessions but with the partitioning powers as a whole, found favour only with Russia. Catherine was actively promoting economic development within her dominions through a policy of free trade anyway; Polish needs complemented Russia's. Giving them most-favoured-nation status was a powerful means of tightening Polish dependency on Russia. Under the terms concluded on 8 March 1775, Polish–Russian trade was to be free of all customs duties; their merchants could travel and trade freely between the two states. Three days later, the treaty with Austria followed. Polish exports would incur a 4 per cent duty, while all goods crossing Habsburg lands would be subject to a 1 per cent transit levy. No duties would be levied on salt. Poles would impose no more than a modest half-ducat per barrel on their beloved Hungarian wine imports, which Maria Theresa agreed 'to facilitate as much as possible'. Otherwise, Austrian exports to Poland could attract at most a duty of five-twelfths of a per cent. Clearly, these terms were very much to the advantage of Austria, but in an age when protectionism and mercantilism were still the norm, the settlement was not an excessively harsh one for Poland.

This left the most important trade area of all – that with Prussia, principally along the Vistula, Poland's major export channel. The

---

34. J.A. Wilder, *Traktat handlowy polsko-pruski z roku 1775* (Warsaw, 1937), pp. 61–3, 170–4 and *passim*.

treaty imposed by Frederick on 18 March was punitive. Prussian exports to the Commonwealth could attract only a duty of 2 per cent. Likewise, Polish exports of raw and finished products would pay only a duty of 2 per cent – but re-exports would pay 12 per cent. But the bulk of the trade going up and down the Vistula was not bound for Prussia at all – it was transit trade, which was also to be subject to a duty of 12 per cent; on the other hand, Prussian goods taken across Polish territory would pay the same 2 per cent levy as their exports. Frederick reserved the right to charge whatever rates he wished on Polish commodities 'which are useful for the factories of his Prussian Majesty's lands'. The clause relating to Danzig was so open-ended as to be meaningless – it would be liable to the same transit duties 'as foreigners'. Frederick had been subjecting Polish trade to harassment and arbitrary impositions for years. His treaty excited the most clamours and opposition, with protests and pleas fired off to St Petersburg and London – but all to no avail. Much as the British disliked the pressures Frederick imposed on Danzig, there was little they could do.[35] Increasingly irritating as the Russians found Frederick, he was still their chief ally.

The negotiation of the commercial treaties proceeded in tandem with the settlement of a wide range of loose ends predominantly concerned with the rights of Polish subjects in the ceded territories. The basic principle adopted was that the status of new subjects would 'not be inferior to that of existing subjects' of the Romanov, Habsburg and Hohenzollern dominions. So-called 'sujets mixtes', whose properties lay in the Commonwealth and across the new borders, could fix their permanent domicile in either Poland or in one of the partitioning states, without incurring any legal or other disabilities on the other side of the frontier. There would be no additional tax incurred on revenues drawn across borders. Any Polish noble or townsman resident in the partitioned lands who wished to sell up and remove to Poland could do so freely, with no further penalties, for a period of six years. Analogous rules were drawn up for the regulation of debts, mortgages, inheritances. Outstanding lawsuits were to be settled in the courts of the defendant's country of residence. Provision was made for the delivery of archives and legal documentation to Poland, even for the delivery of monies found in local treasuries prior to 13 September 1772, which was confirmed as the baseline date for the transfer of the ceded territories (none

35. Scott, *British foreign policy*, pp. 192–202.

of these commitments seems to have been observed). Poland and the
three powers promised not to seek recruits in each other's territories.
Only the Polish–Prussian agreement dealt with the delicate issue of
the *starostwa*, the crown properties bestowed by Polish kings in lifetime
tenure on 'deserving' individuals: these had been taken over immediately on 13 September 1772 in the Prussian sector by the Prussian
treasury. Frederick promised their former holders 'equitable' cash
compensation (which never materialised). The issue was not raised
in the Austrian and Russian treaties, because there was no clear
policy.[36] The Austrians were prepared to sell such estates outright
to their old tenants. Russia either confiscated such lands or was
willing to confirm the tenure of existing holders, provided they
proved co-operative.

The constitutional settlement

Russia, Austria and Prussia were determined on the restoration in
Poland of 'calm and good order . . . on a solid and permanent footing' to be secured by their ministers by negotiation with the Sejm,
in the form of statutes which each power, in a demonstration of
solidarity, pledged itself in advance to guarantee. Panin and
Stackelberg were to fret that this guarantee would open what was
meant to have been an exclusive Russian preserve to the influence
of untrustworthy partners. Their worries proved largely misplaced.
Prussia and Austria wanted territory, not control. They began the
evacuation of their troops from the Polish territories proper a fortnight after the Sejm ratified the territorial treaties. Russian troops
remained.

   Benoît and Reviczky played a comparatively minor role in the
tedious constitutional negotiations. The onus fell on Stackelberg,
in accordance with a virtual prospectus of constitutional reform
elaborated by Panin and Catherine in March 1773. The basis of the
constitutional settlement would be the arrangements worked out
by the Sejm of 1767–68: the *liberum veto* would continue to apply to
all business of any significance. Only matters of minor import could
be decided by majority decisions. The kingship would remain elective – however, in order to reduce scope for undesirable (from
Russia's point of view) external intervention, only Piasts, native Poles,

36. For the texts of the 'Acte[s] séparé[s] contenant différentes stipulations'
see *VL* VIII, pp. 39–42 (Poland–Austria), 51–4 (Poland–Russia) and 51–62
(Poland–Prussia).

would be eligible, provided they were not sons or grandsons of a monarch. Close royal relatives would also be barred from a range of key ministerial positions. Stanisław August's position was assured – but, Panin implied, he had infringed 'the true principle of Polish government [which] is the equilibrium of the powers of the three orders, the royal, the senatorial and the equestrian'. The new statutes would remedy this. Thus the king would be restricted by a new, Sejm-appointed council. Royal powers of patronage were to be extensively curtailed.[37]

From early on during the Sejm, Stanisław August began to draw closer to Stackelberg, intending to repeat the co-operation which had enabled him to hold back the worst excesses of the Confederacy of Radom of 1767–68. Much of his public opposition was little more than posturing. Bereft of wider backing, financially dependent on Stackelberg, he always had to back down. The ambassador was determined to manipulate the balance between the king and the 'nation' far more effectively than his predecessors had done. He indulged Stanisław August in one sphere. On 14 October 1773, in the wake of the abolition of the Jesuits, the Delegation set up, with the ambassador's agreement, a Commission for National Education to take control of almost every aspect of schooling, from primary to university level. This was the biggest single concession which the king secured during the Sejm – but any benefits it might confer would be, of their nature, long-term.[38]

At the very outset of its deliberations, the Delegation had agreed in principle to the establishment of an executive council which would effectively control the king. This would be the so-called 'Permanent Council', *Rada Nieustająca*. When, in mid-November, substantial discussions on the form of government finally resumed, the king's efforts to retain his powers of distribution or to have a substantial say in the composition of the Permanent Council proved fruitless. Stackelberg would only agree that the Commission for National Education should be excluded from its jurisdiction. Even so, it took another threat to declare war before the king agreed to accept the Council on 10 December without further conditions.[39]

37. 'Projet d'un plan . . .' sent out to Stackelberg on 24 Feb./7 Mar. 1773, *SIRIO* CXVIII, esp. pp. 345–56. Panin to Stackelberg, 19/30 July 1774, *SIRIO* CXXXV, p. 157.

38. There is a huge literature on the Commission in Polish. Otherwise, the most accessible, and in many ways still most important, treatment remains A. Jobert, *La Commission d'Éducation Nationale en Pologne (1773–1794)* (Paris, 1941).

39. W. Konopczyński, *Geneza i ustanowienie Rady Nieustajacej* (Kraków, 1917), esp. pp. 200–69.

The Permanent Council's remit was only finalised in October 1774. Insofar as it was an executive organ, it was a largely passive one – designed to keep Poland-Lithuania on hold, ensuring existing laws were implemented, but no more. It was a cumbersome committee of thirty-six, drawn in equal numbers from the Senate and the Chamber of Envoys. The king was reduced to the role of its president. Only the primate sat *ex officio*. The others would be elected by a majority ballot in plenary sessions of the Sejm, a third of each complement being re-elected to ensure continuity. The Council had no legislative, judicial, or fiscal powers of its own. Technically speaking, it was not even supposed to interpret the law, but was to refer all vague or contentious legislation (and most Polish laws were, at the very least, vague) back to the Sejm, to which it was fully answerable. The Council, besides meeting in regular plenary sessions, was also subdivided into five departments – of 'foreign interests', 'police', the army, justice and finance. The king chaired only the Department of Foreign Interests. In the plenary sessions, he was given an extra vote, but otherwise he was bound by the majority decision.

Insofar as the Council was allowed any policy initiatives, it was only to prepare parliamentary bills. Since the Sejm would continue to meet under the standing orders of 1768, which restricted majority voting to minor business under the heading of 'economic matters', the *Rzeczpospolita* was effectively condemned to a closed circle of legislative and executive powerlessness. Among the Council's specific tasks were the preservation of the constitutional status quo, the supervision of state expenditure, 'the greatest care to preserve the alliances and treaties of the Commonwealth' and the preparation of a compendium of civil and criminal law (subject to the approval of a future Sejm).

Superficially, this was a committee-style executive of the sort much in favour among the cameralistically inclined governments of Germany and Russia. In reality, it existed to keep Poland in the condition of a 'puissance intermédiaire' – a buffer state, politically as much as geographically. St Petersburg and Potsdam were at one in insisting that the Polish government should exist in the interests of Poland's neighbours. The Austrians would have liked to see the abolition of the veto, while preserving a weak republican form of government; they were even ready to see the throne made hereditary in the house of Poniatowski but were in no position to face down the combined hostility of Frederick and Catherine to such an idea.[40]

40. Ibid., p. 154. Solov'ev, *IR*, pp. 42–3 (Stackelberg to Panin, 23 May 1773).

To Stanisław August, the most damaging aspect of the new Council were the inroads made into his *ius distributivum*, his powers of appointment. From now on, he could appoint senators (including Roman Catholic bishops) and ministers only from among three candidates for each vacancy put forward by the Permanent Council; he lost his right to promote officers; he lost command of the four companies of the royal guard. He kept his right to nominate to most other non-elective local and titular offices as well as to diplomatic posts. A particular blow was the reform of the crown estates, which had been one of the most important tools of royal patronage. Only four such estates, out of hundreds, would remain in the royal gift. As others fell vacant, they would be auctioned off on fifty-year leases to the highest bidder. The Sejm itself awarded 238 such tenures, mainly to Poniński and his hangers-on.[41]

In order to stabilise the amputated *Rzeczpospolita*, order had to be restored to the chaotic finances. On 20 May 1774, the three ministers informed the Delegation that the Commonwealth could budget for 33 million zloties of annual revenues (not quite £1 million sterling!) – enough, supposedly, to cover all civil expenditures and the upkeep of an army of 30,000. This was almost half as much again as the previous budget of 1767–68, of which only between one-fifth and one-third had been collected during the Barist shambles. The projected figures aroused consternation. It was all very well for Austria to tax its new noble subjects at 12 per cent of net revenues or Prussia at 25 per cent,[42] but such levels of taxation were utterly unheard of in Poland proper. Finally, in February 1775, the state budget was set at over 29 million zloties, after Stackelberg threatened to impose it by force. This figure, based on guesswork and wishful thinking, was never fulfilled. Much of the revenue raised over the next two years went in pensions and emoluments to Poniński and his closest associates. The king's own civil list – the first such in Poland's history – at five million zloties, accounted for over one-sixth of putative expenditure. Perhaps the sole positive aspect of the new budget was to remove direct collection of tax monies from the army to civilian officials.[43]

41. *VL* VIII, pp. 91–3. A. Stroynowski, 'Zmiany w strukturze społecznej użytkowników królewszczyzn w Rzeczypospolitej w drugiej połowie XVIIIw.', *Acta Universitatis Lodziensis: Nauki Humanistyczno-Społeczne*, Ser. I, no. 40 (1978), pp. 21–36.
42. Glassl, *Das österreichische Einrichtungswerk in Galizien (1772–1790)* (Wiesbaden, 1975), pp. 171–2; G. Labuda, ed., *Historia Pomorza*, II, p. 636.
43. M.M. Drozdowski, *Podstawy finansowe działalności państwowej w Polsce, 1763–1793* (Warsaw, 1975), pp. 42–85.

Stackelberg regarded as the most difficult part of his brief the still unresolved religious question, not least because Reviczky parted contact with his non-Catholic colleagues. He urged the Poles to give away as little as possible. While Catherine would not contemplate any major concessions as incompatible with her honour and prestige, even during the heyday of Bar, Russians had been making behind-the-scenes efforts to persuade the Protestant nobles' leaders to back down voluntarily. They had got nowhere.[44] Now, the fact of Partition had assisted by removing the great bulk of Polish Protestants to Prussia. The Goltz brothers, who had so agitated for improved rights for Protestants, lost their crown land tenancies, once among the most lucrative in Poland, to the Prussian treasury. The sole Orthodox diocese passed to Russia. A substantial peasant Orthodox minority remained in the Polish Ukraine and in Lithuania, where the chronic tensions between Uniate and Orthodox clergy showed no abatement.

Stackelberg was able to pressure the Protestant leaders, as disorientated as the rest of the Polish nobility by the Partition, into concessions. The dissenters remained entitled to all offices within the state below ministerial and senatorial rank. Three (unspecified) seats in the Chamber of Envoys were reserved to them, one for each province: Wielkopolska, Małopolska and Lithuania. The *iudicium mixtum* set up by Repnin's Sejm to hear disputes between Catholics and dissenters was abolished and its functions were taken over by the chancellors' courts of the Crown and the Grand Duchy. The provisions relating to the dissenters required a further 'Acte Séparé', appended by the Delegation on 15 March 1775 to the Russo-Polish territorial treaty. The same document reaffirmed the 1767–68 principle of cardinal, supposedly immutable laws and *materiae status*, subject to the application of the *liberum veto*. The functioning of the Permanent Council was sanctioned as a cardinal law. So too, was the restriction of the elective monarchy to native Poles. Austria and Prussia had of course guaranteed in advance the constitutional work of the Sejm in the treaties of 18 September 1773, yet the Russo-Polish 'Acte Séparé' of 15 March, which carried an explicit Russian guarantee of the Sejm's entire work, was, significantly, the only one of its kind. Poland had shrunk but Russia was as determined as ever that it should be in sole control.[45]

44. Panin to Volkonskii, 28 Sept./9 Oct. 1770, *SIRIO* XCVII, pp. 144–8; to Saldern, 28 Aug./8 Sept. 1771, ibid., pp. 424–5. W. Konopczyński, *Konfederacja barska*, 2 vols (1991 edn), I, pp. 357–8, 360–1.
45. Kaunitz's memorandum, 3 Jan. 1776, Arneth, *GMT* VIII, pp. 519–21.

Profit and loss

'I am delighted to see you . . . gain glory in peace, such as princes
seek so strenuously in war, by acquisitions which so increase the
happiness of your reign', drooled Henry, congratulating his big
brother on his enlightened diplomacy.[46] This was no consolation to
the Poles. The *Rzeczpospolita* lost at least 4,530,000 inhabitants, getting on for a third of its population: 580,000 went to Prussia;
2,650,000 went to Austria; 1,300,000 to Russia.[47] The territorial losses
were comparable. Of the 283,200 square miles its lands covered at
the beginning of 1772, it lost well over a quarter. Russia took 35,907
square miles. Austria, with 31,622 square miles, was not far behind.
Then came Prussia, with 14,015 square miles. The Russian share
was comparatively underpopulated and peopled predominantly by
a non-Polish-speaking Byelorussian peasantry. Zachar Chernyshev
got his reward as governor-general of the new lands, clumped together into two new *gubernii* of Polotsk and Mogilev.

Habsburg bureaucrats antiquarianised their share into the 'kingdom of Galicia and Lodomeria' after the Latin forms of the medieval Rus' principalities of Halicz/Galich and Włodzimierz/Vladimir.
Polish-speakers predominated in the western half; further east, there
was a substantial Ukrainian peasant element, but dominated by a
still-numerous *szlachta*. Frederick's new province of Westpreussen
was, despite strong German elements, mainly Polish. It may superficially have been the least substantial, but the Austrians were not
merely resorting to political casuistry when they had insisted that
'perfect equality' in the Partition could not be restricted to demography and area. The former Polish Prussia had been the most
prosperous, urbanised and agriculturally advanced region of the
Commonwealth. For all the ravages of Bar and Frederick's own pre-
Partition depredations, he could not help exulting at the value of
his prize. Galicia, apart from the Wieliczka and Bochnia salt-mines,
contained some of the most fertile agricultural land north of the
Carpathians; Joseph thought the lands along the Zbrucz to be possibly the richest in all the Habsburg dominions. The Russians could

46. Henry to Frederick II, 16 Sept. 1772, *PC* XXXII, 21 305.
47. The state of Polish demographic history for the Partition period is such that it
needs to be treated with great caution. Modern historians tend to accept a higher
figure of 14,000,000 for Poland's pre-1772 population, but this has yet to be satis-
factorily meshed with the demographic consequences of the Partitions. The figures
given should be regarded as *minima*. For an overview of the chief sources, see
I. Gieysztorowa, 'Ludność', in A. Mączak, ed., *Encyklopedia Historii Gospodarczej Polski
do 1945 roku*, 2 vols (Warsaw, 1981), I, p. 430.

hardly complain – their share gave them control of the finest hemp production in the region, further enhancing Russia's domination of the naval stores market.[48] In brief, the First Partition deprived Poland of its most valuable lands and economic resources. Its losses were its tormentors' gains.

The partition yielded a final twist. The Austrians had learned not to miss a trick. The Russians were much intrigued to learn, in September 1774, that an Austrian border commissioner had been combing Polish archives for the Commonwealth's titles to Moldavia (in the fifteenth century, a Polish vassal). Joseph could not resist a wedge of territory between Transylvania and Galicia – fertile, providing better communications with the new Polish lands. As field marshal Rumiantsev's men trudged back through northern Moldavia to Poland and Russia, Austrian troops fell in behind. In Constantinople, the Austrian *internuntius*, Franz von Thugut pressed the Turks to agree to an amicable settlement of the new border dispute, helpfully pointing out that they needed all the friends they could get. The small area of land known as the Bukovina did not give rise to the same sorts of repercussions as the Habsburg occupation of Zips – Turkey's territories were in the wrong place. In St Petersburg, Panin shrugged his shoulders, wished the Austrians luck, but pointed out that this acquisition would do nothing to ease the Polish border negotiations with Frederick. Frederick seethed, but on 7 May 1775, by the Convention of Pera, the Turks caved in and gave Austria most of what it wanted. Maria Theresa complained that Austrian policies were dishonourable, but Galicia and the Bukovina remained Austrian.[49]

Continued difficulties

It became rapidly clear that the political settlement was unstable. The Delegation Sejm had operated in a supercharged atmosphere of intimidation and corruption, intrigue and debauch, redeemed (if that is the word) by posturing and despairing obstructionism. The jurisdiction and competence of the new organs, their relationship to existing bodies, including the Sejm and the army and treasury

48. Frederick to Henry, 18 June 1772, *PC* XXXII, 21 033. Arneth, *GMT* VIII, p. 424; U.L. Lehtonen, *Die polnischen Provinzen Russlands unter Katharina II. in den Jahren 1772–1782* (Berlin, 1907), pp. 411–13.

49. A.M. Golitsyn to D.M. Golitsyn, 3/14 Oct. 1774, *SIRIO* CXXXV, pp. 245–6; Arneth, *GMT* VIII, pp. 469–89.

commissions set up in 1764, which still remained in being, were poorly defined. Politics imploded into a factional flux. The king co-operated with the Russians because he had no choice. Stanisław August's factotum, Ksawery Branicki, appointed Grand Crown *hetman* in February 1774, drew his own conclusions. The king was nothing. Reform meant nothing, for Russia would not allow it. An almost nihilistic restoration of the old, unreformed order had more appeal. If he could bring back the old, untrammelled powers of the *hetman*-ship, he would be more powerful than the king himself and answer-able to virtually no one. Real power lay in St Petersburg. During successive missions to the Russian capital in 1771, 1774, 1775 and 1776 Branicki had been able to charm some, not least Catherine, and alarm others – Panin, who may even have had doubts as to his mental stability. But Panin was no longer the force he had been. Branicki knew where his bread would be buttered. Grigorii Orlov's career as the empress's principal lover came to an end in September 1772 – within a few months he had been replaced in Catherine's saddle by Grigorii Potemkin, the great love of her life. And it was to Potemkin that Branicki looked for support.

Branicki was potentially very useful to Potemkin, from February 1774 governor-general of the province of Novorossiia, located be-tween the southern Polish border and the Crimea. As *hetman* and as holder of the vast crown estate of Biała Cerkiew, secured for him by Potemkin's influence, Branicki would be well placed to facilitate future Russian drives into the Balkans. Perhaps even now Potemkin was thinking of securing his own semi-independent principality in the region, 'Dacia', part of the fantastic schemes mooted during the recent war for the dismemberment of the Ottoman empire. It is quite likely that Branicki made more of Potemkin's friendship than it really warranted. St Petersburg seems to have looked on him as a useful, if erratic, counterweight to a king whom it could, after a decade of unsatisfactory relations, never again bring itself to trust.[50]

The links that Branicki forged in St Petersburg stood him in good stead in Poland. Those who were excluded from the spoils of government by the Stackelberg–Stanisław August axis saw him as their link to Catherine. During the Delegation Sejm there was a massive reordering of the party constellations in Poland. The Czartoryskis resented the loss of the king's dependency on them and began to make common cause with their former political opponents.

50. Panin to Stackelberg, 27 June/8 July 1775, *SIRIO* CXXXV, p. 425; Catherine to Stanisław August, 5/16 Aug., ibid., pp. 447–8; vice-chancellor I.A. Osterman to Stackelberg, 7/18 Dec. 1775, ibid., pp. 491–2.

They made their peace with Branicki, with the sprawling Potocki clan and with the Rzewuski family, to form a vocal, dangerous and irresponsible opposition, ready to weave between St Petersburg and Vienna. This was not unwelcome to Catherine, who had finally accepted that playing off political factions against each other was a far more effective means of political management than relying on the dubious out-group of the dissenters.[51]

In order to enhance their value to St Petersburg, the opposition began to agitate among the *szlachta* at the threat to their ancient liberties that the rule of Poniatowski, Stackelberg and the Permanent Council supposedly posed. Adam Czartoryski and Branicki cooked up fantastic plans to depose Stanisław August in favour of the archduke Maximilian of Habsburg; an even more hare-brained scheme to make Louis XVI's younger brother, the comte d'Artois, king was floated. There was a plan to make Adam Czartoryski hereditary monarch. Stackelberg was sufficiently alarmed to suggest to Reviczky that Austrian troops should move into southern Poland to quell a threatened *szlachta* uprising.[52] Stackelberg paid a brief visit to St Petersburg early in 1776. For most of the previous year, his court had intended to withdraw its troops from Poland at the earliest opportunity.[53] He now convinced Catherine not only that the troops had to stay for the foreseeable future, but that serious adjustments needed to be made, by force, if necessary, to the constitutional settlement. The powers of the new bodies had to be defined more clearly and the authority of the Permanent Council enhanced. Russia's ability to manage the Commonwealth was at stake.[54]

The Sejm of 1776

The final act of the post-Partition settlement was played out at the 1776 Sejm. The *sejmiki* witnessed fraught scenes. Russian troops were present at those where trouble was thought most likely. The Prussians promised military assistance, if required. Stackelberg warned Adam Czartoryski he would arrest him if he attempted to

---

51. See e.g. Panin to Stackelberg, 18/29 Sept. 1775, ibid., pp. 468–9; Stackelberg's (undated) despatch of July/August 1778, Solov'ev, *IR* XXIX, pp. 229–30.

52. Ibid., pp. 179–80; Arneth, *GMT* VIII, p. 522.

53. Osterman to Stackelberg, 10/21 Sept. 1775, *SIRIO* CXXXV, p. 468.

54. Solov'ev, *IR* XXIX, pp. 177–80 (includes the Council's instruction to Stackelberg of February 1776).

stand for election as envoy. In the worst violence, at Ciechanów, north of Warsaw, thirty-six *szlachta* were killed by Russian grenadiers; at Słonim, in Lithuania, three Poles were bayoneted to death by Russian troops defending themselves from a mob of angry *szlachta*. Stackelberg worked closely with Stanisław August to secure favourable returns. Even so, many *sejmiki* were split and, despite the Russian military presence, some thirty opposition envoys were returned.

The confederated Sejm declared most of the opposition results null and void. Royal guardsmen surrounded the royal palace, keeping out undesirables. This was an unheard-of affront to Poland's magnates, far more injurious than a mere partition. The Sejm carried the measures that the king and the ambassador wanted. The Permanent Council was given full powers to direct and supervise all ministers and commissions. Disobedience to any directives would be followed by suspension from office. The *hetmani* lost any real power of command over the army, which was now firmly subordinated to the directives of the Council's Army Department. The appointment of all officers was entrusted to the king, who also regained command of his guards regiments. The Council was empowered to interpret the laws, although all its decisions would require the retrospective approval of each Sejm.[55] Most of the pensions handed out by the 1773–75 Sejm were either rescinded or much reduced. The Commission for National Education was given direct control over the much depleted ex-Jesuit estate, hitherto administered by a commission packed by Poniński's cronies. A former Crown chancellor, Andrzej Zamoyski, was instructed to compile a reformed law code.[56] When the Sejm rose on 31 October, the constitutional pacification of the dismembered *Rzeczpospolita* was largely complete.[57]

---

55. *VL* VIII, pp. 526–35.   56. *VL* VIII, pp. 537–8, 543.
57. The history of the 1776 Sejm remains woefully unexplored. See Solov'ev, *IR* XXIX, pp. 177–83; J. Michalski, ed., *Historia Sejmu Polskiego* (Warsaw, 1984), I, pp. 377–8.

CHAPTER FIVE

Interlude

The szlachta and the Partition

As the first rumours of partition broke across the Commonwealth, Ignacy Twardowski, palatine of Kalisz, wrote: 'We are finished . . . those cut off by the partition, once free, will become slaves. The thought brings tears to my eyes, for in large measure, I, too, will succumb to this fate under the Prussian yoke.'[1] He cried not only for his country's losses, but his own lucrative crown estate of Nakło, about to fall into the maw of the Prussian treasury. August Czartoryski, also reduced to tears, at least conceded that he and his countrymen had brought the disaster on themselves.[2] Twardowski's letters to his patron, Jerzy Mniszech, betray no sense of guilt. The Partition is a test sent from God; or it is a plot hatched between king Poniatowski and the Russians, to introduce royal absolutism; and the main worry is what will happen to the crown leaseholds cut off behind the new borders.[3]

A once-enthusiastic confederate, Józef Wybicki, concluded that, for all its heroism, suffering and self-sacrifice, Bar had proved a destructive and dangerous cul-de-sac. The Poles' own attachment to a woefully misunderstood conception of freedom, rather than the machinations of their neighbours, had been their undoing. The szlachta ought to co-operate with the king to improve their form of government, strengthen themselves sufficiently to become a worthwhile ally and take advantage of divisions among the partitioning

1. 29 Apr. 1772, B.Cz. 3868, p. 203.
2. T. Konopka, *Historia domu naszego: raptularz z czasów Stanisława Augusta*, M. Konopka, ed. (Warsaw, 1993), p. 149.
3. Twardowski to Mniszech, 28 May, 3 June, 2 July, 27 Aug. 1772, B.Cz. 3868, pp. 267, 280–1, 341, 506; cf. Zofia Lubomirska to Mniszech, 17 May, 16 Sept., 27 Oct., 13 Dec., ibid., pp. 243–4, 531, 650–1, 843.

powers to forge international connexions that would help confer genuine security.[4] Such considered analysis was rare in the wake of the Partition. It was exceptional, too, in envisaging a possible future recovery of the lost lands.[5] The great bulk of reactions to the First Partition remained cast in a traditional, moralistic mode. The vices of men were responsible, rather than the shortcomings of the Commonwealth itself.[6]

Popular, run-of-the-mill *szlachta* opinion scarcely saw deeper. The instructions issued by the *sejmiki* to their envoys were almost invariably compiled by small caucuses of activists, often after the elections were over and most electors had staggered home after the boozing and brawling that were an inseparable part of these occasions. But those who drew them up knew they could not put forward anything unacceptable to their constituents without provoking uproar. Not only did the *szlachta* become rapidly reconciled to the Partitions but they showed no inclination whatever to change their ways. Self-criticism is difficult to come by. The parish-pump world of Polish politics remained as it always had. Despite the trauma of losing a good third of their territory, population and resources, the Polish–Lithuanian nobility tried to carry on as if nothing had happened.

Between 1773 and 1788 – the year in which the growing divisions between the three partitioning powers did finally burst into the open to provide an opportunity for reform – there were eight rounds of pre-Sejm *sejmiki*: in 1773, 1776, 1778, 1780, 1782, 1784, 1786 and 1788. A trawl through 117 *instrukcje* of thirty-one constituencies reveals a stubborn conservatism.[7] In this nation where every adult male noble considered himself to be a legislator, not one instruction in 1773 gave any indication as to how Poland might be rescued from its plight, beyond recommendations to despatch embassies to powers which had concluded treaties which either guaranteed, or could be construed to guarantee, Poland's territorial integrity.[8] Foremost among these were, of course, the partitioning powers themselves. The 1660 treaty of Oliva allowed the appeals to

4. J. Wybicki, *Myśli polityczne o wolności cywilnej* [first published 1775–76], E. Rostworowski, ed. (Wrocław, 1984), esp. pp. 87–9 and Pt III *passim*; E. Rostworowski, 'Myśli polityczne Józefa Wybickiego, czyli droga od konfederacji barskiej do obiadów czwartkowych', *Wiek Oświecenia* 1 (1978), pp. 31–52.
5. Wybicki, *Myśli*, pp. 213–14.
6. B. Wolska, *Poezja polityczna czasów pierwszego rozbioru i sejmu delegacyjnego 1772–1775* (Wrocław, 1982), *passim.*
7. For a breakdown of the manuscript sources of the instructions, see Appendix.
8. Kalisz-Poznań, Kraków, Łęczyca, Łomża, Nowogródek, Wołkowysk instructions.

extend to France, a highly unlikely Sweden and an even less plausible England. It was all too characteristic of a legalistic frame of mind which sought security in pacts and agreements rather than in native strength.

When it came to practical suggestions of what the Poles themselves could do, the *sejmiki* were at a loss. There was much hand-wringing, breast-beating and invocation of Providence; expressions of hope in the capacity of the king and the Sejm – both starved of effective power by the nobility for decades – to pull something out of negotiations with the three powers. The *sejmik* at Nowogródek in Lithuania, which returned Tadeusz Rejtan, was unique in informing its envoys that they were to oppose the partition 'even at the cost of their lives and fortunes'; but it was utterly at one with all the other *sejmiki* in failing to offer any practical solutions to Poland's problems or even in considering that any such problems, beyond the actions of foreign powers, existed. That of Łęczyca argued that the Sejm should not meet at all in the present circumstances, but it could only grudgingly bring itself to admit that something might have been lacking in the Commonwealth's old laws. The Kraków *sejmik*, after supposedly giving its envoys *carte blanche* to work for Poland's salvation, showed its true convictions by insisting that 'matters of state' should not be subjected to majority vote; in other words, the *liberum veto* would stay. At Łomża, the *szlachta* were concerned at the prospect of the conversion of Poland's 'ancient liberty . . . into slavish servitude' – code for fears that the three powers might strengthen royal government. The Sieradz *sejmik* urged the full preservation of Poland's frontiers, laws and liberties, without offering any suggestion how. The county of Różan deplored anarchy, injustice and oppression – not for bringing about the Partition, but for producing the 'regicides' who had attempted to abduct the king.

Virtually every *sejmik* condemned the kidnap attempt and the act of interregnum in florid terms, often at greater length than the lamentations over the Partition. Of course, the 1773 *sejmiki* are no reliable guide to noble opinion: they took place against a background of intimidation, plundering foreign armies, shock and dislocation. Some had to be coerced to meet, after breaking up or refusing to assemble. No *sejmik* actually welcomed the Partition. Only one, Zakroczym in Mazowsze, managed to avoid even the most elliptic reference to it. But nowhere is there any sign that the *szlachta* were looking to break with the old ways that had brought them to the abyss. Faith, freedom and liberty were everywhere, with no hint of considering anew what they might mean.

This remained true between 1776 and 1788. The Partition largely
slipped from sight, save as a regrettable point of reference in particular instances. No *sejmik* gave thought to what could be done to
prevent a recurrence. At Radziejów in 1776, where the palatinates
of Brześć Kujawski and Inowrocław met jointly, the *szlachta* strongly
implied that a future Partition might be averted by the full preservation of the status of the Roman Catholic faith and a ban on
all anti-Catholic writings. Constituencies close to the new Prussian
border exhibited the greatest consciousness of the threat from their
neighbour, primarily conceived in economic terms. The counties
of Mazowsze bewailed the adverse consequences of the commercial
treaty, complaining of high tolls and arbitrary exactions by customs
officials. But no solutions were proposed – beyond demands for the
treaty's renegotiation or repeal.[9]

The *szlachta* were equally exercised by the number of serfs who
fled across the border to Prussian territories – and looked to the
establishment of joint Polish–Prussian boundary courts to provide
redress.[10] Further south, the palatinate of Lublin made similar complaints and peddled similar solutions to the problem of serf runaways to Galicia.[11] Otherwise, the Lublin *sejmik* saw the new border
as an injustice to the clergy: those in the lands lost to Austria were
continuing to draw on their revenues in Poland, while those on the
Polish side were being prevented from enjoying their revenues from
properties in the ceded territories. This was most unfair.[12] The
sejmik was concerned for a few dozen villages of the old palatinate
of Bełz, most of which had been taken over by Austria: they had no
local chancery or court which they could properly call their own,
and no formal mechanism for the election of deputies to the Tribu-
nal or envoys to the Sejm.[13] The inconveniences, not the fact, of
Partition were questioned.

No *sejmik* proposed any action to recover the lost lands. Even if
utterly unrealistic, such a suggestion would at least have indicated
that *szlachta* society was not reconciled to what had happened. But
the will to transform the state from a libertarian support system
into a machine capable of playing a positive role in its own defence
was absent. The *szlachta* wanted no more taxation, or, if it had to be

9. Ciechanów 1780, 1782; Czersk, 1782; Łomża, 1778, 1782; Nur, 1776; Wizna,
1778, 1780, 1782; Sochaczew 1776, 1784; Wyszogród, 1788; Brześć Kujawski and
Inowrocław, 1776, 1778, 1782, 1784, 1786, 1788. Similar complaints also came from
further afield, viz., Sandomierz, 1776, 1778, 1780; Lublin, 1786.
10. Brześć Kujawski and Inowrocław, 1782, 1786; Różan, 1780, 1788; Łomża, 1782.
The problem of serf runaways in general exercised almost all the *sejmiki.*
11. 1780 instruction.   12. 1784, 1788 instructions.   13. 1784 instruction.

paid, it was to be levied on clergy, or townsmen, or Jews; or extra funding should be found from the state treasuries' surpluses, or by cutting or abolishing the salaries of civilian officials. The 1776 instructions of Brasław, Kowno and Żmudź in Lithuania reveal an exceptional sophistication of discussion of the impact of taxation, but this is more likely to reflect their domination by royalist magnates than the maturity of the local electorates.[14] Otherwise, the feeling that the army should be increased in size and should be used more extensively in the preservation of law and order was balanced by pressure for makeshift expedients designed to spare the *szlachta*'s purses. In February 1779, Stackelberg put Poland's entire monetary stock at 120 million zloties against an annual trade deficit of 20 million. He warned that within a few years the Commonwealth was in serious danger of being reduced to a subsistence existence.[15] The Mazowsze *sejmiki* complained of the shortage of good-quality coin and the economic oppression of Prussian tolls and tariffs. But if the *Rzeczpospolita* was to be modernised, then more taxes would have to be found; and the *szlachta* gave no indication of appreciating this.

Frederick's economic war

The nobility's reluctance to take on fresh burdens was understandable. Polish and other historians have yet fully to capitalise on Jan Wilder's pioneering work on the impact of the Polish–Prussian commercial treaty of 1775 and to integrate its findings into primarily political and diplomatic treatments of the Partitions.[16] Yet the economic consequences for Poland of Frederick's acquisition of 'Westpreussen' (as it was officially styled from September 1773) were such that it is hardly surprising that many landowners feared further fiscal burdens. Whereas Russia and Austria settled for a greater or lesser freedom of trade with the Commonwealth, Frederick

14. S. Kościałkowski, *Antoni Tyzenhauz*, 2 vols (London, 1970–71), I, pp. 91–135, 148–50.

15. Stackelberg to Panin, Mar. (?) 1779, quoted in J.A. Wilder, *Traktat handlowy polsko-pruski z roku 1775* (Warsaw, 1937), p. 150.

16. J.A. Wilder, *Traktat handlowy polsko-pruski z roku 1775: gospodarcze znaczenie utraty dostępu do morza* (Warsaw, 1937). The new study by H.-J. Bömelburg, *Zwischen polnischer Ständegesellschaft und preussischem Obrigkeitsstaat. Vom Königlichen Preussen zu Westpreussen 1756–1806* (Munich, 1995) largely corroborates Wilder's conclusions and stresses the damage inflicted by Frederician mercantilism not merely on Poland, but on the Hohenzollern lands.

deliberately set out to turn it into a supplier of cheap raw materials, a captive market for Prussian manufactured goods and to eliminate any Polish industry which might rival his own.

The great bulk of Poland's imports and exports, up to 80 per cent – mainly cereals, followed by timber – was conducted along the Vistula and through Danzig. Frederick so squeezed this economic jugular that many of his own merchants and officials warned that his policies would not only harm the Poles, but would threaten the commerce and markets of East Prussia, Silesia and Pomerania. Königsberg's prosperity was largely based on servicing the Polish hinterland. Silesia's eastern trade, extending as far as the Balkans and Russia, was conducted via Poland. Frederick conceded that the worries had economic justification, but he was more interested in the emasculation of his despised neighbour by fiscal means.

It was not enough that the terms of the commercial treaty were grossly weighted in Prussia's favour – Frederick positively encouraged abuses. He had announced in the treaty that his officials would draw up a new tariff to serve as the basis for customs officials' calculations – but when the tariff was published on 24 May 1775, many of the valuations were set at artificially high levels. Customs officials were urged to make the highest possible assessments. In January 1776 the standard 2 per cent Prussian import duty was unilaterally raised to 5 per cent (later lowered to 4 per cent). Fines were imposed for incorrect documentation (all of which had to be in German); weights and measures were manipulated, arbitrary road and river tolls and administrative charges were imposed, so that transit duties reached not the specified 12 per cent but could be as high as 50 or 60 per cent. The import of Polish grain was periodically banned. Prussian customs inspections along the Vistula between the Polish border and Danzig amounted to bureaucratic mugging. Perhaps the only commodity on which the Prussians did not systematically exploit the Poles was in the export of salt – largely because they faced competition from Austria and Russia in the supply of this essential commodity – in which, of course, Poland had been almost entirely self-sufficient before 1772. Contemporary economists such as Johann Büsch, Joannes von Müller or Karl August von Struensee saw in Poland a textbook case of ruination by mercantilist fiscalism.[17]

Frederick's economic war crippled Poland, it did not destroy it. Smuggling flourished on a massive scale. Much of Poland's western

17. Wilder, *Traktat*, chs 3, 4, 5.

overland trade, sufficient to make it the chief factor behind the economic prosperity of Saxony and Leipzig, was diverted from Silesia and through Austrian territory, where it attracted only transit charges of 0.5 per cent. The founding of Kherson in 1778 offered the prospect for landowners in the south-east of an export outlet via the Black Sea, although, by the same token, it tied them more closely to Russia. The Russian army was a major customer. Individual studies of the *latifundia* of great magnates show that these were able, by the sheer scale of their production and by recourse to unpaid serf labour and services, to preserve high levels of income.

Magnates such as the Czartoryskis, the Lubomirskis or the Potockis could sell to Russia or to Austria, not least from estates they held behind the new frontiers. They had access to bankers and brokers in Danzig, Leipzig or Riga who provided them with the credit to enable them to import luxuries and maintain a lifestyle of conspicuous consumption – although passing through Warsaw in 1778, former ambassador Nikolai Repnin was struck by the dullness of even the greatest magnate palaces, compared with what he had known in the 1760s.[18] Even so, those who set the pace of Polish politics, who determined political programmes and commanded the masses of noble clientele, were cushioned from the economic aftermath of the First Partition in a way that their lesser brethren were not – even if it was largely by ruinous borrowing.[19]

The szlachta *and change*

The *szlachta* would welcome improvements which they felt would benefit them directly. Their instructions abound with demands for the maintenance and repair of roads, the reconstruction of archival buildings and courts, for the cleaning up of rivers. These homespun lawgivers, so anxious not to allow their king or parliament any real powers, still looked to them to furnish the mundane, material services for which they withheld the means to provide and over which they showed themselves reluctant to take the initiative locally.

18. Repnin to Panin, 27 Nov., quoted in Solov'ev, *IR* XXIX, p. 232.
19. W. Kula, *Szkice o manufakturach*, 2 vols (Warsaw, 1956), II, ch. 15; *idem, An economic theory of the feudal system* (London, 1976), pp. 132–3, 141–50; Z. Guldon, *Związki handlowe dóbr magnackich na prawobrzeżnej Ukrainie z Gdańskiem w XVIII wieku* (Toruń, 1966), pp. 39–46, 54–8, 72–4, 108–11, 128–35; J. Kasperek, *Gospodarka folwarczna ordynacji zamojskiej w drugiej połowie XVIII wieku* (Warsaw, 1972), pp. 145–52; J. Reinhold, *Polen/Litauen auf den Leipziger Messen des 18. Jahrhunderts* (Weimar, 1971), ch. 3.

Nothing exercised them more than the maintenance of the status quo. The most common demands of their *sejmiki* were over control of runaway serfs and domestics and for the regulation of artisanal and seasonal workers' wages. There was much concern lest the new bodies set up by 1773–75 Sejm, particularly the Permanent Council and its constituent departments, should exceed their powers.

What rankled the nobility most about the Delegation Sejm seemed to be less its assent to the partition, more the other injustices which accompanied it: the pensions for Poniński and his fellow-collaborators; the irregular courts and extraordinary commissions which they had set up to enrich themselves and pursue their private interests. These continued to raise *szlachta* hackles for years afterwards. The Permanent Council, the closest that Poland had ever had to an effective central executive, was an especial subject of mistrust, in part because of the circumstances of its creation, but in part, too, because it represented the novel phenomenon of a reasonably effectively functioning central executive body. Unable to control it, the opposition were determined to portray it as the instrument of absolutism and foreign domination.

The years 1775 to 1788 saw two major reform initiatives in the Commonwealth: the attempted systematisation of law and legal procedure; and the elaboration of a wide-ranging programme of educational reform, at secondary and tertiary level by the Commission for National Education. The Sejm of 1776 had authorised ex-chancellor Andrzej Zamoyski to draft a new, clear code of laws, 'basing himself, above all, on natural justice'.[20] This was not a concept with which the wider masses of nobility were particularly familiar. Word got around that Zamoyski was working towards far-reaching social changes, notably in the sphere of serf–seigneur relations. The *sejmiki* of 1778 and 1780 were uniformly hostile. The new Code was to permit nothing at variance with ancient laws and privileges and its provisions were to be made subject to the scrutiny not merely of the Sejm but of the constituencies. Better still, it was to be rejected altogether – which was precisely what the Sejm of 1780 did. Such social conservatism was scarcely unique to Poland, but it hardly boded well for the future. If the *szlachta* nation had any hope of survival, then it would have to change.

'Our country's only hope lies in a good education', observed Stanisław August's younger brother, Michael Poniatowski, bishop of Płock and president of the Commission for National Education in

1781.[21] Like most grandiose statements about the value of education, this was one of optimistic desperation. The curriculum elaborated for secondary and higher learning by the Commission in its 1784 Regulation was a remarkable achievement. Gone was the fixation with an ossified humanist, Latin-based learning and Aristotelian logic-chopping. All colleges were expected to teach a programme based on Poland's own literature and history. Over six or seven years, it built up to embrace foreign languages, the natural sciences, geography, and the 'moral sciences' – in effect, courses in mutual responsibility, duty and patriotism, love of country and of one's fellow-man. Religion and the classics occupied a far lesser place than they had done in the first half of the eighteenth century. The programme was not entirely new – the Piarists and the Jesuits had been implementing something like this in individual schools and colleges since the 1740s and 1750s. A comparable curriculum had been taught since 1765 in the Cadet Corps which Stanisław August had set up. But only the abolition of the Jesuit Order in 1773 provided the etiolated Polish state with the resources from which to launch the re-education of the wider *szlachta* nation.

'Enlightened' Poland included the king and his entourage; it included members of the opposition, such as Adam Czartoryski and Ignacy Potocki; it included poets and educators, laymen and individual clergy – bishops, ex-Jesuits, ambitious seculars, headed by the uncomfortably radical Hugon Kołłątaj, rector of the Jagiellonian University at Kraków. These men and their friends talked and wrote about natural law and serf emancipation; they drew on Montesquieu and Rousseau and talked the language of the physiocrats and their expectations of a brave new future. In short, they lived in an enlightened universe of their own. They and their like were to be found in the corridors of power of virtually any European state – but the Polish corridors did not lead to any machinery which could translate ideas and ideals into reality. Certainly, the *szlachta* were very interested in education – throughout the whole of Stanisław August's reign there is scarcely a *sejmik* instruction which does not discourse about it, particularly about the need to make the same sort of education available to all nobles, rich and poor alike. The Commission for National Education was by and large welcomed – the 1776 *sejmiki* insisted (successfully), moreover, that it should be given control over the ex-Jesuit estate from the discredited commission set up to administer it by the Delegation.

21. Quoted in K. Mrozowska, *Funkcjonowanie systemu szkolnego Komisji Edukacji Narodowej na terenie Korony w latach 1783–1793* (Wrocław, 1985), pp. 128–9.

Yet there is little sign that the Commission's intentions were understood or appreciated. Of the 20,000-plus nobles who studied in the secondary schools and colleges of the Crown between 1782 and 1792, barely 15 per cent (on the most optimistic reckoning) completed the entire seven years course – a drop in the ocean of *szlachta* youth.[22] Moreover the *szlachta* increasingly had their doubts as to the new-fangled education. Latin and all that went with it was a much bewailed casualty. The language and literature of the Roman Republic was all the education that the true, liberty-loving nobleman required. He could use its constructions, cadences and examples in the courts, at the *sejmik* and the Sejm. Throughout the 1780s, the Commission for National Education had to fight a constant battle against unauthorised schools teaching the old classical curriculum.[23]

Stanisław August's reign saw an astonishing revival in the Polish language, the vigour and beauty of Polish poetry, of letters and the theatre. The presence of even a comparatively modest court and the patronage that went with it helped transform Warsaw, by the late 1780s, into a major European city, with a population approaching 100,000. Its grand aristocratic salons and the king's informal 'Thursday dinners' encouraged flirtation with ideas of social change and new cultural departures. The mainly Warsaw-centred periodical press, the senior classes of the national schools and the lecture halls of the universities of Kraków and Wilno, sought to break with old shibboleths. Particularly in the educational sphere, bitterly antagonistic politicians such as Ignacy Potocki or Adam Czartoryski on the one side, Michał Poniatowski and Joachim Chreptowicz on the other, were able to co-operate. It was possible to argue about serfdom and emancipation, about equality of men, not just of nobles, to a degree unthinkable before the mid-century. Perhaps some 2,000 persons in Poland were reasonably abreast of the latest ideas of the French, British or Italian Enlightenments.[24] But the machinery for translating these ideas into action did not exist. It could only come into being if the *szlachta* nation at large decided that it should do so: and, for all the glittering achievements of Stanislavian culture, there was little sign of that necessary political wind of change.

22. Ibid., pp. 223–45 and *passim* for a searching analysis of educational progress in late eighteenth-century Poland.

23. Ciechanów *sejmik* instruction, 1778; Nur instruction, 1782; Mrozowska, *Funkcjonowanie*, pp. 191–200.

24. B. Grochulska, 'The place of the Enlightenment in Polish social history', in J.K. Fedorowicz, ed., *A Republic of Nobles* (Cambridge, 1982), p. 249.

The king, the opposition and Russia

There is no mystery to this. The dead hand of Stackelberg's proconsulate would not permit it. The Russian court had determined that, once the proceedings of the Delegation Sejm were over, it would reassert in full its old influence over the *Rzeczpospolita.* In August 1777, Stackelberg reported that 'Poland has become a sort of Russian province'.[25] Yet although he and his court appreciated that Stanisław August had come to be their most reliable ally in Poland, they could never forget how, in his early reign, he had set out to make a reality of royal power and reform. His approaches to confederate the Sejmy after 1776 were studiously rejected. Stackelberg played the king and his supporters off against the opposition, insisting on offices and honours for even the most vociferous of Stanisław August's critics. Unless the ambassador firmly stood behind the king, the latter could never be sure that the *sejmiki* would continue to return favourable royalist majorities. Repeated approaches to St Petersburg by Ksawery Branicki, Ignacy Potocki and Adam Czartoryski, angered by the ambassador's balancing act, to have him recalled failed. Even Branicki's marriage to the stunning Alexandra Engelhardt, Potemkin's niece, in 1781, proved less of an advantage than he hoped. For as long as Stackelberg kept the lid clamped down on Polish politics, Catherine and Potemkin would keep him in post.

Under such circumstances, there was no possibility of the king's building up an effective platform of political revival. He was certainly able to construct a substantial party following across the Commonwealth, paying particular attention to the local power-brokers among the middling nobility. But this following was entirely non-ideological and tied together by royal patronage. Stackelberg would not and could not have permitted a party dedicated to political reform. Art, culture, learning, the pleasures of monarchy, were all that Stanisław August was allowed to enjoy. The king was under few illusions. He had learned the hard way. If there was to be any chance for Poland to survive and perhaps even flourish, there was no alternative to collaboration with Russia.

This was dangerous: associated with the gut commitment among the nobility to Catholicism and their ancient freedoms, was an equally deep-rooted russophobia. It ran far more deeply than any hostility towards Prussia or Austria. It may have been that Russia could with

25. Panin to Stackelberg, 31 Mar./11 Apr. 1773, *SIRIO* CXVIII, pp. 378–9. Stackelberg to Panin, quoted in Solov'ev, *IR* XXIX, p. 193.

some plausibility, at least in its own eyes, have presented itself as
the 'protector' of Poland against the Habsburgs and Hohenzollern.
Without Russia's restraining hand, they would have undoubtedly
grabbed more in the Partition, but it was Russia which ruled the
Polish roost; it was Russia which had framed the constitution, Russia
which by the very fact of its ascendancy posed the biggest threat to
Sarmatian liberties. At the same time, however, Russia demonstrated
its inability to prevent the Austrian and Prussian border encroach-
ments or to restrain the economic war which Frederick II waged
against the Commonwealth. Worse still, in the 1780s, Russia began to
restrict, often surreptitiously, the cross-border commercial freedoms
it had set up in 1773–75. Polish subjects with lands on both sides
of the border were subjected to arbitrary impositions by Russian
officials. The new boundaries had completely failed to stem the
flow of Russian serf refugees to Poland. Russian troops and officials
roamed the borderlands at will, forcibly deporting runaways and
native Polish subjects indiscriminately.[26] In 1781, Potemkin even
secured favourable 'corrections' to the borders in the far south-east,
adjacent to his fiefdom of Novorossiia.[27] Russia's 'protectorate' was
a very limited one.

It was the opposition magnates who were free to exploit this
rich, emotive reservoir of russophobia. Polish politics in the 1780s
were a surreal world of struggle over patronage, over access to the
Permanent Council; in Branicki's case, over the restoration in full
of the old, irresponsible *hetman* powers. The deaths of the old
Czartoryski brothers, Michael and August, in 1775 and 1782 did
nothing to reduce factional bitterness. A younger generation ached
to remove the king and Stackelberg in order to indulge their libertarian fantasies of a magnate playground under indulgent Russian
supervision. Branicki would revel in his army, Adam Czartoryski
would build his schools and museums, Ignacy Potocki would shape
a physiocratic utopia and play the European statesman. Russia would
deprive Stanisław August of his last vestiges of power, or simply get
rid of him. Both Branicki and Adam Czartoryski were suspected of
harbouring monarchic ambitions.

26. Instruction of the *sejmik* of Połock, 1778; Stanisław August to the comte de
Monet, 8 Oct. 1783, in E. Mottaz, ed., *Stanislas Poniatowski et Maurice Glayre. Correspondence relative aux partages de la Pologne* (Paris, 1897), pp. 172–5.
27. My thanks to Dr Zofia Zielińska for bringing this territorial 'rectification' to
my notice. Text of the demarcation treaty of 5/16 Jan. 1781 in *CTS* XLVII, pp. 409–13,
makes it clear this was an adjustment completely separate from the First Partition.
It seems to have been ratified by the Sejm of 1782 on the nod, *VL* IX, pp. 4–5.

In 1780 Catherine deemed Poland sufficiently stable to withdraw the great bulk of her troops. A couple of regiments remained in the Ukraine to safeguard magazines and supply routes. The opposition savagely denounced the presence of these leftovers, even as Branicki or Ignacy Potocki travelled to St Petersburg – the real capital of Poland-Lithuania – to intrigue with Potemkin and other Russian bigwigs. It was a political game which Polish magnates had played for years: to stir up anti-Russian feeling to demonstrate that they would be more useful to Russia than their monarch. Apart from frustration at being kept out of power, little united this opposition. The extensive estates of many of its leading families, the Potockis, Czartoryskis, the Rzewuskis and Lubomirskis, in the Austrian sector led to its being styled, rather misleadingly, 'the Galician party'. But they appreciated that the real keys to control of Poland lay in St Petersburg, not Vienna; on the other hand, Vienna discreetly encouraged their activities, in order to demonstrate that it, too, possessed influence in Poland – and it, too, was therefore a potentially valuable ally to Russia.[28]

Exploitation of national emotions and the near-paranoid fear of any form of effective government allowed this opposition to block a range of royalist-inspired reforming initiatives: Zamoyski's Code was but the most spectacular casualty. Efforts by the king to modernise and improve discipline in the army were frustrated by successive Sejmy; his chief collaborator, general Komarzewski, was demonised. In 1785, Ignacy and Stanisław Potocki even accused Komarzewski of intending, with the king's connivance, to poison Adam Czartoryski. The ensuing uproar was only superficially appeased by a general, if frosty, reconciliation at the 1786 Sejm. Politics after the First Partition were as divorced as ever from the practical realities of the Commonwealth's problems. Factional leaders, assured of toleration or even support from Vienna and St Petersburg, were able to indulge in the most irresponsible political adventurism. Political inclinations apart, the Czartoryskis and Potockis, or Sapiehas and Ogińskis were perforce as much subjects of the Habsburgs or the Romanovs as citizens of Poland. In Byelorussia and Galicia they had to behave; in Poland, assured of their new rulers' support, they could amuse themselves.[29]

28. J. Michalski, *Polska wobec wojny o sukcesję bawarską* (Wrocław, 1964), pp. 154–5.
29. Prussia does not feature in these observations, largely because the great territorial magnates had hardly any hereditary estates there.

Realignments

What, then, were the international prospects for Poland in the aftermath of the First Partition? Only a few months after the end of the Delegation Sejm, the continued Austrian and Prussian frontier usurpations led Russia's vice-chancellor Ivan Osterman to contemplate the likelihood of further annexations by all three powers.[30] True, the close unity which Prussia, Russia and Austria observed during the process of Partition did not last. The mistrust between Prussia and Austria had never disappeared. Frederick's economic harrying of the Commonwealth and Danzig caused increasing irritation in St Petersburg. These tensions bubbled into the open during the War of 1778–79 over the Bavarian Succession, which once more pitted the Habsburgs and Hohenzollern against each other.

Here was that rupture in relations which Wybicki had felt Poland could exploit to its own advantage. Frederick's minister for foreign affairs, Friedrich Ewald von Hertzberg, proposed a solution which would have done credit even to Kaunitz's imagination. Austria was to be given Bavaria; it would then restore western Galicia, with the Wieliczka salt-mines, to Poland; which, in turn, would cede Danzig, Thorn and the richest districts of Wielkopolska to Prussia; for good measure, Saxony would cede Lusatia to Prussia, in exchange for the reversion of Ansbach and Bayreuth. Frederick congratulated Hertzberg on his zealous ingenuity and got on with blocking Joseph II's designs on Bavaria.[31] Catherine played the arbiter, giving Frederick far less support than he hoped. He fleetingly considered the possibility that Austria might be made to disgorge Galicia to Poland. The Austrians flirted with the possibility of exchanging Galicia for Bavaria with their tame Bavarian elector Karl Theodor – but he really did not want to become king of Galicia and Lodomeria. Kaunitz even mooted the possibility of allowing Poland to recover all its old territories – as part of a fantastic coalition involving Austria, Turkey, Sweden, France and Poland against Prussia and Russia. Neither Joseph, nor Maria Theresa, nor the French attached any credibility to the idea.[32]

Poland was unable to draw even minimal profit from the war. Schemes of exchange or conquest were made above its head. Its army in 1778 barely exceeded 16,000 men – of no practical value to

30. Osterman to Stackelberg, 3/14 Sept. 1775, *SIRIO* CXXXV, p. 460.
31. Michalski, *Polska wobec wojny*, pp. 9–10.
32. Ibid., pp. 12–13, 106, 110–11, 121–3. Michalski suspects that Kaunitz's plan to restore the old Polish state was a ploy to demonstrate to France Austrian determination to go to war if necessary.

any of the protagonists.[33] Both Prussia and Austria appreciated that it might be possible to set up confederacies in the Commonwealth which might prove of some embarrassment to their opponents – but this was tempered by concern that the confederacies might be used to introduce undesirable reforms. Frederick toyed with the idea of instigating an uprising against the Austrians in Galicia. Stackelberg deflected Stanisław August's proposals for a Confederacy to recover Galicia. Given the closeness of opposition magnates such as Adam Czartoryski to the Austrians, and the effective role of their Galician properties as security for their good behaviour, it is difficult to see how such a Confederacy could have been put together. That, of course, merely underlined one of the crippling consequences of the Partition.[34]

The short, unglamorous conflict saw the final break-up of the harmonious concert between Prussia, Austria and Russia which the First Partition had supposedly brought about. The Peace of Teschen of May 1779, secured through Catherine's mediation, enabled her to add her own guarantee to the Imperial Constitution. Although Russia's influence in Germany could hardly be exercised in the same brutally direct fashion as in Poland, the new guarantee could not but tighten Russia's grip on the Commonwealth, just as that grip made Russia's influence in the Empire as important as that of France.[35] Russia's ascendancy in central and eastern Europe was beginning to resemble hegemony. Both Prussia and Austria vied for her favours. In August 1777, Frederick had renewed his alliance with Russia to 1788 – in part, to pre-empt any closer alliance between Russia and Austria. But his alliance meant less and less to Catherine. She had not allowed herself to be drawn into the Bavarian conflict militarily, partly because she wished to umpire relations between Prussia and Austria, and partly because she needed to keep an eye open for Turkish revanchism.

Had France been in a position to give the Porte support, such was the resentment at the humiliation of the peace of Kutchuk Kainardji of July 1774 that it might well have declared a fresh war against Russia much sooner than it did. Given Russia's ambitions in the Balkans, given Russia's determination to annex the Crimea (so much for its 'independence', accorded at Kutchuk Kainardji, not

33. M.M. Drozdowski, *Podstawy finansowe działalności państwowej w Polsce, 1764–1793* (Warsaw, 1975), pp. 90–1.
34. Michalski, *Polska wobec wojny*, pp. 84–102, 110–14, 116, 125–42, 154–5.
35. K.O. von Aretin, 'Russia as a guarantor power of the Imperial Constitution under Catherine II', *Journal of Modern History* 78 (1986), pp. S141–S160.

that anyone had taken Russian protestations about this seriously), and given, too, that Frederick wanted a strong Turkey to act as a counterweight against Austria, the Prussian alliance was becoming an embarrassment to Catherine. Vienna, not Potsdam, was a useful ally in the Balkans. The Austrians themselves were so impressed by Russian power as to be persuaded that they had little choice but to co-operate with Russia, even if that meant, in practice, accepting a subordinate role; an alliance with Russia might, however, have the merit of isolating Prussia.[36]

On 8 May 1779, a second grandson was born to Catherine – Constantine. Part of the afterbirth was the so-called 'Greek Project' – the grandmother's plan to endow him with a throne of his own in Constantinople. Potemkin was enthusiastic – he, too, was planning his future career-moves. For a time, he seems to have nourished hopes of acquiring the duchy of Courland, but from there he graduated to thinking about becoming king of Poland. Since the Delegation Sejm had conferred Polish nationality on him, he could even pass for a Piast. But the Balkans beckoned. He finally fixed his ambitions on the creation of his own principality of 'Dacia', carved out of Moldavia, Wallachia and the Polish Ukraine, where he was busily taking advantage of his naturalisation to make massive land purchases. He came to own more property in Poland than in Russia.[37] The Romanov empire would thus acquire a huge swathe of client states along its western borders – Poland and Courland, already in the bag; Germany was in its place; and, from a seemingly toothless Muslim bear which had only to be skinned, 'Dacia' and a 'Greek Empire'.[38] Catherine's successes in foreign policy had, after all, been so dazzling. And the young emperor, Joseph II, was so keen to meet her. He even travelled all the way across Poland to Mogilev in her new Byelorussian territories in June 1780, so as to pay court to her. He did not bother to call on Stanisław August. Amid much mutual appreciation, the ground was cleared for the renewal of the old alliance; a final possible obstacle was removed

36. H.L. Dyck, 'Pondering the Russian fact: Kaunitz and the Catherinian Empire in the 1770s', *Canadian Slavonic Papers* 23 (1980–1), pp. 451–69.

37. Solms to Frederick II, 4 May 1779 and Frederick's reply, 22 May, *PC* XLIII, 27 371; Eustachius von Goertz to Frederick, 11, 19 Oct. and Frederick's reply of 2 Nov., ibid., 27 639. I. De Madariaga, *Russia in the age of Catherine the Great* (New Haven, 1981), p. 399.

38. I. De Madariaga, 'The secret Austro-Russian treaty of 1781', *Slavonic and East European Review* 38 (1959–60), p. 114; H. Ragsdale, 'Russian projects of conquest in the eighteenth century', in H. Ragsdale, ed., *Imperial Russian Foreign Policy* (Cambridge, 1993), pp. 82–102.

with Maria Theresa's death on 29 November 1780.[39] In May and June of the following year, Joseph and Catherine secretly agreed a defensive alliance, to run for eight years, directed in the first instance against the Porte; they guaranteed each other's territories; they guaranteed Poland's territory and constitution.

Russia's alliance with Prussia was 'no longer worth the paper it was written on'. Frederick appreciated this even before he learned of the treaty two years later.[40] It blighted his final days. In May 1782, he produced some 'Considérations sur l'état politique de l'Europe'. He foresaw that a belligerent Joseph, allied to Russia, would destroy what he had built: 'thirty years from now, there will be no . . . Prussia, no house of Brandenburg'. Even the wretched Poles might get something back.[41] He consoled himself by continuing to apply his economic thumbscrews to the Commonwealth. Any chances of mending his fences with Russia disappeared in 1785, when he placed himself at the head of the *Fürstenbund*. This Imperial 'League of Princes', designed to restrain Joseph II's adventurism, had the effect of casting Frederick in the unwonted role of defender of German liberties. The boost to his prestige infuriated Catherine, whose new-found influence in the Empire was commensurately pushed back. Frederick died just after two in the morning on 17 August 1786. The Russian ambassador, Sergei Rumiantsev, refused to attend the funeral.[42]

The value of Catherine's new alliance was amply demonstrated by Joseph's support for her outright annexation of the Crimea in 1783, sealed by the Convention of Ainali-Kavak of 8 January 1784. Such was Ottoman despair and anger that few European observers doubted that a fresh conflict in the Balkans could be long delayed. Once again, Stanisław August sensed an opportunity: if only he could persuade Catherine that Poland could offer genuine support in any new conflict, beyond merely functioning as a supply depot for Russia's armies in the Balkans, he might be able to secure the empress's consent to further reform. He hoped to expand his army to 45,000: the 1775 laws had capped the Crown army at 30,000, but had said nothing about Lithuania's. Even so, he would still need Russian subsidies, while the administration of such a force might

39. De Madariaga, *Russia*, p. 384; D.E.D. Beales, *Joseph I* (Cambridge, 1987), I, pp. 435–8.

40. De Madariaga, 'Secret Austro-Russian treaty', pp. 114–15.

41. *Testamente*, pp. 246–50.

42. J.P. LeDonne, *The Russian empire and the world, 1700–1917. The geopolitics of expansion and containment* (New York, 1997), pp. 245–6.

open the door to further reform. Better still, if Poland did prove useful, perhaps it might be rewarded with Moldavia. In 1786, news came that the empress would be visiting her southern provinces and the Crimea in the following year. Stanisław August began to work for a personal appointment with her.

The prospects held out by a fresh Ottoman–Russian conflict also exercised the minds of the opposition. They were only too ready to assist Russia – provided that they, not the king, were to benefit. In the spring of 1787, Catherine was at Kiev. She spent a few days on her barge moored off the Polish bank of the Dnieper at Kaniów, where on 6 May Stanisław August paid his respects. He was graciously received. Ignacy Potocki and Ksawery Branicki were cold-shouldered, even by Potemkin. Catherine made no commitments, but with war on the horizon, the tried and tested means of keeping Poland quiet lay in the Poniatowski–Stackelberg condominium, not in the irresponsible politicking of the opposition. Ignacy Potocki's appeals to Joseph II fell on equally stony ground.

Another Turkish war: Polish restiveness

Whatever the parochialism of Polish politics, they remained a politics based on mass noble participation – what the contemporary Piarist educator, Antoni Popławski, called '*szlachta* democracy'.[43] It was inconceivable that this kind of polity could remain quiescent for long. The Polish nobility may have been culturally or politically short-sighted, but their active parliamentary tradition rendered them combustible material. The perfect conditions had developed for the frustrated opposition to play its patriot games. In October 1787, Turkey at last declared war on Russia – one of those long-awaited events which took everyone by surprise. In February 1788, Austria formally joined in on Catherine's side. In June, Gustav III of Sweden opened hostilities against Russia. In Poland, Stanisław August's determination to hold with Catherine was easily portrayed as a black act of betrayal, even by the very politicians who continued to knock on St Petersburg's doors. Ksawery Branicki kept his nose clean by serving as a volunteer on the Russian side in the long siege of Ochakov, while keeping up the heat in Poland through his allies and intermediaries.

43. A. Popławski, *Zbiór niektórych materyi politycznych* ('A compendium of Political Materials') (Warsaw, 1774), pp. 240–3.

This Turkish war was going to be a very different affair from the last one. General Suvorov only just beat off the Ottoman attack on the fortress of Kinburn in October. The siege of Ochakov dragged on for over a year, from October 1787 to December 1788. Joseph II's attempt to capture Belgrade was a fiasco.[44] In Poland, there was a growing sense that it had to be now or never, if Russian tutelage was to be shaken off. Raw emotion, not calculation, was at work. Stanisław August differed. He insisted that, if Poland were to survive intact, it had to stick with Russia. Almost as soon as the Turkish war erupted he appealed to Catherine to agree to a Confederacy which would allow him to increase the army, join her anti-Turkish alliance and permit some strengthening of the central government. He hoped to secure Moldavia and direct access to the Black Sea. He was ready for a perpetual alliance with Russia. He hoped that Russia would finance and arm the enlarged army, since it was highly unlikely the *szlachta* would do so. Polish officerships would be modelled on those of Russia. Poland would conclude no alliances without Russia's approval.[45]

Such a treaty would have heightened Poland's dependence on Russia and perhaps even paved the way for its absorption. Stanisław August knew well that he rendered himself open to such a charge. Yet he felt he had little choice. No one in Poland was more aware of how fragile the Commonwealth's situation was. No one was more sceptical of the *szlachta*'s inability to face up to the reforms that would be necessary to convert it into a genuinely independent state. The growing popularity of the self-seeking 'patriot' opposition programme could only have strengthened this conviction. The international crisis was a threat as much as an opportunity. Russia had effectively broken with Prussia – and that made Prussia a greater danger than ever. Frederick William II had, it is true, called a halt to the most glaring customs and commercial abuses encouraged by his illustrious predecessor but that was largely because they hit the Prussian economy as badly as the Polish. Punitively high tolls on such staples as timber and cereals remained. There was no relief for Danzig. Worse, rumours were sweeping the country that the Prussians intended to exploit Russian distractions to acquire further territories from Poland. 'There is no other way', wrote Stanisław August to his resident in St Petersburg, Augustyn Deboli, 'in which we can escape from our present degradation and from

44. De Madariaga, *Russia*, ch. 25.
45. E. Rostworowski, *Ostatni król Rzeczypospolitej* (Warsaw, 1966), pp. 129–33.

that paralysis which leaves us helpless at every frontier usurpation by our neighbours.'[46]

Ksawery Branicki and the wealthiest of the Potocki clan, Felix, had their own proposals. In May 1788 they suggested that the Commonwealth should cease to be a monarchy altogether, to become a republic – ruled by magnate oligarchs such as themselves (Potemkin was not impressed by Branicki's platitudinous bombast that every monarch was a potential despot).[47] Catherine had to be careful to avoid another Confederacy of Bar. Yet she could not trust the king – the balance between him and the opposition had to be maintained. In June 1788, Aleksander Bezborodko, her chief adviser after Potemkin, proposed restricting the Polish 'alliance' to 12,000 National Cavalry, to serve under Russian commanders – in effect as hostages for the good behaviour of their civilian brethren. Their costs would be paid only after the war was over. A confederated Sejm was acceptable, but it was not to carry through any further reform. There should be no territorial gains for Poland. If nothing else, their prospect would give Prussia an excuse to seek fresh Polish territory, in the name of the preservation of the balance of power.[48]

In March, Prussia's foreign minister, Hertzberg, had proposed his own solution to the Turkish war to Catherine – another exchange that would, miraculously, leave everyone much better off. Turkey would cede Wallachia and Moldavia to Austria; Bessarabia and Ochakov to Russia; but it would be sure of the safety of all its provinces south of the Danube, for they would be secured under a perpetual guarantee by Prussia, Austria and Russia. In return for its new gains, Austria would restore Galicia to Poland, which would then gratefully pass Danzig, Thorn and the palatinates of Poznań and Kalisz to Prussia. Catherine turned this flight of diplomatic fantasy down flat. Leaving aside its lunatic implausibility, neither she nor her embattled ally Austria wished to see any further growth in Prussian power. In May the Russians informed Vienna that they would join with them to prevent any Prussian expansion in Poland, by force, if necessary. But Hertzberg did not give up: 'Thorn and Danzig, Danzig and Thorn' was to be the Prussian refrain over the next few years, to be secured via more or less labyrinthine exchanges involving minimum force and expenditure.[49]

46. Quoted ibid., pp. 131–2. J. Michalski, 'Polen und Preussen in der Epoche der Teilungen', *Jahrbuch für die Geschichte Mittel- und Ostdeutschlands* 30 (1981), p. 47.
47. Rostworowski, *Ostatni król*, pp. 136–8.   48. Ibid., pp. 138–41.
49. R.H. Lord, *The Second Partition of Poland: a study in diplomatic history* (Cambridge, Mass., 1915), pp. 75–81; T.C.W. Blanning, *The origins of the French revolutionary wars* (Harlow, 1986), pp. 52–3.

In June, Adam Czartoryski, Ignacy Potocki and some of their closest associates assembled at the Hanoverian spa of Pyrmont. They rubbed shoulders with the Prussian queen and crown prince. Far from being alarmed at rumours of Prussian territorial designs, Ignacy Potocki saw possibilities in them. Most of the opposition magnates owned territories either in Galicia or in the south and east of Poland. They could market their produce via Austrian, or even Russian territories. Potocki mulled over the possibilities of ceding Danzig, Thorn and parts of Wielkopolska, a price worth paying for assistance against the despotic designs of Stanisław August. He does not seem to have gone as far as actually putting such proposals to the Prussians.[50] His musings reflected unpleasant reality: saddled with a crippled economy, a weak army and an ineffective central government, Poland had nothing to offer any prospective ally – other than further territory. The announcements that the Prussians were to make in October and November 1788, not only offering an alliance, but declaring the Commonwealth to be at liberty to settle its own affairs, were to confirm to those looking to Berlin that they had chosen the right path.

The Prussian option was not merely for political malcontents. In late December 1788, the reforming cleric, Hugon Kołłątaj, penned his 'Remarks on the intervention in the Commonwealth's interests of two great powers . . .'. This tract of staggering naivety demonstrated blind belief in the goodness and altruism of Frederick William II. Kołłątaj dismissed any suggestions that this royal 'friend of humanity' harboured any territorial ambitions against Poland. But he also passionately denounced the moral and political consequences of a Russian alliance. It was folly to believe that Russia, with its interests along the Black Sea littoral and its 'Greek' ambitions in the Balkans, would be able to resist the lure of further Polish territory, particularly in the Ukraine. The king's policy, of holding with Russia, for fear of the alternatives, would inevitably prepare the way for Poland 'to be a Russian province'. Russia would allow neither reform nor expansion of the army – whereas the Prussian link promised to confer true independence and sovereignty.[51]

Of course, this was wishful thinking. But such were Poland's dilemmas that wishful thinking was all that was left – the alternative, as Kołłątaj pointed out, was absorption, one way or another, by Russia. Wherever the Poles turned, they could grasp only at straws.

50. Rostworowski, *Ostatni król*, pp. 142–3.

51. Kołłątaj's authorship has been established by Z. Zielińska, *Kołłątaj i orientacja pruska u progu Sejmu Czteroletniego* (Warsaw, 1991), pp. 27–41. Text of 'Uwagi nad wpływaniem do interesów Rzeczypospolitej dwóch mocarstw . . .', ibid., pp. 63–108.

Stanisław August may have looked to Russia for protection against Prussia, but Russia's word was no more its bond than that of any other state, or no more than it had been in the past. Of the partitioning powers, only Austria was sympathetic towards the Poles, largely because it had the most pressing interest in not seeing any further strengthening of Prussia. But Austria had the least influence in Poland, and it had its own besetting internal problems, which became ever more acute as the war against the Porte progressed. It had little choice but to follow in Russia's wake. Joseph II's social reforms made the *szlachta* intensely suspicious, while Prussian blandishments made Galicia seem that part of the lost territories most liable to be recovered.

The Poles had reams of excellent advice, home-grown and external, about how to comport themselves. No less a figure than Jean-Jacques Rousseau had taken it upon himself to counsel them, after being persuaded that not only the Corsicans, but the Poles too, still had the chance to set up an uncorrupted form of government. His *Considérations sur le gouvernement de la Pologne*, completed in 1771, offered a programme for the education of society in virtue, praised the *liberum veto* if due safeguards were introduced against its 'abuse', warned against an over-mighty executive, advised keeping an elective monarchy and stressed the need for the noble electorate to keep firm control of all legislative processes. Though not meant for publication, the *Considérations* circulated widely in manuscript. A Polish translation appeared in 1789. Their enlightened utopianism, which could so easily be made to chime in with Poland's own political traditions, won most adherents among those who sought genuine reform. But it offered no solutions to the Commonwealth's foreign policy dilemmas. Stanisław August's own preference was for an English-style parliamentary monarchy. In 1787, Stanisław Staszic daringly suggested that Poland could be saved only by the adoption of 'oświecony despotyzm' – enlightened despotism (in any country but Poland, Staszic's 'enlightened despotism' – he is one of the first to have used the term – would have passed for constitutional monarchy). Such notions found as little echo as Józef Wybicki's pleas for stronger government in the mid-1770s.[52]

The pressure of the opposition, the refusal of St Petersburg to come down firmly in favour of a royalist-led Confederacy, the

52. J. Fabre, *Stanislas-Auguste Poniatowski et l'Europe des Lumières* (Paris, 1952), pp. 255–68, 343–4; B. Leśnodorski, 'La pensée politique de Rousseau en Pologne', *Annales Historiques de la Révolution Française* 34 (1964), pp. 497–514. S. Staszic, *Uwagi nad Życiem Jana Zamoyskiego*, S. Czarnowski, ed. (Wrocław, 1951 edn), pp. 60–70.

consciousness of dramatic shifts pivoting around the Turkish war, all contributed towards an exceptionally febrile atmosphere at the *sejmiki* of August 1788. A bare majority of royalist envoys was returned. As for their instructions, in many respects they remained true to conservative type. But there was clear awareness of the international scene – the great majority insisted that Poland should stay neutral in the wars: a rebuff to the king's hopes for a Russian alliance. The breakthrough, such as it was, occurred over the army. There was universal support for its expansion. Most *sejmiki* would not pin themselves down to a figure, though levels of 30,000 to 40,000 were mentioned.[53] Such modesty was realistic – the *szlachta* remained as reluctant as ever to pay taxes, and where these were to be levied, they were, in the first instance, always to be on non-noble-owned properties: the church was seen as a suitable source of new money.

The nobility showed virtually no conception of the administrative infrastructure necessary to run an up-to-date army. On the contrary, the Permanent Council was bitterly attacked for its supposed abuses; and, within the Permanent Council, the Army Department, which had so effectively curbed the *hetmani*, was singled out for especially vitriolic criticism. Ministers and civilian officials were widely expected to take salary cuts or even serve gratis, out of pure patriotic virtue. The resultant 'savings' would help pay for the army's expansion. If necessary, the army could be stiffened by a revival of the (mythical) *popisy*, the local military reviews of the noble feudal levy. As far as possible, the administration of the army was to be decentralised, removed from Warsaw and subjected to the closer control of the *hetmani* and their allies in the provinces. Whatever enlightened pastimes the *szlachta*'s leaders practised, they knew that the easiest way to mobilise their followers was to invoke a liberty-laden past and raise a hue and cry against *absolutum dominium*.[54]

53. Sochaczew, Sandomierz, Lublin.
54. The most searching analysis of the 1788 instructions is J. Michalski, 'Sejmiki poselskie 1788 roku', *Przegląd Historyczny* 51 (1960), pp. 52–73, 331–67, 465–82.

CHAPTER SIX

The Second Partition

The partitioning powers: disagreements

Russia's wars with Sweden and Turkey between 1788 and 1792 seemed to hold out the *Rzeczpospolita*'s last opportunity to assert its sovereignty. Something else, more basic but at least as important, happened during this period – a painful appreciation that politics might consist of more than an unruly scrum over places and preferments. The envoys and senators assembled for the Sejm in October 1788 had to try to teach themselves what government really meant. It was enough to furnish Poland with a new Constitution in May 1791; it was not enough to save it from destruction.

Catherine II's consent, in June 1788, to an alliance with Poland was not welcome in Berlin, where Hertzberg feared that it would be a block to Prussia's expansion – the very reason why Stanisław August had so eagerly sought it. In September, the minister in Warsaw, Ludwig von Buchholtz, was ordered to let Stackelberg know that it could only be construed as an unfriendly act. Hertzberg advised Frederick William to build up something which did not yet exist – a pro-Prussian party among the Poles.[1]

Hertzberg's plans for a chain of territorial exchanges which would benefit everyone except the Porte had served only to convince the Austrians that Poland had to be preserved intact. Kaunitz continued to take the line that any gains from Poland would work to the disproportionate advantage of the old enemy. As early as January 1788, he had urged on Catherine a triple alliance of Russia, Austria and Poland in order to recover West Prussia for the Commonwealth.

1. Despatches to Buchholtz of 3, 16 September 1788, cited *in extenso* in W. Kalinka, *Sejm Czteroletni*, 2 vols (Warsaw, 1991 edn), I, pp. 87–90. Kalinka's work, first published in 1881, remains the standard work on the Four Years Sejm.

128

How serious he may have been was another matter (it so often was with Kaunitz) – he may have simply intended to bring home the need to keep Prussia firmly in check. Catherine did agree, on 12 May 1788, to a joint Austro-Russian declaration reaffirming the commitment to Poland's territorial integrity. It may well have been Austrian pressure which prodded her to accept Stanisław August's alliance proposals.[2] However, in the face of Berlin's opposition to her putative alliance with Poland, she backed down. This was no time to irritate the Prussians. On 28 September, Stackelberg received orders to fob the Poles off.[3] It was too late.

Frederick II had played the international scene with masterly dexterity, making his moves only when convinced the diplomatic kaleidoscope was in his favour. Frederick William and Hertzberg hurled themselves into turbulent waters, flailing about in the belief that they had to emerge with something. Their successful intervention in Holland in September 1787 against a francophile democratic movement had allowed them to break Prussia's diplomatic isolation and clinch, in August 1788, a Triple Alliance with Britain and the Dutch Republic. Frederick William and Hertzberg fully appreciated that, while the British Prime Minister, William Pitt, opposed Prussian expansion, he was also concerned at the growing power of Russia and its rapprochement with France, signalled by the commercial treaty of January 1787. Hertzberg convinced himself and his master that a combination of bluff, blackmail and deceit could round off the Frederician legacy.[4]

Prussia's tilt towards Poland

While individual magnates had been flirting with the Prussian option since their rebuff at Kiev and Kaniów the previous spring, the weaving together of a viable Prussian party was no easy undertaking. Prussia's tariff and toll offensive, despite some mitigation of the worst excesses, was hardly calculated to win Polish confidence. Rumours of Prussian territorial designs refused to die down. The

2. Ibid., I, pp. 55–7.   3. Ibid., I, pp. 92–5.
4. R.H. Lord, *The Second Partition of Poland* (Cambridge, Mass., 1915), pp. 64–95; J. Michalski, 'Dyplomacja polska w latach 1764–1795', *HDP* II, p. 614; J. Dutkiewicz, 'Prusy a Polska w dobie Sejmu Czteroletniego w świetle korespondencji dyplomatycznej pruskiej', in H. Kocój, ed., *Cztery lata nadziei* (Katowice, 1980), pp. 26–53; J. Black, *British foreign policy in an age of revolutions 1783–1793* (Cambridge, 1994), pp. 142–71; J.P. LeDonne, *The Russian empire and the world, 1700–1917. The geopolitics of expansion and containment* (New York, 1997), pp. 297–9.

instruction to Buchholtz of 30 September was despatched before Hertzberg could have learned of Catherine's retreat over the Polish alliance. Buchholtz was to protest against the plan and offer Prussia's own alliance in its stead. This move, Hertzberg made clear, was to divide the Poles and lead a substantial number of them to set up a breakaway Confederacy, which would invoke Prussian assistance. It was emphatically not intended to favour the confederation of the Sejm – one of the first actions the Sejm took – for this might pave the way to undesirable reforms.[5] The Sejm held together, but the Prussian offer, conveyed on 13 October, caused a sensation. Prussia now named a new ambassador, Girolamo Lucchesini, the most adroit of Frederick II's cosmopolitan diplomatic appointees, to supervise Buchholtz and manipulate the Sejm. The truth was, however, that the Prussian initiative had sparked off a train of events which no one could control.

The Sejm's 177 envoys were primarily well-to-do independent country gentlemen, steeped in Poland's libertarian culture, touched only to a degree by fashionable enlightened ideas, utterly innocent of the labyrinthine twists of international diplomacy. Patriots who mythologised themselves into legislators, the sterile years of the later 1770s and 1780s had not at all prepared them for such a role. For over a decade the magnate opposition had played on the russophobia which they had imbibed in their mothers' milk. The use by Russian troops of their Ukrainian territories as a transit route to the Balkans and the attendant excesses fired up the envoys' simmering resentment. When the Prussian offer of alliance was put, they felt that they were being taken seriously by a major power for the first time. The mood swung in favour of Prussia – Frederick William suddenly emerged as Poland's protector. Stanisław August smelled a very large rat, but his warnings were ignored. Revelling in a sense of new-found freedom and sovereignty, on 20 October, the Sejm rapturously ordained the expansion of the army to 100,000 men. Such mundane matters as paying for it appeared mere trivia. Stackelberg reckoned such an army would require expenditure of at least 50 million zloties, at a time when the Polish state could barely raise 18 million. 'They are children, happy enough today, but when they have to pay for these men, they will sorely regret it.'[6]

A month later the Prussians dramatically raised the stakes. Lucchesini and Buchholtz warned that if the constitutional guarantee was not thrown over, Prussia's newly found influence would

5. Kalinka, *Sejm*, I, pp. 120–1.
6. Ibid., pp. 150–1, with similar comments by other diplomats.

prove unsustainable. On 20 November a fresh note was read to the assembly: Frederick William II understood his guarantee of 1775 to apply purely to Poland's independence – not to its internal form of government, which the Poles were free to change as they saw fit.[7] Any hope Stanisław August now had of preserving the Russian connexion was destroyed. The Sejm pressed for the withdrawal of all Russian forces and magazines from the Commonwealth's territory. On 19 January 1789, the hated Permanent Council was abolished. Catherine, already fighting on two fronts, faced with the prospect that even Prussia and Britain might turn on her, swallowed these humiliations. She would restore her position as soon as the Turkish war was over. Russian troops were withdrawn, even though this meant setting up new and much lengthier supply lines to the Balkan theatre. In April 1790, Stackelberg was recalled, to be replaced by the more discreet Jakov Bulgakov.[8]

The envoys were caught up in a veritable auction of magnate bids for their support by ever more 'patriotic' proposals. This was the first Sejm whose participants felt truly able to have their own say. The result was an effusion of speeches, motions and addresses, usually driven by what individuals deemed important, rather than by any logical programme. The marshal of the Sejm, Stanisław Małachowski, was reluctant to try to impose any discipline on proceedings precisely because he did not dare jeopardise this unwonted 'freedom'. The Sejm fumbled its way into the dual role of legislature and executive. On 6 December 1788, it voted to remain in session indefinitely.

The Prussians welcomed the abolition of the Permanent Council as a promising step towards the creation of a profitable anarchy. Otherwise, they found themselves in the position of having to make the best of a bad job, reluctantly endorsing reforms for fear of undermining their own position. They secretly intrigued against the expansion of the army.[9] As talk of replacing an elective with a hereditary monarchy became more common, Lucchesini made encouraging noises – and discreetly urged opponents of the idea not to give way.[10] Like his Russian counterpart, he encouraged envoys to filibuster and delay with their flights of patriotic garrulity. Abroad, Berlin did what it could to keep its new protégé within bounds. In

7. Ibid., pp. 210–14.
8. Ibid., pp. 277–90, 303–48; II, 63–4, 193. *AGS* I, Council Sessions of 23 Oct./ 3 Nov., 30 Oct./11 Nov., 6/17 Nov., 14–16/25–27 Dec. 1788; 10/21 May 1789, cols 627, 629–30, 632, 647; 692.
9. Kalinka, *Sejm*, I, pp. 157–8.
10. Z. Zielińska, *'O sukcesyi tronu w Polszcze' 1787–1790* (Warsaw, 1991), pp. 87–9.

Constantinople, the Prussians sabotaged Polish efforts to conclude a commercial treaty. Lucchesini warned Genoa and Hesse-Cassel against extending loans to the Commonwealth. Poland, which had virtually no armaments industry worth the name, and had hitherto relied on imports from Russia, turned to Prussia for help. Prussia obliged by selling over 30,000 overpriced and sub-standard muskets.[11] Frederick William proved extremely reluctant to implement the offer of the alliance made in October 1788: his ministers dreamed up an ingenious variety of excuses. Yet, as the Poles edged towards reform, the Prussians had to follow.

Towards reform

In November 1789, a comprehensive system of local administration was laid in the shape of elected commissions of the peace.[12] Determined, if necessarily ad hoc efforts were made to boost revenues. The resilience of the economy in the face of the tariff pressures imposed by its neighbours is both a surprise and a mystery, but Stackelberg's warnings of the 1770s, that the fiscal campaign against Poland would reduce it to little more than subsistence level, proved unfounded. Exports of grain, timber and livestock continued – sufficient, indeed, to lead the British government to give serious consideration to Poland as an alternative raw materials supplier to Russia.[13] Overland routes via Habsburg territories and rising cereal prices helped mitigate the impact of Prussian tolls. During the Sejm, Warsaw recovered the old prosperity of Poniatowski's early reign, even if much of it was underpinned by a perilous reliance on foreign credit. In practical terms, this translated into a greater willingness to endure the higher levels of taxation which the expansion of the army and government inevitably entailed.

In April 1789 the Sejm voted a land tax, the so-called 'Perpetual Offering' ('offering' – *ofiara* – looked better than 'tax' – *podatek* – to the *szlachta*). This 10 per cent levy on net landed income (20 per cent for religious institutions), much influenced by the fashionable

11. Kalinka, *Sejm*, I, 361–2, 435; II, p. 32. Lord, *Second Partition*, p. 168; E. Rostworowski, 'Sprawa zaplecza przemysłowego dla armii na Sejmie Czteroletnim', *Kwartalnik Historyczny* 63, no. 4 (1956), pp. 44–63; Michalski, 'Dyplomacja polska', p. 643.

12. Kalinka, *Sejm*, I, pp. 440–3; W. Szaj, 'Organizacja i działalność administracyjna wielkopolskich komisji porządkowych cywilno-wojskowych (1789–1792)', *Studia i materiały do dziejów Wielkopolski i Pomorza* 23 (1976), pp. 85–102.

13. Black, *British foreign policy*, pp. 280–2.

physiocratic elixir of the *impôt unique*, was intended to solve Poland's fiscal deficiencies almost at a stroke. It was a sad disappointment. It was widely expected to return at least sixteen million zloties from across the Commonwealth – the actual returns by 1791–92 stabilised at around nine million zloties; net returns were more likely to have been closer to 6 per cent than to 10. A range of supplementary fiscal measures had to be put in place. Yet all this, too, was an unavoidable part of a learning process. In 1788, customs officials, the most numerous part of the fiscal administration, numbered little over 1,000 persons – this in a state nearly the size of France and a population of some eight million. Within the space of barely two years, this same state, with virtually no fiscal or executive tradition, was trying to put in place the sort of administrative structures which elsewhere in Europe had taken decades, if not centuries, to evolve.

It was an impossible task: between 1789 and 1790 basic annual tax revenues rose from around nineteen to over forty million zloties. This was probably less than 10 per cent of British tax levels, or less than a half of Prussian. Measured against an international background, Poland's financial endeavour amounted to a mere blip. Measured in a domestic context and against the disabilities imposed from abroad, a doubling of taxation within the space of two years, assessed and raised mainly by unpaid amateurs, appears remarkable. But it was not enough to pay for the army of 100,000 so enthusiastically voted for at the outset of the Sejm. Barely half that magic figure was to be raised.[14] Progress on reform in general was so slow that in October 1790 the shamefaced Sejm decided that it could only justify its further prolongation by agreeing to the election of a fresh cohort of envoys who would take their seats alongside the old members.

The real sticking-point went to the heart of constitutional change: how was the *Rzeczpospolita* to have an effective government while preserving old *szlachta* freedoms? It was in response to yet another Prussian excuse – that Frederick William could not possibly proceed to an alliance with Poland until he knew what sort of reformed state he would be dealing with – that on 7 September 1789 the Sejm set up the Deputation for the Reform of the Form of Government.[15] Although this body never completed its task, it made enough progress to render it impossible for the Prussians to put up further excuses without losing all credibility. Frederick William agreed to

14. By far the best treatment of Polish finances in this period remains R. Rybarski, *Skarbowość Polski w dobie rozbiorów* (Kraków, 1937). See especially pp. 71–4, 272–348, 441–65.

15. Kalinka, *Sejm*, I, pp. 230–1, 344–5, 470–4. Lord, *Second Partition*, pp. 112–27.

content himself with an outline set of constitutional principles, accepted by the Sejm in December 1789. They gratifyingly combined conservatism with utopianism. Wider social reform was rejected; the pre-eminence of the *szlachta* was reasserted; the decisions of future Sejmy would be bound by the mandatory instructions of the *sejmiki.*[16] The treaty was signed on 29 March 1790.[17]

International complications

Prussia looked for acquisitions from Poland and the humbling of Austria. Frederick William and Hertzberg hoped that Austrian difficulties in the war against the Porte and the domestic unrest engendered by Joseph II's reforms would allow the Habsburgs to be browbeaten into ceding Galicia to the Poles, who would then deliver Danzig, Thorn and parts of Wielkopolska to their Prussian benefactors. The Austrians would be compensated by the Turkish cession of Moldavia and Wallachia, and Turkey would be reassured by a Prussian guarantee of its remaining European territories. Ideally, the whole operation would be transacted without war, but if it came to the crunch, Prussia would fight. Russia would be kept in check by Sweden and by a British fleet off St Petersburg. To deal with the Habsburgs, Frederick William began a major military build-up in Silesia from the summer of 1789. To strengthen their hand, in January 1790, the Prussians concluded an alliance with the Porte (not that they let it know of their plans for giving away its territories).[18] The following month, Joseph II died. The Habsburg monarchy seemed on the verge of revolt and dissolution. Even the newly expanding Polish army could be used to invade and foment discord in Galicia, while Prussian troops invaded from Silesia.[19]

Not least of the difficulties facing this scheme was the reluctance of the *szlachta* to involve themselves in anything smacking of offensive warfare. The enthusiasm of Ignacy Potocki, Stanisław Małachowski and a few of their friends found little echo. In the treaty of 29 March, the Prussians settled for a defensive alliance: the 12,000 Polish troops specified would at least act as some form of shield against Austrian

16. Kalinka, *Sejm*, I, pp. 483–98; E. Rostworowski, 'Marzenie dobrego obywatela, czyli królewski projekt Konstytucji', *idem*, *Legendy i Fakty XVIIIw.* (Warsaw, 1963), pp. 291–9; Zielińska, 'O sukcesyi', pp. 92–3.

17. *CTS* L, pp. 489–95.   18. Lord, *Second Partition*, pp. 76–7, 117–20.

19. Kalinka, *Sejm*, I, pp. 479–83.

attack while Prussian troops fell on Habsburg territories from Silesia. The *szlachta* wanted the treaty because they saw in Frederick William 'the gendarme of the Commonwealth, readily and freely performing the duty' of protecting it from Russia.[20] The agreement did nothing to settle the continued commercial and toll disputes between the two states, beyond allowing for continued negotiations. The lack of progress on this front continually reawakened Polish suspicions of Prussian motives. Prussia was saddled with an open-ended commitment to defend the Commonwealth's territorial integrity, in the first instance with a force of 14,000 men.

Three months after the treaty's signature, a damning report by general von Kalckreuth on the state of the Polish army showed that the reciprocal Polish commitment to defend Prussia was worthless – though since Prussia was simultaneously trying to sabotage its ally's reforms, it could hardly complain.[21] All that the treaty, which did not rule out 'the amicable resolution of certain controversies . . . concerning particular [stretches of] frontier', gave Prussia was the hope that it would retain its influence in Poland and realise its territorial claims in the future. Ignacy Potocki, the chief Polish negotiator, could not prevent the closure of even this loophole, when, in September 1790, the Sejm decreed the perpetual inalienability of all Polish territory. Within six months of its signature, the treaty of Warsaw had become utterly useless to the Prussians.[22] As for Poland, Potocki's adventurism had threatened to embroil it in war, despoil it of yet more territory and failed to settle what really mattered to *szlachta* purses – the commercial disputes with his new Prussian friends. The result was growing disenchantment and a drift back in sentiment towards Stanisław August. Loathing of Russia remained as strong as ever.

Of necessity, Poland's foreign policy remained one of drift. The king and the small corps of professional diplomats he had painstakingly built up over many years were marginalised. The Sejm's Deputation for Foreign Affairs functioned erratically, allowing itself to be dominated by aristocratic dilettantes. Of the partitioning powers, only Austria was seriously interested in shoring up the Commonwealth's territorial integrity as a potential ally against Prussia. However, increasing Austrian pressure during Joseph's later reign on

---

20. Ibid., II, p. 24.

21. Ibid., pp. 113–14; Lord, *Second Partition*, pp. 128–33; Michalski, 'Dyplomacja polska', p. 615.

22. Text of the treaty of Warsaw in *CTS* L, pp. 489–95. See also Kalinka, *Sejm*, II, pp. 183–95 and Lord, *Second Partition*, pp. 112–27.

the Galician 'sujets mixtes', in terms of taxation and social reform, did nothing to endear the Habsburgs to the Poles. The Foreign Affairs Deputation made no effort at all to cultivate good relations with either St Petersburg or Vienna – *szlachta* opinion would have been enraged. Flights of diplomatic fantasy ruled. Ignacy Potocki and Stanisław Małachowski toyed with the idea of a Hohenzollern succession in Poland. In March 1790, Ignacy's cousin Piotr Potocki arrived in Constantinople and began (vainly) to negotiate an alliance, which he hoped would recover for Poland not only Galicia, but also Byelorussia and even Kiev.[23]

The prospect of war spreading to include Prussia and its Polish ally was very real. Potemkin and the Council of State were confident that there would be little difficulty in occupying and even annexing the Polish Ukrainian palatinates if it finally came to a breach.[24] In late June 1790, with 300,000 hostile Prussian and Austrian troops facing each other across the frontier, last-ditch negotiations to avert a war were opened under British mediation at Reichenbach in Silesia. It said something for Poland's real international weight that its diplomats were not invited to the talks (although Lucchesini was a participant). Hertzberg made an attempt to implement a partial version of his exchange plan. Austria would restore a substantial portion of northern Galicia, including the salt-mines and the towns of Brody, Zamość, Tarnów and Rzeszów; Austria would keep Belgrade and the Banat from the Porte. The Prussians would, of course, persuade the Poles to cede them Danzig and Thorn.

The attempt to re-edit the First Partition fell through in part because Lucchesini assured Frederick William that the Galician restoration was far too limited to win the Poles' assent and in part because Joseph's successor, Leopold II, also found the proposed exchange unworthwhile: there was also the small matter of securing the Turks' agreement. But above all, it was Britain's role which was crucial. If the Austrians were ready to accept the *status quo ante bellum*, Britain would not back any Prussian offensive against Austria. Loath though he was to give up the recently captured Belgrade, Leopold II took the point. The alternative was collapse. The Convention of Reichenbach of 27 July killed off Hertzberg's exchange schemes and destroyed his standing with Frederick William. The Prussians had spent a vast amount of money to mobilise their war machine in order not to finish off their old enemy. Austria was

23. Michalski, 'Dyplomacja polska', pp. 642–3, 661–5.
24. Lord, *Second Partition*, pp. 128–44. *AGS*, session of 11/22 Apr. 1790, cols 774–6.

wracked by war and revolt from Belgium to Hungary and faced with the growing prospect of conflict with a lunatic France. Prussia had bottled out: it was not strong enough to embark on an aggressive foreign policy on its own. It had not even got anything from Poland. 'I cannot contain myself for shame and grief', complained Hertzberg.[25]

Pitt fretted about Russia. Its continued expansion towards the Black Sea and its regrettably closer relations with France (not yet soured by the Revolution) threatened a fresh, nightmarish, diplomatic revolution. If Russia gained access to the Black Sea and the eastern Mediterranean then it might prefer to export its naval stores and industrial raw materials to France instead of Britain. The Anglo-Russian commercial treaty of 1766 lapsed in early 1787, just as Russia was forging a most-favoured-nation relationship with France. In this context, Pitt showed great interest in a reinvigorated Poland, as an alternative supplier to Russia, as well as a potentially lucrative export market. He accepted the urgent necessity of putting its commercial relations with Prussia on a more favourable footing – and, to this end, he was most insistent on the Polish cession of Danzig and Thorn. After all, they could offer little else.[26] These plans inevitably ran up against the adamant refusal of the Poles to cede any more territory, against Prussians' reluctance to surrender their lucrative commercial exactions and, above all, against Catherine's own determination.

Pitt was ready to take Britain to war against Russia. Frederick William was prepared to play along. He was convinced that an over-extended Russia would back down in the face of military and naval demonstrations. He managed to persuade himself that the Austrians would not only not support Russia, but might even line up against it. On 21 and 22 March, the British Cabinet resolved to send thirty-nine ships of the line into the Baltic forthwith. Frederick William ordered the deployment of 88,000 men in East Prussia, within striking distance of Russian Livonia. Pitt tried to convince the Poles to join in. Frederick William tempted them with the prospect of recovering not only the lands they had ceded to the Russians in 1772 but the vast territories they had surrendered at Andrussovo in 1667 – in return, inevitably, for the cession of Danzig, Thorn and parts of Wielkopolska.[27]

25. Lord, *Second Partition*, pp. 141–52; Black, *British foreign policy*, pp. 257–62.

26. Ibid., pp. 49–52, 272–86. I. De Madariaga, *Russia in the age of Catherine the Great* (London, 1981), pp. 392, 400–1; LeDonne, *The Russian empire*, pp. 298–9.

27. Lord, *Second Partition*, pp. 153–65, 170–8; Z. Libiszowska, *Życie polskie w Londynie w XVIII wieku* (Warsaw, 1972), pp. 118–32; Black, *British foreign policy*, pp. 270–99.

The *sine qua non* for Pitt was that Russia should restore the hard-won fortress of Ochakov to Turkey. Catherine's advisers were sufficiently concerned to urge concessions. In March 1791, Potemkin suggested that Prussia could be bought off with a fresh Partition of Poland, an offer that would surely have been taken up, had it been made sooner.[28] Catherine would not budge. She had made peace with the Swedes, at Verela, on 14 August 1790. Anglo-Prussian sabre-rattling left her unmoved. In London, her ambassador, Semeon Vorontsov, orchestrated a brilliantly successful press campaign against Pitt's policy. Public opinion could not understand why the ministry was so set on risking a major war over a distant object on the shores of the Black Sea. By early April, it was clear that the Commons would not vote supply. Pitt ordered his minister in Berlin to tell the Prussians that Britain would not deliver its planned ultimatum to Russia, nor make its fleet available in the Baltic.[29] The international effort to restrain Russia had crumbled. On 4 August, Austria signed a definitive peace with Turkey at Sistova. On 11 August, the Russians and the Turks concluded an armistice at Galatz, leaving the former in possession of Ochakov and the adjacent territory of Yedisan. Catherine had faced down Britain and Prussia and was poised to make peace on her own terms.

The Third of May

Poland's opportunities were narrowing fast. In November 1789, the Sejm had had to accept the limitations inherent in a republican system of government unfamiliar with the nuts and bolts of administration and fiscality. The 100,000 army quota was suspended: provisionally, the Commonwealth, which had so far managed to increase its army to 45,000, would aim to put together one of 65,000.[30] Confused as reformers were over the nature of the constitutional changes they wanted, they nevertheless could agree that one sacred cow at least had to be slaughtered. Interregna and royal elections were fundamental to the traditional *szlachta* vision of the perfect Commonwealth. After two months of furious debate in August and September of 1790, the Sejm resolved to put the question of elective versus hereditary monarchy to the *sejmiki*. Marshal Małachowski and his allies recommended the restoration of the Wettin dynasty.[31]

28. Lord, *Second Partition*, pp. 179–84.   29. Black, *British foreign policy*, pp. 300–28.
30. *VL* IX, pp. 162–3. Kalinka, *Sejm*, I, p. 440.
31. *VL* IX, p. 183. Zielińska, 'O sukcesyi', *passim*.

The fresh round of instructions which were issued by the *sejmiki* of November 1790 convinced Ignacy Potocki and those opponents of the king who saw in the Rousseauesque 'National Will' the true basis of reform that the *szlachta* nation was not perhaps as mature as they imagined. Some three-quarters of the assemblies agreed to the succession of the elector Friedrich August III of Saxony but were overwhelmingly opposed to the restoration of full-blown hereditary rule. Most *sejmiki* were opposed to any tinkering with the social order. There was intense suspicion of proposals mooted by Ignacy Potocki's associate, Hugon Kołłątaj, for admitting townsmen into the legislature and emancipating the serfs. Many wanted to scrap the new-fangled Commission for National Education. At the same time, there was a clear impatience at the failure to complete the reformation of government. It remained embarrassingly true that, beyond the Sejm's endorsement of the 'Principles of the Form of Government' of December 1789, virtually nothing tangible had been achieved. Not until 24 March 1791 did the exhausted Sejm finally approve a law on the *sejmiki*, providing a mechanism for the expression of the national will. Their envoys would be constrained by binding instructions in response to any future legislative proposals by the king and his ministers.[32]

By March 1791, however, a parallel, clandestine track of constitutional reform was being beaten out. The lamentable pace of change and a realisation that the favourable international conditions would not last for ever had convinced Ignacy Potocki, Adam Czartoryski, Stanisław Małachowski and Hugon Kołłątaj that genuine constitutional progress could not come about via the Sejm's laborious official machinery, but through a deal with the king. Stanisław August seemed a safer bet to the majority of envoys than either those who wanted to restore the old anarchy or dabble in the ideas of the French Revolution, whose progress the Warsaw press was reporting with uncensored gusto.

On 24 April, the Sejm dispersed for Easter, in order to reassemble on 2 May, when it was to discuss treasury business. The king and Potocki intended to use the support of around a hundred royalist and reform-minded envoys who had stayed behind to push their new Constitution through on 5 May, before significant numbers of conservative opponents returned. News of some sort of plot began to leak on 30 April. The Prussian chargé d'affaires, Friedrich Goltz (Lucchesini was at the Sistova talks), wrote anxiously to his court

---

32. *VL* IX, p. 238. Kalinka, *Sejm*, II, pp. 438–45.

that he suspected a *coup d'état*. On 6 May, Hertzberg ordered him to do everything he could to stop it. 'A well-ruled Poland might be dangerous, even ruinous, for Prussia.'[33]

The rumours had led the conspirators to bring their *coup d'état* forward to 3 May. Kołłątaj mobilized the Warsaw citizenry. Troops under Stanisław August's nephew, prince Józef Poniatowski, surrounded the royal castle, where the Sejm was meeting. Despite the objections of a small minority, the new Constitution was enthusiastically acclaimed. The *liberum veto* was finally abolished in favour of majority voting. A new executive, the so-called 'Custodial Council of the Laws' (*Straż Praw*), was set up, with provision to ensure it did not arrogate excessive powers to itself. A ministerial countersignature was necessary to validate any monarchic decision, although the ruler could not be held to account. Any minister could be dismissed by a two-thirds majority vote of the envoys and senators. The Sejm would meet as and when necessary. The mandatory power of *sejmiki* instructions was put aside. Townsmen were given a consultative voice on commercial and economic legislation. Ennoblement was made easier. On Stanisław August's death, the throne was to pass in hereditary succession to Friedrich August III.[34]

The Commonwealth now had something it had lacked for over a century: the embryo of an effectively functioning government. Although there were serious divisions of opinion in the country at large over the Constitution, its opponents felt isolated and demoralised. A highly effective combination of reformist propaganda, celebratory festivities and adroit use of royal patronage stiffened the joy and relief at a great breakthrough. To committed reformers, the Third of May was to serve as the basis of further change. To many, perhaps most, after three years of fraught debate, surely this was as much as Poland needed. Such was the tenor of the official proclamation of the Constitution on 7 May: 'Our country is saved; our freedoms assured; we are a free and independent nation; we have shaken off the bonds of slavery and misrule.'

Among the cautious was the king – less from personal inclination than from an acute consciousness of the limitations of *szlachta*

33. E. Rostworowski, *Ostatni król Rzeczypospolitej* (Warsaw, 1966), p. 231.

34. There is a vast literature in Polish on the subject. Otherwise, see J.T. Lukowski, 'Recasting Utopia: Montesquieu, Rousseau and the Polish Constitution of 3 May 1791', *Historical Journal* 37 (1994), pp. 65–87. The best translation, although it deliberately plays up the Constitution's 'liberal' aspects, remains that made by the Polish minister in London, Franciszek Bukaty, in *The Annual Register* for 1791, pp. 177–200.

society.[35] His appointment to the Custodial Council of Ksawery Branicki as minister for the army was dictated not just by a misguided desire to keep a notorious troublemaker inside the government tent, but also by a wish to reassure domestic society and, most of all, St Petersburg that the 'Polish Revolution' was very different from the French.[36] This desire not to offend reflected both Poland's continued weakness and the continuation of old habits. The Constitution's preamble spoke of 'the present circumstances of Europe and this fleeting moment which has restored our fate into our own hands'. There was a feeling that, provided only minimal dissent emerged, and that doubters were won over by persuasion, rather than force, all would be well. And Poland still had its Prussian alliance.

The neighbours and the new Constitution

The delicacy of the situation was underlined by the reaction of the Saxon elector to the offer of the succession. The Wettins had never reconciled themselves to the loss of the Polish crown. The possibility of their restoration had been the subject of discreet unofficial negotiations between reformers and the long-serving Saxon minister, August Franz Essen, since the start of the Sejm. The sober reluctance of the Saxons to take at face value the encouraging noises from Poland, even occasionally from Frederick William (against, naturally, suitable compensation in Polish territory), contrasted sharply with the naive optimism of Polish diplomacy, which gave the Saxons no advance warning of the offer formally made in the Statute of Government. Without the imprimatur of Catherine the Great, Friedrich August III would only prevaricate.[37]

From Russia, there came ominous silence. The new Constitution had largely restored the conduct of foreign affairs to Stanisław August, yet he was very reluctant even officially to notify the Russians of the reform. It is still not clear why this was so. Concern at an embarrassing Russian response? Fears that any active overtures

35. W. Smoleński, *Ostatni rok Sejmu Wielkiego* (Kraków, 1897), pp. 55, 94–5, 110–11, 133–5. Full text of the Proclamation in A. Grześkowiak-Krwawicz, ed., *Za i Przeciw Ustawie Rządowej* (Warsaw, 1992), pp. 24–9.

36. J. Wojakowski, *Straż Praw* (Warsaw, 1982), pp. 96–100.

37. Zielińska, *'O sukcesji'*, pp. 48–104, 201–6; Michalski, 'Dyplomacja', pp. 672–5.

to St Petersburg would be ill-received by the *szlachta* nation? A cautious wait-and-see policy? Or just a failure of nerve? Stanisław August finally wrote to inform Catherine of the Constitution on 24 December, a delay which could only be interpreted as a major snub. He received no response.[38] Poland's minister-resident, Augustyn Deboli, had no doubt as to what Catherine and her advisers really believed. From St Petersburg, he sent a stream of frantic messages urging the government to show more energy in building up its army and forming wider alliances, to concentrate less on constitutional minutiae and pay greater heed to the very real threat that Russia posed.[39]

Deboli was right to be alarmed. The assertion of Polish independence ran counter to the central thrust of almost a century of Russian foreign policy. The insults and massive logistical inconveniences visited on Russia by the Four Years Sejm were not to be lightly shrugged off. Even a passive Poland was a threat. The Sejm began to work for a much closer integration with the Commonwealth of its vassal duchy of Courland, which Russia had treated as its own dependency for decades. Even more outrageously, it took active steps to set up a native Orthodox metropolitanate, which was finally to sever all links with Russia and its Most Holy Synod.[40] For the time being, Catherine was ready to remain a spectator – but she expected the Poles themselves to invoke her assistance against this revolutionary innovation. On 27 May, she made clear to Potemkin that, as soon as peace talks with the Turks at Jassy were completed, Russian troops would be redeployed against Poland. She had to be sure, too, that Prussia was not behind the reform. The Council of State agreed with the empress (not that it was likely to do otherwise) that if the new form of government – which Catherine somewhat flatteringly described as 'absolutist' – took hold, 'it cannot not be dangerous to neighbouring powers, Russia included'.[41]

The Austrians begged to differ. A stronger Poland could be a barrier against Prussia. On 23 May, Kaunitz wrote to St Petersburg to urge acceptance of the Constitution. Leopold II hoped that his own tilt towards Prussia, marked by the seeming calls to a crusade against France in the Circular of Padua (6 July) and the Declaration

38. Ibid., p. 646; Smoleński, *Ostatni rok*, pp. 238–9, 245–6.

39. e.g., Deboli to Stanisław August, 5 Apr., 13 May, 10 June, 30 July, 9 Aug., 2 Dec. 1791 AGAD/ZP 421, ff. 16, 67, 84, 121, 141–3, 244.

40. Smoleński, *Ostatni rok*, pp. 83–8, 328–9.

41. Solov'ev, *IPP*, p. 558. *AGS*, 8/19 and 12/23 May 1791, cols 852–3. De Madariaga, *Russia*, pp. 420–2.

of Pillnitz (27 August), could help secure Poland's position: he and Kaunitz looked to insert a joint guarantee for the new Constitution into their putative alliance with Prussia.[42] But the more Austria became entangled with France, the less it could do to preserve Poland. This was not lost on Catherine, to whom in November 1791 Kaunitz suggested a joint declaration of support for the 3 May Constitution: a reformed Poland would provide the ideal buffer state – strong enough to bridle Prussia, but too weak to threaten its neighbours. Catherine, instead, encouraged Austria and Prussia to arms against France: their embroilment in the west would give her a free hand to restore her version of order to her Polish backyard.[43]

The Russians need not have worried about the Prussian attitude. Officially, Frederick William congratulated the Poles.[44] Hertzberg, in semi-retirement, praised the moderation of the Statute of Government to the Berlin Academy and expressed private alarm to Lucchesini:

> The Poles have dealt a fatal blow to the Prussian monarchy, by introducing a hereditary throne and a constitution better than the English . . . I foresee that, sooner or later, Poland will take West Prussia from us, perhaps even East Prussia. How can we defend our state, exposed from Memel to Teschen, against a numerous and well-ruled nation?[45]

This was even more flattering than Catherine's accusations of absolutism. But such reactions demonstrated how dramatically the new Constitution had changed Poland's international position.

Partition was, however, made more likely by the very lack of support in Poland for Russian intervention. Even those who had doubts about the new Constitution did not want the Russians back. There were only three politicians of any standing ready to play that card: Felix Potocki, general of the Crown artillery, the richest magnate of the Polish Ukraine and a long-standing Russian client; Ksawery Branicki, Crown *hetman* and minister for the army; and Seweryn Rzewuski, field-*hetman* of the Crown, held captive in Russia from

42. Solov'ev, *IPP*, pp. 564–5; Smoleński, *Ostatni rok*, pp. 236–8; Lord, *Second Partition*, pp. 205–28; T.C.W. Blanning, *The origins of the French revolutionary wars* (Harlow, 1986), pp. 83–9.

43. Lord, *Second Partition*, pp. 222–4, 235; De Madariaga, *Russia*, pp. 427–8.

44. Frederick William II to Stanisław August, 23 May 1791 in Chodźko, pp. 253–4.

45. Quoted in E. Rostworowski, *Ostatni król*, p. 238. Cf. J. Van Horn Melton, 'From Enlightenment to Revolution: Hertzberg, Schlözer and the problem of despotism in the late *Aufklärung*', *Central European History* 12 (1979), pp. 106–8, 112–13, 116–17.

1767 to 1772 for his defence of Catholicism, now ready to invoke its assistance in defence of ancient republican liberties. Their posturings during the Sejm had cost them much support. Rzewuski and Potocki felt so isolated that they preferred to reside in Vienna. Early in October, at Potemkin's invitation, the two malcontents left to join him at Jassy in Moldavia, where he was to conduct peace talks with the Turks. They arrived on the 16th, the day he died of fever.[46]

In Warsaw, Branicki persuaded Stanisław August – whose belief in avoiding trouble by offending no one was becoming unmanageable – to give him leave to travel to Jassy in order to sort out his wife's claims on the Potemkin estate. Deboli despairingly pointed out that this would only facilitate Branicki and his cronies' plots for Russian intervention.[47] On 15 November, the malcontents were joined by Catherine's chief foreign policy adviser, Alexander Bezborodko, with reassurances of support. Before he returned to Warsaw in December, Branicki laid plans to confederate Lithuania, under the direction of Szymon Kossakowski: an ex-Barist confederate, a general in the Russian service and brother of Józef, the bishop of Livonia, another malcontent. Russian intervention would enable them to become the dominant political force in the Grand Duchy. Rzewuski and Potocki remained in Jassy, oblivious to appeals and orders from king, Sejm and Custodial Council to return. Their dismissal from office on 27 January 1792 left them unmoved. They did not recognise the authority of a government which had buried 'Polish liberty'.[48] By then, Bezborodko had formally brought the war with the Porte to an end, securing Yedisan and Ochakov, with the peace of Jassy, on 9 January.[49]

Bezborodko remained concerned that a Russian invasion might yet trigger Prussian assistance for Poland under the treaty of March 1790; in turn, that might bring Britain into the war. Catherine agreed that Prussia and Austria should be apprised of Russia's intentions beforehand – but she was determined to invade Poland regardless. Indeed, by December 1791, it seems highly likely that she had finally decided that, at the very least, she would annex the Ukraine. Her immersion in the history of Russia's ancient and medieval past inclined her to a *réunion* policy. Her new toy-boy, Platon Zubov, and his ally in the College of Foreign Affairs, Arkadii Morkov, were pushing for the annexation of the Polish Ukraine,

46. Smoleński, *Ostatni rok*, pp. 149–59, 173–87.
47. Deboli to Stanisław August, 28 Oct., 8 Nov. 1791, AGAD/ZP 421, ff. 203, 206–11.
48. Smoleński, *Ostatni rok*, pp. 193–228.
49. Ibid., p. 303; De Madariaga, *Russia*, p. 429.

with rich pickings for themselves. Only if Prussia and Austria showed themselves hostile to Catherine's plans would she contemplate offering them a share in the Polish spoils.[50]

At Jassy, the malcontents insisted to Bezborodko that, although they were assured of mass *szlachta* support, they also needed the backing of 100,000 Russian soldiers. In mid-March, they removed to St Petersburg to finalise their triumphant return. Astonishingly, Stanisław August allowed Branicki to join them, yet again supposedly to tidy up Potemkin's inheritance. During early April, Potocki and Rzewuski put together an act of Confederacy which would be proclaimed in Poland, appealing 'to the great Catherine, who reigns so gloriously and with such justice over an empire which is our neighbour, friend and ally', whose treaty obligations surely obliged her to come to the defence of long-standing liberties. By some remarkably selective interpretation, the authors concluded that 'the fatal examples of Paris' had led a 'misguided mob' to impose the triumph of monarchic despotism over republican liberty on 3 May. Moreover, they assured their future audience that they would not permit the loss of 'even the smallest scrap of the Commonwealth's territory'. Much of the text was based on Potemkin's own papers and a schedule of twenty-three articles drawn up by Catherine herself, positing, in outline, the restoration of the constitutional status quo of 1768 and 1775.[51] The Act proclaimed the abolition of the 3 May Constitution.

The lack of any further firm detail reflected the failure of Branicki, Rzewuski and Potocki to agree among themselves. The first two wanted a restoration of the old *hetman* powers in differing degrees; Potocki wanted to convert Poland into a kingless federal republic of provinces under Russian protection. The three almost came to blows over the issue. For the time being, they made do with their Act of Confederacy, to which, with ten other supporters, they put their signatures on 27 April. It was post-dated to 14 May and supposedly set up in the township of Targowica, just inside Poland's border with the Russian Ukraine. The invasion was set to take place four days later.[52]

50. Solov'ev, *IPP* (Catherine's memorandum of 4/15 December), pp. 565–7, 592; Smoleński, *Ostatni rok*, p. 253; Lord, *Second Partition*, pp. 252–5; De Madariaga, *Russia*, p. 430; cf. Catherine II to major-general M.V. Krechetnikov, 8/19 Dec. 1792, *SIRIO* XLVII, p. 473.
51. Chodźko, pp. 262–74; Smoleński, *Ostatni rok*, pp. 305–13; Lord, *Second Partition*, pp. 274–6. A copy of Catherine's articles is to be found in *SIRIO* XLVII, pp. 303–5.
52. W. Smoleński, *Konfederacya Targowicka* (Kraków, 1903), pp. 27–31; Lord, *Second Partition*, pp. 249–53.

Austria and Prussia were too distracted in the west to be likely to cause difficulties. In July 1791, the Austrians had successfully insisted on including a joint guarantee of 'the free constitution' of Poland, in a preliminary agreement which envisaged the possibility of future co-operation against France. Leopold and Kaunitz were almost desperate to preserve Poland, preferably under Wettin rule. The Commonwealth, as a 'puissance intermédiaire' stabilised under a hereditary dynasty owing its position to the protection of the neighbouring powers, would give the Habsburgs security in the rear. The preservation of Poland's territorial integrity would reassure the Habsburgs against what they feared more than France – the further expansion towards the Austrian borders of their own allies. On 7 February 1792, in Berlin, the July understanding was converted into a much closer defensive alliance against French aggression and ideological subversion. If war erupted, Austria's possessions in the Netherlands would be at risk; it was extremely doubtful if Austria would be able to cope without Prussian help. At Prussian insistence, the commitment to Poland was significantly diluted: the two signatories would endeavour to preserve Poland's territory and independence, but maintain not 'the' but 'a' free constitution.[53]

To Leopold, the changed article represented an acceptable concession, for the preservation of the Commonwealth was not called into question.[54] Catherine played along with this ingenious diplomatic elasticity. Her letter of 28 February to Kaunitz finally confirmed what he must have long suspected: the new Constitution was quite unacceptable. She tartly reminded the Austrians that they themselves were committed by treaty to the preservation of the previous form of Polish government. On the other hand, she was sufficiently conscious of Austrian sensitivities to assure them that she had no intention to partition the Commonwealth.[55] Before the letter reached Vienna, Leopold II unexpectedly died on 1 March. His successor, Francis II, was much more eager for a Prussian rapprochement than his father had been. Since, on 20 April, the French gratuitously declared war on Austria, the change of monarch probably made no difference as far as Poland was concerned. Austria simply could not afford both to protect Poland and defend itself from France.

53. Preliminary convention of Vienna, 25 July 1791, *CTS* LI, pp. 187–8; treaty of Berlin, 7 Feb. 1792, ibid., p. 293.

54. P.W. Schroeder, *The transformation of European politics 1763–1848* (Oxford, 1996 edn), pp. 91–3.

55. Lord, *Second Partition*, pp. 208–16, 233–36; De Madariaga, *Russia*, pp. 430–1.

Fresh realignments

The crucial push for partition came, unsurprisingly, from Prussia. Its politicians could not risk the emergence of a strong Poland. Frederick William, quite unperturbed by his own earlier insistence to the Poles that they should undertake reforms in order to secure his alliance, told Lucchesini that the *casus foederis* could not apply to a form of government not in existence when the alliance was first concluded. His ministers thought this self-evident.[56] For all the tensions which had accumulated between Prussia and Russia since 1787, relations had never been severed. Even as they first goaded the Poles against the Russians, the Prussians tried to persuade Catherine that she could recover her old influence in Poland if only she realigned with them and ditched Austria. In December 1790, Hertzberg told the Russian minister, Maxim Alopeus, that Prussia would endorse Russia's territorial claims against Turkey (another Prussian ally), in return for Danzig and Thorn. In October 1791, the Prussians began to moot the possibility of a direct alliance with Russia, quite distinct from their hoped-for arrangements with Austria.[57]

Their overtures confirmed Catherine's conviction that the Prussians would not be a serious obstacle. On the contrary, the French dimension promised a new and far more lucrative variant of Hertzberg's old exchange schemes. Barely a week after the conclusion of Prussia's February 1792 alliance with Austria, news arrived from Heinrich-Leopold von Goltz, the ambassador in St Petersburg, that Catherine was set on invading Poland. She would agree to a partition, if necessary, to obviate opposition from Prussia and Austria. Frederick William had intended, in the event of war with France, to seek compensation for his trouble in the Rhineland duchies of Jülich and Berg. But on 16 February, he and his ministers decided it would be much simpler to go for Polish territory. The left bank of the Vistula would do very nicely.[58]

Agreement on the Second Partition was to be reached far more swiftly and directly than on the First. The ice had been well and truly broken, a spate of exchange proposals from the Balkans to Belgium had familiarised politicians with the idea of shunting borders and toppling sovereigns by appending signatures to pieces of

56. Smoleński, *Ostatni rok*, pp. 253–5; Dutkiewicz, 'Prusy a Polska', pp. 45–7.
57. Kalinka, *Sejm*, I, pp. 228–9; Solov'ev, *IPP*, pp. 534–6; *AGS* (9/20 Dec. 1790), col. 820; Lord, *Second Partition*, pp. 161–2, 232–4.
58. Ibid., pp. 235–40, 257–9.

paper. Yet amid the fevered atmosphere of diplomatic mistrust, coyness and caution could not entirely be discarded. Austria might not have liked the prospect of its new friend Prussia's aggrandisement in Poland, but it had its own expansionist plans: that hardy, grief-bringing perennial, the exchange of Bavaria for strategically inconvenient Belgium, was once again under consideration. Karl Theodor, who loathed his electorate, was ready to swap it for Austria's Netherlands, if a royal title was thrown in. Prussia's opposition had been crucial to blocking the scheme on previous occasions. The up-and-coming Anton Spielmann sensed an opportunity to make his mark and ease out the geriatric Kaunitz. On 21 March, with the new ruler's blessing, he began the demolition of the chancellor's policies. He told the Prussian envoy in Vienna that, provided Austria obtained commensurate territory elsewhere, it would not oppose Prussian expansion in Poland. A month later came the French declaration of war – to Frederick William's delight. He expected to deal almost as easily with these democrats as he had with the Dutch in 1787. On 24 April, he ordered preparations for war, complaining at Austrian time-wasting. A series of ministerial conferences at Potsdam between 12 and 15 May resolved to send some cautious feelers to Russia over Polish territory.[59]

Russian invasion: the Confederacy of Targowica

The Commonwealth survived long enough to fête the first anniversary of its new Constitution. But during March and April, Catherine had sent orders to general Mikhail Kakhovskii to concentrate 100,000 troops on Poland's eastern and south-eastern borders, ready to invade on 18 May.[60] On that day, the Russian minister, Jakov Bulgakov, delivered the announcement of the Russian troop entries, first, to the grand chancellor of Lithuania, Joachim Chreptowicz, then to the king and the primate and finally to his Prussian and Austrian colleagues. He made pre-printed copies available for public consumption.[61]

The war was over in two months. The Poles had no chance. They had brought their army up to 57,000 men, but only 45,000 were

59. Ibid., pp. 261–6, 310–12; Blanning, *Origins of the French revolutionary wars*, pp. 114–19; Schroeder, *The transformation*, pp. 97–8.
60. *SIRIO* XLVII, pp. 241–44, 245–55 (14/25 Mar., 1/12 Apr.); similar orders to major-general Mikhail Krechetnikov, 2/13 Apr., ibid., pp. 256–68.
61. Smoleński, *Ostatni rok*, pp. 393–400. Text of the declaration in Chodźko, pp. 274–81.

field troops. They were mainly inexperienced, poorly armed and equipped, easy meat for Kakhovskii's veterans. The commander in Lithuania, Ludwig of Württemberg, who owed his appointment to being prince Adam Czartoryski's son-in-law, resigned on grounds of ill-health when postal intercepts showed he was following Frederick William's directions not to put up too much resistance.[62] His wretched men were pushed remorselessly back onto Warsaw. The Crown troops under Józef Poniatowski gave a better account of themselves, but they, too, were constantly forced back. Frederick William II's letter of 8 June, informing Stanisław August that he could scarcely be expected to abide by his alliance, since he had not been consulted on a Constitution which had so provoked Russia, can have been no surprise.[63] He thoughtfully sent a copy to St Petersburg. The Austrians and Saxons sent their regrets. In Warsaw, the Austrian chargé d'affaires, Benedict de Caché, hastened to quash all rumours that Francis II would intervene to defend Poland.[64]

The Russian invasion also punctured the bubble of self-delusion created by the Poles' own emotions and rhetoric of the past four years. The Sejm certainly reacted positively, with calls to arms, appeals for volunteers and substantial votes of extraordinary taxation. But as international reality battered its way into the *szlachta* homeland, old habits reasserted themselves. On 22 May, the Sejm invested Stanisław August with full powers of command over the army, reserving only confirmation of a final peace treaty to itself.[65] This unprecedented decision was tantamount to dumping the responsibility for handling an impossible situation onto the king. On 29 May, the Sejm adjourned indefinitely: the great majority of envoys and senators returned to their homes.

On 19 June, the Custodial Council proposed to salvage Poland's situation by offering the succession to Catherine's second grandson, the thirteen-year-old Grand Duke Constantine. The move was poorly received in St Petersburg, where it was treated as a ploy to excite the jealousy of Austria and Prussia against Russia.[66] The speed of the Russian advance cut the Polish government off from huge swathes of manpower and tax resources; negotiations for a major loan with Dutch bankers collapsed when the Targowica leaders announced that they would not honour any such agreements. On

62. W. Smoleński, *Konfederacya Targowicka* (Kraków, 1903) pp. 45–7.
63. Text in Chodźko, pp. 292–3.
64. Smoleński, *Konfederacya Targowicka*, pp. 48–51. *AGS*, session of 14/25 June 1792, col. 922.
65. *VL* IX, p. 447.   66. *AGS*, session of 21 June/2 July 1792, cols 922–7.

23 July, the king called an extraordinary meeting of ministers, which accepted the inevitable. By eleven votes to three (with one abstention) it endorsed the decision to ask for the unconditional ceasefire which the Russians were demanding and for Stanisław August to comply with Catherine's demand that he accede to the Confederacy of Targowica. He did so the next day. A night of rioting followed in the angry capital. On 26 July, Józef Poniatowski, faithful to the orders of his commander-in-chief, concluded an armistice. During the next fortnight, he and dozens of officers resigned their commissions. Leading reformers, including Hugon Kołłątaj, Ignacy Potocki and Stanisław Małachowski, fled to Saxony. The king was left to face the music.

Stanisław August intended to do what he had done in 1767, 1773 and 1776: come to an arrangement with the Russians and rescue what he could. This was the basis on which the ministerial council of 23 July had opted for accession to Targowica; the émigrés in Dresden expected him to succeed and were confident that, sooner or later, they would be reinstated in the country and in office. Their expectations were totally unrealistic. In St Petersburg, neither king nor the reformers had an iota of credibility. Poland was to be ruled through Targowica. It took a second, unconditional act of submission to the Confederacy for the king to begin to win Catherine's approval, only to be blighted by postal intercepts to Dresden, revealing his continued attachment to the 3 May Constitution.[67] The Targowica leaders themselves did not want the king's accession, fearing that he might turn their Russian patrons against them. But 'government' by Targowica was an irrelevancy. The Confederacy, proclaimed in the wake of the advancing Russian armies, attracted pitifully little support. Most accessions were secured by force or the threat of confiscation of property. The Confederacy was an opportunity for its leaders to embark on an orgy of self-enrichment, settling old scores and enmities, some stretching back to the Barist years and the 1773–75 Sejm. The institutions set up by 3 May ground to a halt. The Confederacy's leaders, even as they looked over their shoulders to St Petersburg for guidance which never seemed to come, were unable to agree among themselves. Mass revulsion swept the country against them. On top of all this came the exactions, contributions and billetings imposed by the invading Russian troops.[68]

67. *AGS*, sessions of 26 July/6 Aug., 2/13 Aug. 1792, cols 937–9.
68. Smoleński, *Konfederacya Targowicka*, pp. 269–99, 322–7.

Partition and compensation

If there was any doubt in Catherine's mind about a further partition, Targowica's inability to create any kind of order in the Common-wealth settled the issue. With regard to Prussia and Austria, she was determined to retain the greatest possible freedom of manoeuvre. Rather than join their dual alliance of February 1792, she preferred to negotiate an extension of her existing alliance with Austria and a wholly separate alliance with Prussia: she could then play them off against each other. On 14 July, the Austrian alliance was reaffirmed in St Petersburg, with an agreement to restore the Polish constitu-tion of 1773: the commitment it contained to preserve Poland's territorial integrity was nothing more than a sop towards Kaunitz's concerns.[69] More revealing was the second 'Secret and Separate Article' of Russia's defensive alliance with Prussia of 7 August: the two states agreed to endow Poland with a form of government 'approaching' that elaborated in 1768, 1773 and 1775 – the Russian negotiators clearly had Catherine's twenty-three-point programme in mind – but if measures to restore the old form of government failed, then she and Frederick William reserved the right 'to concert other, more effective measures in order to satisfy their respective interests and the mutual tranquillity of their states'.[70]

The gesture towards Kaunitz in the July treaty was unnecessary. On 29 May, Anton Spielmann, with Francis II's express approval, sent his agreement to a proposal from Frederick William II's minis-ter, Schulenburg. Since it was inevitable that Russia would annex Polish territory, Austria and Prussia, too, were entitled to seek 'com-pensation'. Prussia would do so in Poland, regulating the extent of its claims by reference to Russia's. Austria would exchange Belgium for Bavaria and the Upper Palatinate. Kaunitz was horrified. This territorial wheeze had no chance of success, not least because Karl Theodor's heir, Karl, duke of Zweibrücken, was as firmly opposed to the exchange as he always had been. The old chancellor's efforts to persuade Francis II to repudiate the plan led to his being cut out of all important business. On 19 August, he resigned.[71]

Kaunitz's forebodings were justified. Spielmann's dealings with Schulenburg produced only a non-binding understanding. On the other hand, in July, both Austria and Prussia received independent

---

69. Text of treaty in *CTS* LI, pp. 359–76. See esp. the 'Article Séparé', pp. 374–5.

70. Treaty of St Petersburg, 3/14 July 1792, *CTS* LI, pp. 407–11.

71. Lord, *Second Partition*, pp. 312–20; T. Cegielski and Ł. Kądziela, *Rozbiory Polski 1772–1793–1795* (Warsaw, 1990), pp. 250–2.

assurances from St Petersburg of support for their 'compensation' demands – though neither knew that the other had this assurance. Admittedly, neither could be sure that they could trust Russia. Catherine was egging them both on to war against France, while claiming that her hands were too tied by Jacobinism in Poland to be able to assist them with anything more than a half-million-rouble subsidy – a sum both found totally inadequate. The mutual mistrust was as palpable as in the build-up to the First Partition, and scarcely more helpful to Poland. With nothing definite signed, Catherine might yet want to keep any Polish booty for herself alone. Even so, the protestations of support for the Bavarian–Belgian exchange reiterated in Vienna by Catherine's ambassador, prince Andrei Razumovskii, were enough to encourage the Austrians to demand more. Their ambassador in St Petersburg, Ludwig Cobenzl, maintained that Russia was very cool to any Prussian acquisitions in Poland.

By the time Spielmann and Schulenburg came to discuss the details of the exchanges and indemnities at Frankfurt-am-Main and Mainz in July (the occasion was Francis II's imperial coronation on the 14th at Frankfurt), the Austrians had realised that, whatever the strategic benefits of acquiring Bavaria, their chronically hard-up monarchy would sorely miss the more lucrative Belgian revenues. So, Spielmann and vice-chancellor Philipp Cobenzl demanded more: Lusatia (which was Saxon); or, alternatively, the margravates of Ansbach and Bayreuth, recently reverted to Prussia. Schulenburg stonewalled. His ministerial colleagues, Finckenstein and Alvensleben, were strongly against the Austrian acquisition of Bavaria and were determined to hang on to Ansbach and Bayreuth. Frederick William vacillated, ready to throw in the two Franconian duchies, if only he got more out of Poland.

The talks between Schulenburg, Spielmann and Cobenzl yielded no positive results, beyond allowing the Austrians to ascertain the extent of Prussian claims on Poland: besides Danzig and Thorn, the palatinates of Poznań, Gniezno, Kalisz, Brześć Kujawski and the western third of Sieradz – the wealthiest areas of the Commonwealth, removing the awkward triangle of territory jammed between Silesia and West Prussia. As for the Prussians, they convinced themselves that only a direct agreement with Russia would yield them satisfactory compensation. Their treaty with Russia of 7 August was a step in the right direction. On 8 August, Philipp Cobenzl conceded that if Russia wanted territory in Poland, Austria would not stand in the way. On the 24th, the Russian vice-chancellor, Ivan Osterman, officially informed the Austrian and Prussian ambassadors that Catherine approved the principle of indemnities against France at Poland's expense. On 28 September, Frederick William sent a rescript to Goltz in St Petersburg, officially laying down the full extent of his claims, as already expounded to the Austrians at Mainz.[72]

These diplomatic exchanges led the Austrian State Conference to consider, for the first time, the possibility of acquiring territory from Poland (sittings of 27 August and 7 September). But it was still a second best. Francis II instructed Spielmann, on 12 September, to drop the Ansbach–Bayreuth option and seek additional territory not from Poland but from France – Alsace, no less. A week later, in a fresh round of negotiations at Frankfurt, Spielmann, on his own initiative, threw in an additional demand for Lorraine. The deposition of Louis XVI on 10 August only confirmed that France was surely falling apart. Austrian troops had invaded from Belgium, the Prussians had taken Longwy and Verdun, the road to Paris was open. On 20 September, the democratic rabble brought the duke of Brunswick's Prussians to a grinding halt at Valmy. Spielmann's pipe-dreams evaporated. The allies were cleared out of France. Of the Prussians' 42,000 troops, barely 20,000 recrossed the frontier at the end of October and half of those were sick or wounded. French troops poured into the Rhineland, capturing Frankfurt, Speier and Mainz.

A humiliated Frederick William resolved to take his revenge out on the Poles. On 8 October, he formulated a new set of territorial demands: the Prussian frontier would be advanced to Częstochowa in the south, along the upper Vistula to Rawa, then due north to the southern tip of East Prussia at Soldau. Poland, in the west, would be little more than an insubstantial bridgehead across the Vistula around Warsaw. On 17 October, he wrote directly to Catherine, to inform her that he would undertake no further actions against France until his indemnities were settled. Exactly one week later, at his headquarters in Merle, he warned Spielmann that Austria could count on no more help from him until he received his territorial *arrondissement* from Poland.[73] On 6 November, Austria suffered a catastrophic defeat at Jemappes. Belgium lay open to the French.

Catherine was so furious at her allies' failures that she was ready to deny them any territorial compensation. Bezborodko and Alexander Vorontsov calmed her down. Poland was ungovernable; the

---

72. Lord, *Second Partition*, pp. 326–42; De Madariaga, *Russia*, p. 433; Cegielski and Kądziela, *Rozbiory Polski*, pp. 252–7.
73. Lord, *Second Partition*, ch. 15.

news of French successes was supposedly boosting Jacobinism throughout the Commonwealth. Warsaw seethed with rumours of a 'Sicilian Vespers' against Russia and Targowica. A deputation from the Confederacy, thanking Catherine for her assistance, went on to admit that if Russian troops were withdrawn from Poland, Targowica would collapse.[74] Partition was the only solution.

The simplest way to proceed was by a direct deal with Prussia, gasping for a share, refusing to fight against France unless she secured it. Any additional agreement with Austria – due for compensation elsewhere – would only complicate matters. Poland, Bezborodko noted on 13 December, was to be reduced to a harmless buffer state. On the 16th, vice-chancellor Osterman informed Goltz that Catherine accepted all Prussian claims. The empress herself laid down her counter-claim: everything east of a line almost due north from the Austrian border on the Zbrucz up to the Dvina at the eastern tip of Courland. Frederick William was delighted. For the first time, his Cabinet ministers told him on 27 December, Prussia would become 'a coherent kingdom'. True, the sheer extent of Russia's claim, four times the size of their own, disconcerted them, but they raised no serious objections.

The treaty itself was drafted by Arkadii Morkov, who followed, as far as possible, the form and wording of the partition conventions of 1772. Doubtless this helped Goltz, who could never quite believe that Catherine would not change her mind at the last moment, rush through the negotiations in six days. The document was signed on 23 January 1793. Where the conventions of 1772 had spoken of Polish factionalism and anarchy, the new agreement spoke of 'the same spirit of insurrection and dangerous innovations, which now reign in France . . . ready to erupt in Poland' constraining Russia and Prussia to protect their subjects 'from the effects of a scandalous and often contagious example'. The acquisitions as such were justified by the need for compensation for their exertions against the French threat. Articles II and V expounded the territorial claims in only the sketchiest manner, in far less detail than the 1772 conventions. There was a loose commitment to help secure the Bavarian exchange for Austria.[75]

Like its antecedents, the 1793 treaty insisted on the need for Polish assent. The same tried and trusted means would be used: a

74. Bulgakov to Osterman, 31 Oct./10 Nov. 1792, in Solov'ev, *IPP*, pp. 590–1. Cf. the instruction to ambassador J.J. Sievers, 22 Dec. 1792/2 Jan. 1793, ibid., pp. 592–5. Lord, *Second Partition*, pp. 384–5.

75. Bezborodko's notes of 2/13 Dec. in Solov'ev, *IPP*, p. 592; Lord, *Second Partition*, pp. 389–93; treaty of St Petersburg, *CTS* LI, pp. 451–8.

terrorised parliament and plenipotentiary Delegation. To make sure, the Sejm would be held not in sullen, 'jacobin' Warsaw, but in the sleepy Lithuanian backwater of Grodno. To carry out the task, Catherine recalled an old helpmate from semi-honourable retirement, Jakov Sievers, a cultured, able Estonian German, well suited to dress up her designs in the language of humanity, generosity and beneficence to the perjured Poles.[76]

The Grodno Sejm

On 16 January 1793, Ludwig von Buchholtz announced the impending entry of Prussian troops into Poland, a friendly precautionary measure against the spread of revolutionary ideas.[77] On 24 January, Prussian troops entered Wielkopolska, massacred a small Polish garrison in the town of Kargowa and occupied Thorn. They waited until 8 March before beginning a blockade of Danzig, which remained as hostile as ever to the joys of Hohenzollern rule. It finally capitulated on 4 April. Even some of Targowica's leaders, who had rejected all rumours of partition as scaremongering, realised what was afoot. Russia and Prussia had bound themselves not to make any public declaration of their plans until at least 5 April. This enabled Sievers, who arrived in Warsaw on 9 February, to affect ignorance and surprise at the Prussian troop entries; he even allowed Targowica's principal representative in Warsaw, field-*hetman* Piotr Ożarowski, to issue a formal declaration of protest against the Prussian invasion, although he also warned him against undertaking any armed resistance. Sievers' emollience was enough to inspire the wildest hopes, even once it had sunk in that Russia was going to annex Polish land, that Catherine was opposed to Prussia's doing so.

A spate of major bankruptcies among the capital's leading bankers only compounded the general sense of despair and bewilderment. The king found himself saddled with debts of some 30 million zloties (approaching £1,000,000 sterling) and virtually no income. He had to beg the ambassador for funds, while once again playing for time in the straw-clutching hope of a favourable turn of events. On 15 March, Felix Potocki left Grodno for St Petersburg, on a pointless mission to persuade the empress to grant a fresh republican Constitution and preserve the Commonwealth's territorial integrity.[78]

76. Sievers' instruction of 22 December 1792/2 January 1793 is a classic of the genre. Solov'ev, *IPP*, pp. 592–5. On Sievers' career, see R.E. Jones, *Provincial development in Russia: Catherine II and Jakob Sievers* (New Brunswick, 1984).

77. Chodźko, pp. 297–99.

78. Smoleński, *Konfederacya Targowicka*, pp. 357–67, 388–400.

Sievers arrived in Grodno on 21 March. On 7 April generals von Möllendorf and Krechetnikov proclaimed the formal annexation of the Prussian and Russian shares of Poland and ordered the inhabitants to take oaths of loyalty. On 9 April, Sievers and Buchholtz delivered identical notes to the General Council of the Confederacy, announcing the Partition and demanding the calling of a Sejm.[79] On 17 April, Seweryn Rzewuski issued a formal protest and retired to the safety of his Galician estates, bewailing the loss of Polish territory but consoling himself that Polish freedom had been salvaged from the horrors of the 3 May Constitution. With Ksawery Branicki domiciled in St Petersburg after November 1792, leadership of Targowica passed to men like Ożarowski in Warsaw and the Kossakowski brothers in Grodno, whose main purpose was to profit as much as they could personally from the lucrative business of aiding and abetting the dismantling of their Commonwealth. The Kossakowskis hoped to separate Lithuania from the Crown entirely, or even see the remnant of the Commonwealth converted into an autonomous Russian province, in which they would wield vice-regal powers. Sievers' priority was to push through the territorial cessions.

It was on bishop Kossakowski's advice that Sievers resuscitated the Permanent Council at the end of April, so that it, rather than Targowica, could issue (with the king, its president) the official proclamations for the extraordinary Sejm and *sejmiki*. Such was the reluctance to participate that almost all the restored Council's sessions were technically inquorate, including that of 3 May(!), which issued the proclamations.[80] All known supporters of the 1791 Constitution were barred from participation at the *sejmiki*, which met on 27 May. Assemblies were not held in the newly annexed lands. As in 1773, Prussian and Russian troops attended in support of the partitioning powers' stooges. Where between 1776 and 1788, 177 envoys were normally elected, only 134 were returned in 1793. Sievers put the average 'cost' of an envoy at between 200 (in Lithuania) and 500 (in the Crown) ducats – a bargain, he thought.[81]

79. Text in Chodźko, pp. 306–9. The Grodno Sejm still awaits comprehensive treatment. The following is based largely on Z. Mann, *Stanisław August na Sejmie ostatnim* (Warsaw, 1938); Ł. Kądziela, *Między zdradą a służbą Rzeczypospolitej* (Warsaw, 1993); and J.J. Sievers, *Jak doprowadziłem do drugiego rozbioru Polski* (reprint of *Drugi rozbiór Polski z pamiętników Sieversa*, Poznań, 1865), B. Grochulska and P. Ugniewski, eds (Warsaw, 1992).
80. The council's quorum was fifteen, excluding the king; the 3 May 1793 session counted fourteen. Ł. Kądziela, 'Efemeryczna Rada Nieutająca z wiosny 1793 roku', *Wiek Oświecenia* 9 (1993), pp. 175–86.
81. Sievers, *Jak doprowadziłem*, pp. 95–7.

The Sejm opened on 17 June. Sievers' initial confidence, that he could settle all business within a fortnight, rapidly evaporated, as small groups of envoys entrenched themselves in procedural wrangles and foot-dragging, discreetly encouraged by the king. It is still far from clear how much of the resistance and obstruction was genuine, how much was a performance designed to distance individual actors from the destruction of their own country. The king's best hope was the same as in 1773, and just as illusory, that other powers, notably Austria and Britain, would exert pressure against partition. Britain could do nothing and, in any case, was now involved in war against France. The Austrians, furious at getting nothing in Alsace or Bavaria and being cut out of the Polish deal, encouraged opposition at the Sejm, in the hope that this would produce such confusion that Russia and Prussia would let them back into their game. The fall-back hope for the Poles was to drive a wedge between Russia and Prussia – a line which Sievers encouraged, simply as a means of ensuring the more rapid settlement of his demands and increasing Polish dependency on Russia.[82]

Sievers handled any opponents in the usual manner: confiscations, house arrests, expulsion from Grodno, or just sending troops into the debating chamber. He refused to allow anything other than open voting. The public were barred after 21 June. Yet opposition was constant, not least because the Sejm's marshal, Franciszek Bieliński (on a Russian retainer of 500 ducats per month), commanded virtually no authority. Only on 11 July did the Sejm finally set up a thirty-two-man Delegation to negotiate with Sievers, and only on the 17th did it give it the plenipotentiary powers on which the ambassador insisted. Even so, its brief was restricted to dealing with Russia. As far as possible, the Sejm tried to ignore Buchholtz, whose powers of persuasion were limited by the absence of Prussian troops.

As in 1773, the grounds of opposition were pre-eminently legalistic and procedural. There was the occasional ringingly principled rhetoric, not least from Stanisław August, but his practice of giving way whenever Sievers threatened to confiscate his revenues or not cover his debts only completed his discreditment. Sievers had dragged the Polish horse to water and made it drink. On 22 July, the Delegation finally signed the treaty of territorial cession with Russia; the Sejm gave its confirmation on 17 August. More than 96,560 square miles and over 3,000,000 inhabitants were signed away.[83]

82. Cegielski and Kądziela, *Rozbiory Polski*, pp. 271–8.   83. *CTS* LII, pp. 83–90.

Only on 2 September, and with the threats of a widening of the
Prussian share, with Russian troops surrounding Grodno castle and
Russian officers packing the debating chamber, did the Sejm accord
the Delegation plenipotentiary powers to talk with Buchholtz. Even
so, the Sejm insisted on tacking on preconditions, notably the conclusion of a favourable commercial treaty. Berlin insisted on agreement
to the treaty of cession pure and simple, without strings. On 22 September, Sievers' cossacks ran four of the most obstreperous envoys
out of Grodno. The Sejm went on virtual strike. The envoys refused
to speak. Sometime after nine in the evening, Sievers sent a message
through a frustrated general Rautenfeld that no one, not even the
king, was to leave the chamber until unconditional powers were
accorded the Delegation. The Sejm maintained its silence. Finally,
around three in the morning on 23 September, marshal Bieliński
decided that silence meant consent. He asked three times for the
Sejm's agreement. Each time, silence. Bieliński noted in the official
record that the assembly had agreed unanimously to grant the necessary powers to the Delegation. Its members signed the treaty of
cession with Buchholtz on 25 September. It was Frederick William
II's birthday. He had just been given 22,400 square miles of territory
with over 1,100,000 subjects.[84]

84. Ibid., pp. 137–46.

CHAPTER SEVEN

The Third Partition

A new settlement?

The Grodno Sejm was to remain in session for another two months. Like the Warsaw Sejm of 1773–75, it had to frame an acceptable constitutional settlement. Any concessions that the Poles managed to secure could be nothing more than the paper trappings of what was but the simulacrum of a state. The diplomatic butchery had cost the Commonwealth almost half its territory and population. The *Rzeczpospolita* was reduced to a fragile column of 83,000 square miles, jammed between Galicia, East Prussia and the Baltic. Where the population had numbered some 8,000,000, now it was at best half of that figure. Warsaw was little more than thirty miles from the new Prussian border.

Fears of fresh Prussian economic exploitation and territorial usurpations achieved what Catherine wanted – they pushed Poland ever further into her embrace. All hope of any form of sovereign existence disappeared. Stanisław August and his chief collaborator, the new Crown grand marshal, Fryderyk Moszyński, could only aspire to set up that ideal of the 'état bien policé', orderly and efficient in its internal administration. Sievers' priority was to carry through an alliance which would complete the rump Commonwealth's total dependence on Russia. The treaty of 'constant friendship, indissoluble union and defensive alliance' of 16 October, though couched in the diplomatic phraseology of equals, was, as one envoy dared to point out, nothing more than a *pactum subiectionis*.[1] To defend this province, Russia had the right to install its troops at

---

1. Ł. Kądziela, *Między zdradą a służbą Rzeczypospolitej. Fryderyk Moszyński w latach 1792–1793* (Warsaw, 1993), pp. 266–7.

will. Wherever Polish units were stationed alongside numerically superior Russian ones, Russian officers would always be in command. Sievers attached no importance to such face-saving formulae as 'in case of necessity', 'after prior agreement with the Polish government'. The *de facto* viceroys of Poland, the Russian ambassadors, would always get what they wanted. In grateful return for the new obligations Catherine and her successors were assuming, the little Commonwealth promised never to conclude any agreements with other powers, nor undertake any foreign policy initiatives, without Russia's consent. Polish and Russian diplomats would always work towards common goals – in other words, Poland's diplomatic corps was reduced to a Russian subsidiary service.[2]

The October treaty was a mechanism to allow Russia to do as it wished in Poland. The constitutional settlement was to provide the formal channels. It harked back to Stanisław August's Kaniów proposals of 1787, although, given the massive reduction in size of Poland-Lithuania, it meant a hugely deeper dependence on Russia than the king could possibly have envisaged those six years previously. The new arrangements, finalised by the Sejm on its very last day, after a marathon fifteen-hour overnight sitting on 23–24 November, aimed to provide a firm executive and a trouble-free legislature. By Article XV of the treaty of alliance Russia had guaranteed the new constitutional arrangements in advance. This time, Poland was deemed sufficiently inoffensive to leave scope for changes in the constitution in the future – subject, naturally, to Russia's consent. A unicameral Sejm of 108 envoys and 62 senators would convene every four years. The day-to-day administration would be headed by the re-established Permanent Council. For all the official obloquy heaped on the Four Years Sejm, the local commissions of the peace which it had set up were allowed to survive largely intact; although townsmen lost their limited rights to representation in the new parliaments, most of the other concessions granted them in 1788–92 remained in place. The tripartite division of law into cardinal, *materiae status* and 'economic matters' introduced in 1768 was largely reaffirmed, with one crucial difference. *Materiae status* could be altered by a three-quarters majority of the Sejm (instead of the 1768 unanimity requirement). The Cardinal Laws, which included the totality of noble privileges as they stood before 1788, not least 'full dominion' over the peasantry, were to remain immutable. All other business was to be decided by a simple majority. The central

2. Text of treaty in *CTS* LII, pp. 165–74.

commissions set up by the Four Years Sejm survived. It was a matter of particular relief to Stanisław August that he managed to preserve the Commission for National Education.

All this was window-dressing. Catherine herself admitted that 'Poland' was a purely provisional entity, whose final incorporation into Russia was only a matter of time.[3] The newly annexed Ukrainian lands gave it a military boulevard into the Balkans for the inevitable future conflicts with the Ottoman Porte. The bridgehead over the Vistula constituted an excellent forward supply base which would permit far more effective intervention in European politics than at any time in the past. No longer would Russia be faced with the embarrassing logistical problems which had so impaired the effectiveness of its armies during the Seven Years War. Russia was, after all, since 1779, a guarantor of the Holy Roman Empire. The threat to that venerable old pile posed by the French Revolution opened up new prospects for the western spread of Russian influence.

From the partitioning powers' Polish perspective, the French Revolution was excellent news. The subversive threat of Jacobinism was the perfect pretext for any form of intervention in the Commonwealth. The Second and Third Partitions did not require the production of the erudite justificatory tomes which had accompanied the First. Catherine was able to urge Prussia and Austria on against France in the west, while assuring them she was fully occupied combating the monster of revolution in Poland. Targowica imposed a stringent censorship from the moment it established itself in Warsaw. French citizens and diplomats were subject to police supervision and harassment. The revolutionary government's chargé d'affaires, Descorches, was expelled in July 1792, almost as soon as he arrived. The import of French literature was restricted, French travellers were subjected to stringent checks, in tandem with similar measures imposed in Russia.[4] Such was the flummery deemed appropriate to make respectable the execution of a state by diplomacy.

In truth, the 'revolution of 3 May' was as far removed from the French prototype as it was possible to be. Poland was an overwhelmingly agrarian society, dominated by a predominantly conservative nobility. Stanisław August and the majority of the reformers

3. R.H. Lord, 'The Third Partition of Poland', *Slavonic and East European Review* 3 (1924–25), p. 481.
4. W. Smoleński, *Konfederacya Targowicka* (Kraków, 1903), pp. 271, 274–5, 337–8, 368–72, 409–10; J. Łojek, 'Series librorum prohibitorum z 1793 roku', *Przegląd Humanistyczny*, no. 3 (1965), pp. 125–32; J.J. Sievers, *Jak doprowadziłem do drugiego rozbioru Polski* (first publ. 1865), B. Grochulska and P. Ugniewski, eds (Warsaw, 1992), pp. 43–4.

were as favourable towards the early revolution as 'liberal' opinion
anywhere in Europe – rather less enthusiastic than Charles James
Fox in England. The September massacres and the trial and execution of Louis XVI caused as much revulsion in Warsaw as they did
in St Petersburg, London, Vienna or Berlin – indeed, in Warsaw,
they helped break fashionable society's boycott of the Russian em-
bassy's social events.

There were, however, two potential flashpoints – the capital and
the army. Warsaw was no hotbed of bourgeois sedition – on the
contrary, its leading citizens had been pathetically grateful for the
crumbs thrown them in 1791. Yet the very duration of the Four
Years Sejm had politicised its inhabitants to an unprecedented
degree. Their radicalisation, if such it can be called, was accomplished
above all by the Russian army of occupation under general Igelström
– some 30,000 men across 'Poland', about half of them in Warsaw
and its immediate environs. These troops had to be supplied and
maintained – and the bulk of the burden was put on the local
populace. The Russians took what they wanted. The hardest hit
were the peasantry and the urban poor, particularly during the
winter of 1793–94. This was not so much radicalisation as aliena-
tion – but, in such circumstances, it was hardly surprising that the
news from Paris, which, for all the censorship measures, could not
be suppressed, aroused enormous interest. The French declaration
of 19 November 1792, promising revolutionary aid to all oppressed
people, was too readily taken at face value. The joint Russo-Prussian
declaration of 9 April 1793, informing the Commonwealth of the
Second Partition, had conjured up the spectre of a Sicilian Vespers
against the forces of occupation. The conduct of the empress's
troops now threatened to make this a reality.

The second combustible element was the army. It had dwindled
to some 36,000 men by the time the Grodno Sejm had ended, but
its fate remained unresolved. Arrears of pay were a major obstacle
to a simple demobilisation. In principle, the Sejm had decided to
reduce the army to around half that size, but had failed to set
definite figures. The Russians wished to incorporate some 20,000
men into their own forces. Despite the traumas of the 1792 war, the
army and its officers felt betrayed, not beaten. It was the younger
and poorer element among the officer corps, represented above all
by general Tadeusz Kościuszko, which was to prove most attracted
by the French option – not out of a desire for social reconstruction
as such, but because France seemed to be the only power in Europe
to offer any hope of an escape for Poland from its miseries. The

French straw was a feeble and illusory one to clutch, but it was the only one there was. The alternative was the meek acceptance of the loss of independence and nationhood.

Years later, general Igelström was to admit that, during the winter of 1793–94, he received orders from St Petersburg to provoke disturbances in Warsaw which would furnish a pretext for the final incorporation of Poland into the Russian empire. His appointment as Sievers' successor caused alarm among the Poles. He had a long-standing reputation for brutality: in 1767, on Repnin's orders, he had overseen the arrest and deportation of the Rzewuskis and bishops Sołtyk and Załuski to Russia. Unlike Sievers, he was closely associated with Catherine's lover, Platon Zubov, with Alexander Bezborodko and Arkadii Morkov, the men who had been most active in pushing for the Second Partition and who now looked to topping up their gains with fresh spoils.[5] Sievers' determination to make of Poland an orderly vassal state contributed to his own undoing. Catherine was furious that he allowed the Poles even the tokens of independence – such as the right to consultation over the entry of Russian troops, or limited concessions to Polish officers' rights of seniority when serving alongside their Russian counterparts. She took as a personal insult his consent to the restoration of the *Virtuti Militari* medal instituted by Stanisław August during the 1792 campaign and banned by Targowica. Stanisław August had to suffer the humiliation of publicly proclaiming a new ban on the wearing of the medal and sending a cringing apology to the empress.[6] Alliance with Russia did not just mean loss of independence, but grovelling subservience and grateful acceptance of the most extreme indignities. The outbreak of insurrection should have caused little surprise.

Insurrection

Plans for a rising had been discussed as early as the autumn of 1792 by Ignacy Potocki, Hugon Kołłątaj and their émigré associates in Dresden and Leipzig. They displayed all the naivety of the confederates of Bar in their faith in a favourable international conjuncture: imminent renewal of war between Russia and Sweden and Turkey; massive military and financial aid from France. French revolutionary

---

5. W. Tokarz, *Insurekcja warszawska* (Warsaw, 1950 edn), pp. 32–6.
6. Z. Góralski, *Stanisław August w insurekcji kościuszkowskiej* (Warsaw, 1988), pp. 21–3.

rhetoric at least provided some excuse for such fantasies. On 26 August 1792, the Legislative Assembly had conferred honorary French citizenship on Tadeusz Kościuszko for his services to 'the cause of liberty and . . . to the liberation of the peoples', a reflection of his role in the war of 1792 and of his distinguished service to the American cause in the War of Independence. When the general travelled to Paris in January 1793 to plead the Polish cause, he promised (utterly unrealistically) to sweep away serfdom and the monarchy, to extend the *szlachta*'s rights and liberties to the rest of the populace, and to deploy the rebuilt Polish army against all three partitioning powers. The French encouraged the idea of an uprising – it would, of course, divert Prussia and Austria – but they refused any definite commitments of aid.[7] Undeterred, on his return to Saxony in March, Kościuszko drew up a fantastic scheme for agitators and landowners in the rump Polish state and in the newly partitioned lands to make clandestine preparations to restore the Polish forces to the magical 100,000 level and to raise a further 100,000 local militia in a *levée-en-masse*. Parallel risings were to be prepared among the Don Cossacks, the Crimean Tatars and in the duchy of Courland.

Marginally less imaginative plans were also being hatched from August 1793 in Warsaw by more conservative circles, headed by major-general Ignacy Działyński and the banker Andrzej Kapostas. They aimed to mount an insurrection directed against the Russian occupation forces in the Polish state and in the lands cordoned off in Russia's share of the Second Partition. Popular participation would be kept to a minimum. They accepted, however, that they needed Kościuszko's co-operation. He warned them that without mass support and international backing, they would fail.[8]

There was virtually no preparation of the sort that Kościuszko hoped for. No matter how much they smarted under the fate of their Commonwealth, the *szlachta* could not bring themselves to subvert the only social order they knew. In any case, by the first three weeks of March 1794, Igelström's network of spies and informers had enabled him to carry out sweeping arrests among the Warsaw conspirators. What triggered the Insurrection was not systematic preparation, but the threat to the Polish army. In February

7. B. Leśnodorski, *Polscy Jakobini* (Warsaw, 1969), pp. 149–52; J. Godechot, 'Robespierre et la Pologne', in A. Zahorski, ed., *Wiek XVIII: Polska i Świat* (Warsaw, 1974), pp. 373–4; S. Herbst, *Z dziejów wojskowych powstania kościuszkowskiego 1794 roku* (Warsaw, 1983), pp. 18–19.

8. K. Bauer, *Blaski i cienie insurekcji kościuszkowskiej* (Warsaw, 1982), pp. 28–31.

1794, the Permanent Council finally announced the reduction of the Crown forces by almost two-thirds, from 23,546 to 8,429, and the Lithuanian forces by almost one half, from just over 12,500 to 6,500. Only private soldiers would have their arrears paid off in cash. The demobilised troops were widely expected to be impressed into the Russian army.[9] At Ostrołęka, north of Warsaw, general Antoni Madaliński, instead of passively awaiting arrest for his involvement in the conspiracy, set out on 13 March on a sweeping march west of the capital, with his brigade of 1,200 cavalry. He intended to join up with troops in Kraków to force Kościuszko's hand. Kościuszko himself slipped into Kraków on 23 March. The following day, with only about 1,000 regulars at his disposal, he proclaimed his Insurrection.

It was, of course, doomed; and, as Stanisław August feared, it brought about the final destruction of Poland. But the king's way was an alternative which would lead only to its slow asphyxiation. Kościuszko's rising generated sufficient national energy to register a protest against the legitimacy of Poland's dismemberment far more effective than Rejtan's despairing actions in 1773 or the hopeless resistance of Polish forces in 1792. His enterprise should have been snuffed out almost immediately. Madaliński had caught the Russians and Prussians off guard. The latter spluttered with indignation at his violation of their new territories and his brushing aside of the light units he encountered; the bulk of Prussian forces were engaged against France. But massively superior, if scattered, Russian forces circled in for an easy kill. Kościuszko resolved to fight his way through to Warsaw. On 4 April, at Racławice, a few miles north-east of Kraków, he defeated general Tormasov. Reinforcements came too late to help the Russians, but their arrival forced Kościuszko to fall back on Kraków.

Racławice was a small encounter, barely enough to register on the European military seismograph. But the moral consequences were vastly greater than its tactical significance. It inspired the Polish units, scattered across the little state and behind the Russian cordon, with a new belief in their ability to win through. Most importantly of all, the news electrified the capital. In the early hours of 17 April, a reconstituted conspiratorial leadership launched a revolt. Three thousand regular troops and 25,000 townsfolk, armed from the state arsenal, launched themselves against Igelström's 7,000 Russians, who were completely unprepared for the savage street fighting that followed. The ambassador himself was lucky to escape alive, and he

---

9. Herbst, *Z dziejów*, pp. 42–3.

could only look on helplessly as the enraged mob lynched his son-in-law. Late on 18 April, he managed to fight his way through to the safety of Prussian detachments west of the city, largely thanks to the deliberate inaction of the Polish general Mokronowski, who was appalled at the prospect of what might follow if Catherine's ambassador were added to the toll of casualties – 2,300 Russians dead or wounded, 2,000 more in captivity, 28 guns taken. Over 3,000 Polish soldiers and civilians were dead or wounded. In Wilno, the Russians were expelled on the night of 22–23 April, less bloodily, but no less effectively. Szymon Kossakowski, grand *hetman* of Lithuania, general in the Russian service, co-founder of the Confederacy of Targowica, was hanged for treason on the 25th. During the summer, the Rising even spread briefly to Russia's particular preserve of Courland. On 27 June, in the port of Libau, Kościuszko's representative, lieutenant-general Heinrich von Mirbach, declared the full incorporation of the duchy into the Commonwealth.[10]

Five years after it was all over, a close associate of Kościuszko, Józef Pawlikowski, produced a pamphlet entitled 'Can the Poles acquire their independence?' His formula was Kościuszko's own: all Poles, of every social station, had to believe in their cause; but that could only happen if they were made free. Serfdom had to be ended. Only then could the nation's full energies be directed towards national liberation and a new Poland be restored.[11] In 1794, however, Kościuszko had to adapt to mundane realities. He knew perfectly well that there was no chance of realising the assurances he had proffered the French in January 1793. The *szlachta* had even less intention of abolishing 'feudalism' in Poland than those who abolished it in France had of discarding the small print which accompanied that much-trumpeted exercise in altruism. Without the *szlachta*, there was no chance of any sort of rising against the partitioning powers. Without the peasantry, any sort of rising was bound to be unsustainable.[12]

Kościuszko tried to resolve this irresolvable dilemma as well as any honourable, reasonable man could. By the Act of Insurrection he assumed dictatorial powers unprecedented in Polish history – but he eschewed specifics: he was fighting 'for the defence of our

10. H. Strods, 'Der Kościuszko-Aufstand 1794 und Kurland', *Acta Baltica* 34 (1996), pp. 123–30.

11. [J. Pawlikowski], *Czy Polacy wybić się moga na niepodległość.* E. Halicz, ed., Warsaw, 1967 edn; first edn [Paris] 1800.

12. A. Woltanowski, 'Tadeusz Kościuszko i pierwszy etap reform włościańskich', *Przegląd Historyczny*, 78 (1987), pp. 19–44.

territorial integrity, the restoration of the sovereignty of the Nation and the encompassing of universal liberty'. In the Polish context, the last phrase did not necessarily mean the liberty of all. Immediately after he proclaimed the Insurrection, he urged, discreetly, the reduction of peasant labour dues to half their normal levels for the duration of the Rising. He dared go no further in trying to kindle peasant enthusiasm, for fear of alienating the seigneurs. Two thousand peasants, armed with scythes, helped break the last Russian stand at Racławice. After the battle, Kościuszko made an ostentatious point of wearing the peasant topcoat, the *sukmana*, and promoted two peasants, Wojciech Bartos and Józef Świstacki, to the rank of ensign. Bartos's landlord agreed to his and his family's emancipation and exemption from all labour dues. He threw in his best cow, a piglet and a sow. Presumably, the family's obligations were allocated to other peasants. In his efforts to persuade the *szlachta* to embark on wide-ranging alleviations of peasant burdens, Kościuszko made little progress. Even the commission of the peace which he set up to administer the palatinate of Kraków showed little enthusiasm or understanding. Most landlords remained stubbornly determined to exact labour services – to them, such exactions were an integral part of 'freedom'.[13]

As the Rising progressed, it was, of necessity, radicalised. To divert the enemy from Kraków, Kościuszko barricaded his army in fortified camp at Połaniec on the upper Vistula. There, he was joined by Ignacy Potocki and Hugon Kołłątaj. They had co-operated with him in drafting the original act of Insurrection. The need to mobilise wider popular enthusiasm led them to issue, on 7 May, the Proclamation of Połaniec. All serfs were declared personally free; those who discharged their obligations and taxes were accorded full freedom of movement; although labour duties remained, they were reduced by between a quarter and a half; no labour duties at all were to be levied on peasants conscripted into the army or their families – landlords who refused to comply were to be summarily tried as enemies and traitors; recalcitrant state officials and bailiffs were to be dismissed; a network of local superintendents was to enforce these new measures, which, in a gesture to reassure the nobility, were to be reviewed by a Sejm to be called after the Insurrection had achieved its aims. In his more optimistic moments, Kościuszko dreamed that such measures might produce 300,000 conscripts and militia; but even at the Rising's height, in September, he had at

13. Ibid.

most 72,000 men under arms – of whom only a minority were regulars. The Proclamation proved no more effective than his earlier appeals. The nobility remained chronically suspicious of social experimentation. Even in Warsaw, the leadership of the Rising was largely dominated by conservatives.

Only occasionally did 'Jacobin' agitation threaten to get out of hand. The violence that did occur against individuals was motivated less by ideology than by an unsurprising desire for revenge and retribution. On 9 May, Warsaw's provisional government, pressed by agitators and an angry street mob, passed sentences of death by hanging (immediately carried out) on four leading members of the Targowica Confederacy: Grand Crown *hetman* Piotr Ożarowski, bishop Józef Kossakowski and two close collaborators of Sievers at the Grodno Sejm, Józef Ankwicz and Józef Zabiełło. By any standards, these men were traitors. On 28 June, the Warsaw mob stormed the prisons and lynched two more *targowiczanie*, bishop Ignacy Massalski and prince Antoni Czetwertyński, along with five lesser collaborators and one innocent official who tried to stop the violence. The king's ailing brother, the primate, Michael Poniatowski, was threatened with a similar fate after a rumour circulated that he was secretly passing information to the Prussians. The threats may well have contributed to his death from apoplexy on 11 August. The king, too, went in fear of his life, almost from the moment the Insurrection erupted, but no physical harm befell him. This was more or less the sum total of Polish 'Jacobinism'.[14] Not that anyone in Poland ever admitted to *Jakobinizm* – that was an epithet bandied about by worried conservatives and indignant outsiders. 'For him,' observed Ignacy Potocki of Frederick William II, 'every Pole who loves his liberty and his country is a Jacobin.'[15]

Yet the tensions and worries which the mere thought of revolutionary radicalism aroused contributed significantly to dampening enthusiasm for the Rising, particularly among the well-to-do. Little is known of what the serfs themselves felt. The chances of rallying the peasantry of the Ukraine and Byelorussia were virtually non-existent. There was too much in the way of social and religious antagonism between them and their Polish masters. In the Ukraine, not only were memories of the great rising of 1768 and its suppression still fresh, but they had been painfully compounded only recently. In 1789, there had been a fresh bout of repressions by

14. A. Zahorski, *Warszawa w powstaniu kościuszkowskim* (Warsaw, 1967), pp. 122–4, 139–41, 179–80.
15. Leśnodorski, *Polscy Jakobini*, p. 210.

Polish landlords, provoked by entirely baseless rumours of a new peasant rising. Already in 1792 prince Józef Poniatowski's troops had learned they could not depend on the Ukrainian peasantry's support against the invading Russians. In Courland, the Lettish peasantry, among the most oppressed in Europe, joined the Rising to settle scores with their German-speaking landlords – but by September, Russian troops restored Russian order.[16] As for the ethnic Polish peasants, after Racławice, most of their militia wanted to go home. They had done what they were supposed to have done, beaten the Russians; and for all the reverence which peasant memory came to afford Kościuszko, in the end, he could offer them little beyond fine words.

Kościuszko hoped to shorten the odds in his favour by emphasising that his quarrel was with Russia alone. During the street battles in Warsaw, Prussian units outside the capital were reassured that no hostile action would be taken against them. This fiction was unsustainable. The uprising gave Frederick William II's ministers and generals fresh ammunition to use in their pleas to disengage from their disastrous, demoralising operations against France. Most of the Prussian high command, who had spent their entire careers fighting the Austrians, failed to see why Frederick the Great's successor was allied to them in the first place.[17] In April 1794, only fresh British subsidies persuaded the Prussians to keep over 60,000 men in the Rhineland. Scenting easy victory in Poland, Frederick William was at first ready to rely purely on the 40,000 or so troops immediately available to him in his eastern territories. In June, he accompanied general Favrat's corps of 17,000 men to link up with general Denisov's 10,000 Russians. On 6 June, Kościuszko, with less than half their combined strength, was brought to bay near the little village of Szczekociny. After five hours of fighting, he had to retreat – this time, to Warsaw. Among his 1,200 dead was the newly promoted and emancipated Wojciech Bartos. On 16 June, Prussian forces occupied Kraków. On 30 June, Austrian troops began crossing into Poland.

Kościuszko had not only hoped that Austria would stay out of the war – immediately after proclaiming his Insurrection, he had sent reassurances to Vienna that he had no intention of extending his

16. W. Kalinka, *Sejm Czteroletni* (Warsaw, 1991 edn), I, pp. 328–43; Strods, 'Der Kościuszko-Aufstand', pp. 125, 127–9.

17. W. Real, *Von Potsdam nach Basel. Studien zur Geschichte der Beziehungen Preussens zu den europäischen Mächten vom Regierungsantritt Friedrich Wilhelm II. bis zum Abschluss des Friedens vom Basel 1786–1795* (Stuttgart, 1958), pp. 50–2, 77–80, 99–100.

activities to Galicia – he even hoped for Austrian assistance. How he proposed to reconcile that with his continued hopes of French support is another matter, but the need to manage Austrian sensibilities was a further constraint against allowing radicalism its head in Poland.[18]

Austria had been horrified by the extent of Prussian gains under the Second Partition – a reaction intensified by the dawning realisation in Vienna that it could expect no real assistance from Prussia in its hopes of attaining that will o' the wisp, the Bavarian–Belgian exchange. The Austrians had assumed that it would be in Catherine's own interests to keep Prussian gains in Poland to a minimum and that, as a matter of course, they would be invited to participate in the Partition negotiations. They were indeed invited to put their name to the January 1793 Partition Treaty – but only on 23 March, two full months after it had been signed. Four days later, Francis II dismissed the two chief architects – some might say dupes – of the policy of rapprochement with Prussia, Philipp Cobenzl and Anton Spielmann. Kaunitz's protégé, Johann Amadeus Franz von Thugut, was made Director-General of the Chancery – in effect, chancellor and foreign minister. His almost pathological prussophobia was much reinforced by the ever sharper deterioration of military relations between Austrian and Prussian commanders on the French front. Möllendorf, who had replaced the duke of Brunswick as commander in the west in January 1794, admirably conveyed the impression that he would rather be fighting on the French side against the Austrians (in August, he initiated secret and wholly unauthorised peace overtures to the French).[19]

To add insult to injury, the Prussians claimed, in September 1793, that unless they received substantial financial support from Austria and their allies, they would be unable to continue the war – precisely because they also needed to consolidate their new Polish acquisitions. Thugut's reaction, on 21 October, was to instruct Ludwig Cobenzl in St Petersburg that he should now look on Prussia as an enemy power. He was prepared to reconcile himself to the Second Partition, and even accede to the January 1793 treaty – provided Austria, too, received appropriate compensation, which, in the present circumstances, meant considerably more than the Bavarian–Belgian exchange. Austria's policy of reforging the old

18. Z. Góralski, *Austria a trzeci rozbiór Polski* (Warsaw, 1979), pp. 62–4, 68–71, 88, 95–6.

19. Real, *Von Potsdam nach Basel*, pp. 80–4, 102–19. K.A. Roider, *Baron Thugut and Austria's response to the French Revolution* (Princeton, 1987), pp. 96–109.

alliance with Britain, not just to sustain the war against France, but
to work towards the isolation of Prussia, ran up against the axiom-
atic British determination to preserve the Low Countries in Austrian
hands as a permanent check against France. Pitt would not agree to
the Bavarian exchange. That left Poland as the sole realistic source
of 'compensation' for Austria. In April 1793, marshal Lacy, of the
Kriegsrat, the War Council, suggested that Austria should take a
great wedge of territory between the Vistula and Bug rivers, then
east to the new Russian border near Pinsk.[20]

Austria did not take immediate advantage of the Rising. It had
only 10,000 troops in Galicia; it needed to square Russia – although
Thugut hoped that Russia would be able to suppress the Rising on
its own and then cut a territorial deal with Austria. The Austrians
also looked to feed their troops in the west with Polish grain and
were reluctant to take measures which might jeopardise supplies.
On the other hand, there was considerable sympathy and support
in Galicia for the Rising. While many Polish nobles, especially from
the border palatinates of Kraków and Sandomierz, chose to remove
to Galicia to escape the rigours of the Rising, there was no lack of
Galician nobles willing to serve in Kościuszko's ranks. The Habsburg
authorities were concerned that Jacobin principles might spread to
Galicia, and, from there, infect Hungary. From Warsaw, De Caché
was sending back increasingly alarmist reports of political radicalism. After their experiences under Joseph II and Leopold II, the
Austrians had more to fear from such ideas than either Prussia or
Russia.[21]

By the end of May, Thugut and Francis II had agreed that the
Rising had to be stopped and that the troops currently stationed in
Galicia had to be strengthened by units in Bohemia and Moravia.
General Harnoncourt, commanding in Galicia, was authorised to
give shelter to any Russian troops crossing into Austrian territory,
but to sweep out any insurgents. Thugut and the *Kriegsrat* accepted
that they could not possibly acquire all the territories proposed by
Lacy in April 1793: but they would take as much as they could of
the palatinates of Kraków, Sandomierz, Lublin and Chełm. Had the
Austrian authorities in Galicia shown a little less dithering, they
could easily have occupied Kraków (which was ready to surrender
to them voluntarily) before the Prussians entered it on 15 June. On
21 June, Thugut wrote to Ludwig Cobenzl in St Petersburg that

20. Real, *Von Potsdam nach Basel*, p. 76; Roider, *Baron Thugut*, pp. 132–9; Góralski,
Austria, pp. 43–7, 57–9.
21. Roider, *Baron Thugut*, pp. 149–51.

Austria's 'compensation' for its efforts against France would have to come from Poland. The Austrian disaster at Fleurus on 26 June, which finally destroyed the allied position in the Netherlands, confirmed, if confirmation were needed, the choice of the Polish option. The Dutch and the British pulled their troops out. The Austrians began the transfer of 20,000 men from Flanders and Brabant to Galicia.[22]

Russia remained the key. Those Poles who counted on Russia being distracted by a revival of the Turkish war were correct, insofar as such a threat was taken very seriously by Catherine – it was, indeed, the main reason why she was not able to deploy much larger forces from the outset against Kościuszko. The State Council, meeting on 20 April/1 May 1794, felt it had no option but to ask for Prussian assistance in suppressing the insurrection.[23] On the other hand, Catherine also wished to limit the inevitable gains Prussia would make – and there was no better instrument for this than Austria. Whereas in 1771–72 Frederick II had been able to play Russia off against Austria to pave the way for his own acquisitions, in 1792, and again in 1794, Catherine was able to assume his role, this time playing Prussia off against Austria. In 1792–93, Prussia had benefited; in 1794–95, it was to be Austria's turn.

Catherine was prepared to concede the Austrian demands, which, if implemented, would destroy the hopes the Prussians were nurturing of consolidating their final frontier along the Vistula. Kraków, if held by Prussia, would be a serious obstacle to any future Habsburg designs on Prussia; in Austrian hands, it threatened to function as a springboard into Silesia. The Prussians actually hoped to outbid Austria for Catherine's affections by proposing the creation of a small principality, a final apology for a buffer state, between Prussia and Russia, which would go to Catherine's lover, Platon Zubov. But Bezborodko, Osterman and Zubov had already decided, by the end of May 1794, on the final removal of Poland, along boundaries very similar to those enforced in 1795.[24] On 22 July, the Russians informed the Prussian and Austrian ambassadors that 'the time has come for the three courts to take measures not only to extinguish the last sparks of the conflagration which has flared up in the neighbouring

---

22. Góralski, *Austria*, pp. 99–104, 123–5, 131–4.   23. *AGS*, cols 978–9.
24. R.H. Lord, 'The Third Partition', pp. 486–8; Góralski, *Austria*, pp. 138–9, 156–8, 163; E. Moritz, 'Die Plaene der preussischen Regierung zur Teilung Polens in der Zeit des Kościuszko-Aufstandes', in G. Labuda, ed., *Węzłowe problemy dziejów Prus* (Poznań, 1971), pp. 57–71.

state, but also to ensure that a new flame should never burn from the ashes'.[25]

Had the Prussians been able to capture Warsaw, they would have been in a much stronger bargaining position – instead, they were to endure an even greater humiliation than at Valmy. Kościuszko was a skilled military engineer. The improvised fortifications which he constructed around the capital were more than enough to hold off the siege which Frederick William II and the Russian general Fersen opened on 27 July. Fersen permitted himself only minimal co-operation – he had no intention of allowing the ace card of Warsaw to fall to a Prussian assault. Harnoncourt, for the Austrians, refused point-blank Frederick William's request for assistance.[26] Prussian heavy siege artillery began to arrive only on 19 August; the following day, a Polish uprising finally ignited in Wielkopolska, threatening to cut the king off from Brandenburg. On 5–6 September, Frederick William II called off the siege. Disease and hunger had reduced his 30,000 troops by almost a half. Ten days later, Kościuszko sent 3,000 men under general Henryk Dąbrowski in a counter-offensive into Wielkopolska, where he compounded Prussian discomfiture by capturing Bromberg (Bydgoszcz) on 2 October, in territory annexed from Poland in 1772. The Prussians feared not only the loss of Thorn and Danzig, but even the humiliating possibility that Dąbrowski might seize Frankfurt.[27]

Such nervousness reflected Prussia's financial and military exhaustion, rather than the facts. Not only were the Poles heavily outnumbered, they were even less well-armed than they had been in 1792. Russian forces had recaptured Wilno on 12 August. On 1 September, Kościuszko had finally authorised his commanders to take on the Austrians.[28] Most importantly of all, on 8 August, the Turks had given the Russians full assurances that they intended no hostilities. On the 18th, Catherine ordered general Alexander Suvorov from his stations in the Ukraine into Poland. It was to prevent the creation of an overwhelmingly irresistible force that Kościuszko decided to attack general Fersen's 12,000-strong corps south-east of Warsaw. Kościuszko, with only 7,000 men, was again heavily outnumbered. At Maciejowice, on 10 October, in a murderous encounter, he suffered his last defeat. The partitioning powers

25. Quoted in T. Cegielski and Ł. Kądziela, *Rozbiory Polski 1772–1793–1795* (Warsaw, 1990), p. 308.
26. Góralski, *Austria*, pp. 160–1.   27. Real, *Von Potsdam nach Basel*, pp. 100–1.
28. Góralski, *Austria*, pp. 167–8.

put about the fashionably romantic and highly convenient story that, as he was captured by the Russians, 'Finis Poloniae! the end of Poland! the great, unfortunate hero cried . . .' Kościuszko always denied it.[29]

On 4 November, Suvorov's troops stormed the poorly fortified Warsaw suburb of Praga on the east bank of the Vistula. The Russians themselves put the number of those massacred at 20,000. Warsaw surrendered the next day. The remaining regular troops were allowed to march out with the honours of war. By the time they reached Radoszyce ninety miles south-west of Warsaw, on 16 November, most of the men had deserted. On 19 November, the senior officers who remained surrendered to the pursuing general Denisov, who escorted them back to Warsaw as Suvorov's 'guests'. On the 22nd, they were all released, after signing assurances that they would not bear arms against Catherine (nothing was said about Austria or Prussia). Only Kościuszko's nominal successor, Tomasz Wawrzecki, refused. He was taken to St Petersburg.[30] On the same day, Ignacy Potocki issued an official circular announcing the end of the Rising. A month later, he and the other civilian leaders followed Wawrzecki to the Russian capital.

If Suvorov had not finished off the Insurrection, famine would have done so. Poland had been so devastated that even before the assault on Praga, soldiers and horses in Warsaw had begun to die of hunger.[31] Stanisław August appealed to Catherine to take his country under her protection. She responded in true enlightened fashion, by ordering Suvorov to remove to St Petersburg the massive holdings, approaching some 300,000 volumes, of Warsaw's Załuski library. The cossacks loading the books cut awkward tomes to size with their sabres.[32] To Stanisław August Catherine wrote that she had done her best to save the Poles from themselves but the matter was now out of her hands. 'All my efforts have been repaid by ingratitude, hatred and perfidy.' Twelve thousand participants of

29. Sirisa [i.e. August Sadebeck], *Polens Ende: historisch, statistisch und geographisch beschrieben* (Warsaw, 1797), p. 9. Cf. Kościuszko to Ségur, 31 Oct. 1803, in Chodźko, pp. 392–3.
30. Accounts of the final days of the Rising are confused. But see M. Żywirska, *Ostatnie lata Stanisława Augusta* (Warsaw, 1975), p. 37 and J. Pachoński, *General Jan Henryk Dąbrowski 1755–1818* (Warsaw, 1981), pp. 120–6.
31. I. De Madariaga, *Russia in the age of Catherine the Great* (New Haven, 1981), pp. 446–7; K. Bauer, *Blaski i cienie*, puts the number slain in Praga at 9,500 troops, 7,000 civilians and Russian losses in dead and wounded at 3,000 (p. 175).
32. The holdings formed the core of the Imperial Library, opened in 1814 to the public, Poles excepted. T. Zarzębski, *Polskie prawo bibliotekarskie 1773–1990* (Warsaw, 1991), pp. 21–3.

the Rising deported to hard labour in Russia were given occasion to reflect on their moral failings.[33]

Elimination

On 19 August 1794, a new Prussian ambassador, Bogislaw Tauentzien von Wittenberg, reached St Petersburg, with instructions to press for the Vistula frontier. In the north, he was to try to secure the entire littoral between East Prussia and the bay of Riga, including Courland. Catherine strung him along, awaiting news from Warsaw. On 30 October, she made clear to him that Kraków and Sandomierz were to go to Austria.

Even though, on 12 September, Thugut formally authorised Cobenzl to begin partition negotiations, leaving it to him to secure the best possible deal for Austria, he and Francis II remained uncertain of their final commitment to Partition. They accepted that Russia would be, in effect, an arbiter between themselves and Prussia. They rejected, in August, direct Prussian approaches for talks. With cheerful mendacity, Thugut accused Frederick William II of negotiating with Kościuszko to preserve a Polish state. Regardless of what the Austrians did, they could hardly make up for having missed out on the 1793 Partition; whatever happened, Prussia would gain territory and resources. Thugut's hope that Russia might still agree to give Austria the full extent of territories proposed by Lacy in April 1793 was only wishful thinking.[34] Partition was the only solution as far as Russia was concerned, the sooner the better. No matter that in November, the Austrians were able to inform the Russians that Möllendorf's adjutant had been holding secret talks with the French in Basel. Osterman and Bezborodko warned Cobenzl that, if necessary, they and the Prussians would carve up Poland by themselves.[35] Cobenzl, on 9 December, reassured the Russians that they could count fully on his compliance.

Bezborodko, Osterman and Markov began discussions with Cobenzl and Tauentzien separately on 15 December. The latter, a soldier rather than a diplomat, beat what he considered to be a

33. Z. Góralski, *Stanisław August*, pp. 232–6, 242; Catherine to Stanisław August, [2 Dec. 1793], quoted in Solov'ev, *IPP*, p. 627. R. McGrew, *Paul I of Russia 1754–1801* (Oxford, 1992), p. 197.

34. R.H. Lord, 'The Third Partition', p. 490; Góralski, *Austria*, pp. 169–73.

35. Real, *Von Potsdam nach Basel*, p. 102; Cegielski and Kądziela, *Rozbiory Polski*, p. 316.

tactical retreat over the inevitable Russian annexation of Courland (which duly took place on 26 April of the following year)[36] but clung stubbornly to his insistence on the Vistula boundary with Austria, from Silesia to the confluence with the river Bug. This would give the Prussians not only Kraków (which they already held) but Warsaw – which the Russians held. On the 19th, at the one and only conference between the representatives of all three powers, Tauentzien stormed out when the Russians warned that they would hand over Warsaw to the Prussians only if they, in their turn, surrendered Kraków to the Austrians. Tauentzien's exit allowed Cobenzl and the Russians to finalise their own arrangements.

On 3 January 1795, Cobenzl, Osterman, Bezborodko and Markov signed two 'Declarations concerning the third partition of Poland', one each for Austria and Russia. They were to have 'the force, value and obligation' of 'the most formal and most solemn treaty'.[37] Austria and Russia, while mutually guaranteeing each other's territories, would invite Prussia to accede after they had exchanged ratifications. Russia's new boundary would follow the Bug and Niemen rivers. It took in Wołyń, which Lacy had hoped Austria could secure. Vienna had to settle for what St Petersburg would grant. The Austrian border would be formed by the Bug in the north, the Pilica in the south, and a short stretch of the Vistula in the centre. Warsaw would become a Prussian frontier town, situated in a snaking rim of territory – 'the remaining part of Poland' – which the two Imperial courts would also guarantee. There was also a secret Declaration. Austria formally acceded to the Second Partition treaty of 23 January – thus bestowing its official recognition on that transaction. But Francis II did so only with regard to Russia's and Austria's interests; and his guarantee extended only to Russia's share of Poland in 1793.

The possibility remained that Prussia might object to the present 'Declarations' between empress and emperor and even resort to hostilities (it was implicitly understood, against Austria): if that happened, Russia would immediately assist its new partner 'with all its strength against the common enemy' (who was, after all, 'secretly' negotiating with those enemies of civilisation, the French). Francis would guarantee Hohenzollern gains under the Second Partition only after Prussia recognised the Third. The Secret Declaration

36. A.V. Berkis, *The history of the duchy of Courland (1561–1795)* (Towson, Md., 1969), pp. 296–9. Acts of submission and incorporation, 28 Mar., 26 Apr. 1795, *CTS* LII, pp. 347–66.
37. 'Déclaration[s] concernant le troisième partage de la Pologne', St Petersburg, 23 Dec. 1794/3 Jan. 1795, *CTS* LII, pp. 285–97.

also carried the understanding that Austria had been short-changed by the Second Partition. Catherine would assist with the Bavarian–Netherlands exchange, now a very dead horse, if only in view of the French occupation of Belgium. More significantly, Catherine signified her consent 'in advance' to the making good of Austrian 'rights' to various territories of Venice usurped by that Republic, and indeed to any other proposals for acquisitions which might suitably secure the desired object of 'compensation' against France.

The principal beneficiary of the treaty was Catherine, and not merely in terms of the territory gained – at over 46,330 square miles, almost half as much again as the combined shares of Austria and Prussia. She also gained some 1,200,000 new subjects. Austria obtained 18,147 square miles of territory, Prussia slightly more, but its 18,533 square miles of largely sandy soils were far less valuable. Austria secured 1,500,000 new subjects, Prussia around a million. Russia held, indeed imposed, the balance. As Osterman pointed out to the Prussians in January, they and the Austrians could acquire territory in Poland purely by Catherine's grace and favour.[38] The Declarations of St Petersburg may have helped ease Austria's way to Campo Formio in their promise of further compensation, but in reality they committed Catherine to nothing. The alliance first concluded between Catherine and Joseph in the autumn of 1782 was explicitly renewed. The Russian commitment to secure additional territory for Austria against Turkey was phrased no more strongly than that to secure it territory from France. The purpose of the Declarations was not to give Russian support for Austrian acquisitions for the future, but to bind the Austrians to furnish their renewed support for Catherine's 'Greek' Project. Cobenzl agreed all the more readily as he did not seriously believe that Project would come to anything. There was no doubt, however, that Russia held the whip-hand over its partitioning partners.[39]

The immediate problem was to fix the Prussians, whose negotiations at Basel with the French had become public and official from the end of December.[40] For the time being, news of the 3 January treaty was withheld from Tauentzien, who fondly imagined he could secure a bilateral agreement with the Austrians which would still leave Kraków in Prussian hands. Catherine would have none of this:

38. Góralski, *Austria*, pp. 206–7.
39. For some penetrating comments on Russia's role, see P.W. Schroeder, *The transformation of European politics 1763–1848* (Oxford, 1996 edn), pp. 144–50. Roider, *Baron Thugut*, pp. 170–2.
40. Real, *Von Potsdam nach Basel*, pp. 122–37.

she insisted that he and Cobenzl continue to negotiate through her, not directly with each other. Tauentzien knew that if Prussia could not get the line of the Vistula, its ministers and generals would have preferred not to have a final partition at all. After the euphoria of the Second Partition had passed and the problems of fighting a nation-in-arms had made themselves felt, it began to dawn on Berlin that it was not merely acquiring additional units of resource, but a population which might not passively accept the joys of Hohenzollern rule. Even in May 1794, as he laid out new territorial variants open to Frederick William II, his finance minister Struensee warned that it would take at least thirty years to assimilate the new Polish subjects into Prussia. His estimate showed how little conception *ancien régime* ministers had of the forces beginning to buffet Europe.[41]

Thugut would have settled for a Polish mini-state, even wholly under Russian control, if it kept Prussia at arm's length; better still, if it rolled back all of Prussia's gains at Poland's expense. This was especially so after news of the Franco-Prussian peace of Basel of 5 April reached him.[42] Catherine, for all the vitriol which she heaped on the Prussians for abandoning the struggle against the Revolution, was not interested. After the failure of Targowica and Kościuszko's Revolt, there was no place for Poland in her vision of Europe. She was an old woman in a hurry to settle the affairs of Europe before the son whom she so avidly despised took over from her. Once she laid down the law to Prussia and Austria, she would be in a position to settle scores with the Turks. In May, the Prussians began to pull their troops back from the Rhine. The Austrians feared they would turn against them. Desultory clashes took place between their units in Poland. Vienna put Bohemia and Moravia on a war footing. On 2 July, it withdrew its last remaining troops from the territories earmarked for Catherine, who now built up her forces around Warsaw to 60,000 men. But the Prussians were so shattered that there was no real prospect of their fighting Russia; likewise, Austria was too dependent on Russia and still too engaged against France to undertake any initiatives against Prussia. Catherine pressed the Austrians to cede a small, exposed triangle of territory between the Vistula and the Bug, east of Warsaw, to Prussia, to help nudge it

41. Moritz, 'Die Plaene', pp. 61–2, 67–8; Solov'ev, *IPP*, pp. 623–4; Góralski, *Austria*, p. 240. See also W.W. Hagen, 'The Partitions of Poland and the crisis of the Old Regime in Prussia, 1772–1806', *Central European History* 9 (1976), pp. 115–28; B. Simms, *The impact of Napoleon: Prussian high politics, foreign policy and the crisis of the executive, 1797–1806* (Cambridge, 1997), esp. ch. 3.
42. Góralski, *Austria*, pp. 234–5; Roider, *Baron Thugut*, pp. 187–9.

into withdrawal from Kraków. The Austrians agreed, a further sign of their subordination.

On 9 August, the Russian and Austrian ambassadors in Berlin informed the astonished Prussian ministers that eight months previously their governments had reached an agreement on the final partition of the Polish–Lithuanian Commonwealth. The Prussians were furious – but helpless. Their country was exhausted and isolated. In May, Austria had formed an alliance with Britain and been given a £4,000,000 loan to reinvigorate its war effort. Russia had mended its fences with Britain in February with a treaty of alliance, converted, on 28 September, into a fully fledged triple alliance which took in Austria. Paradoxically, the closest the Prussians had to a friend was France, which would have welcomed their aid against Austria, had they been in any condition to provide it. On 28 August Tauentzien, in St Petersburg, agreed to surrender Kraków, but insisted that his decision be ratified by Berlin.

Frederick William II had no choice. A final Partition treaty was concluded in St Petersburg on 24 October. It followed the model of the First Partition conventions, in consisting of three separate, largely identically worded, agreements: between Russia and Austria; Russia and Prussia; Austria and Prussia. These were little more than matter-of-fact supplements to the 3 January Russo-Austrian agreement, signifying Frederick William's accession to it and incorporating the frontier amendments. The conventions recognised that the Austrian and Prussian borders in particular were not yet clearly defined and provided for a final delineation (at Austrian insistence) with Russian assistance and mediation. The Prussians agreed to evacuate Kraków within six weeks of the treaty's signature; until then, Catherine's troops would remain in Warsaw and other territories earmarked for Prussia.[43]

Tidying-up

The Declarations of 3 January 1795 spelled out all requisite explanation for the suppression of the Polish–Lithuanian Commonwealth. The neighbour-monarchs,

> convinced by experience of the absolute inability of the Republic of Poland to provide itself either with a [firm and rigorous] government or to live peacefully under the law while preserving any form of independence, in their wisdom and love of peace and the happiness of

43. Treaty of St Petersburg, 13/24 Oct. 1795 (Russo-Prussian text only), *CTS* LIII, pp. 1–8. Cegielski and Kądziela, *Rozbiory Polski*, pp. 322–5.

their subjects have decided on the unavoidable necessity of resorting to . . . a total partition of this republic between the three neighbouring powers.[44]

Since the Commonwealth had ceased to exist, a Sejm to ratify its final eradication could hardly be called. It was a question of implementing what had already been agreed, with no reference but to the three powers themselves. The Prussians began the slow evacuation of Kraków at the beginning of November, and completed it within the six-week deadline, by 4 January 1796. They gave vent to their frustrations (and/or followed their normal practice) by looting the royal castle on the Wawel hill. Austrian troops entered on 5 January. On 10 January the Russians pulled out of Warsaw and Prussian troops marched in, taking the Polish coronation insignia with them.

Other loose ends remained. The most awkward was Stanisław August. The Partition would not be complete unless he abdicated. In January, he was taken under heavy guard to Grodno, away from Warsaw where he was causing irritation by his constant complaints at Russian conduct. The governor-general of Lithuania, his old adversary Nikolai Repnin, warned that unless he stepped down, neither his own future nor that of his family or retainers would be secured; nor would his debts, which had reached 40,000,000 zloties, well over £1,100,000, be redeemed. On 25 November 1795 Poland's last king signed a humiliating receipt for his reign. He had to avow that all his efforts 'to increase the happiness' of his subjects 'or, at least, to diminish their misfortunes' had proved vain: for this, 'the unfortunate insurrection' which had afflicted Poland was to blame. Under the circumstances, only Poland's neighbours could assure his compatriots of 'peace and repose'. Stanisław August not only 'freely and voluntarily' abdicated, but, by entrusting his 'solemn act of renunciation' to the empress's safe-keeping, and appealing to her 'to accord her maternal bounties' to his former subjects, he made her a kind of spiritual legatee of the *Rzeczpospolita*.

Catherine allowed him to retain his 'sacred, indelible' royal title. He was provisionally allocated a Russian pension of 200,000 ducats per annum, most of which he had spent by the following August.[45] His hopes of travel to Germany and to Italy were dashed. The

44. 'Déclaration concernant le troisième partage de la Pologne', 23 Dec. 1794/ 3 Jan. 1795, preamble, *CTS* LII, pp. 287–8.
45. Full text of the 'Acte d'abdication de Sa Majesté le Roi de Pologne' appears as an attachment to the Convention of St Petersburg of 15/26 Jan. 1797, between Russia, Austria and Prussia, *CTS* LIII, pp. 423–5. Żywirska, *Ostatnie lata*, pp. 122–39.

titular king of Poland retained far too much symbolic importance to be allowed to roam revolutionary Europe. He was kept under virtual house arrest in Grodno, though the conditions were much relaxed after Catherine's death on 17 November 1796. In March 1797, he removed to St Petersburg, at the emperor Paul's invitation, and graced his coronation the following month. Paul also released the thousands of Polish captives and deportees – except Stanisław August. Residing in the Marble Palace, he remained, to all intents and purposes, a prisoner of state to the end, which came on 12 February 1798 with an apoplectic fit. Paul gave him a royal funeral. He was buried in St Petersburg's Polish, Catholic church of (who else?) St Catherine. Even in the grave, he continued to bask in his patroness's tolerance and protection.[46]

Stanisław August lived long enough to see the three powers complete the demarcation of what had once been his country. The border delineations between Prussia and Russia, Russia and Austria proceeded smoothly, but, in the south, in the Kraków region, Russian mediation was necessary to sort out the bad-tempered squabbling between the Prussian and Austrian commissioners. As expected, Catherine's decision, on 21 October 1796, on balance favoured the Austrians. Two further agreements – a provisional understanding on 5 December and an 'Acte Définitif' on 31 January 1797 were necessary to implement Catherine's arbitration. The delay would have been greater if news of her death had reached her commissioners in Kraków sooner. The 'Acte Définitif' stressed that the conciliation and arbitration processes had been completed under the guarantee of her successor, Paul. Austria and Prussia were careful to leave no room on this little stretch of border for the sort of disputes which had brought so much grief to the Poles after the First Partition. The number of frontier markers to be erected (138 on each side), their exact distance from and location relative to each other, with specific triangulation instructions, were noted in the 'Acte Définitif'. A final 'Acte de Démarcation' concluded in Warsaw on 19 March 1797 regulated the entire length of the Prusso-Austrian border through the old Polish territories.[47]

46. The 'post-history' of Stanisław August's remains is a macabre and barely credible tale in itself. The body was finally laid to rest on 14 February 1995 in St John's Cathedral, in Warsaw – well away from Poland's other kings, in the Wawel castle in Kraków.

47. Z. Góralski, 'Die Grenzdemarkationen in Polen nach der dritten Teilung (1795–1797)', *Jahrbücher für Geschichte Osteuropas* 19 (1971), pp. 212–38. Texts of Catherine's award and the demarcation agreements in *CTS* LIII, pp. 303–6, 343–50, 429–84; LIV, pp. 23–30.

A sort of death certificate for the Polish–Lithuanian Common-wealth was issued in the shape of the Convention agreed between the three powers in St Petersburg on 26 January 1797. This largely tidied up unfinished business. Russia, Austria and Prussia agreed to set up a joint commission to oversee the repayment of the Polish state debt and of Stanisław August's personal debts. News of the proposal would be published 'in all the gazettes' so that all with legitimate claims could submit them to the Commission which would begin work in Warsaw on 12 May. A similar tripartite commission would begin work at the same time to deal with claims arising from the 1793 Warsaw bank crash. The 200,000 ducat pension paid to Stanisław August by Russia would now be shared equally by all three powers as 'a signal testimony of their regard and goodwill towards him'. Out of his new, joint allowance, he would have to repay two-thirds of what Russia had paid him between his arrival in Grodno and the signature of the present convention. It was not only Frederick the Great among crowned heads who could haggle as well as any fishwife.

In recognition of 'all the inconveniences attached to so-called *sujets mixtes*' the three powers agreed to endure them no more. Those with possessions in more than one state were given five years in which to decide where to make their permanent domicile. They could freely sell up elsewhere. Ecclesiastics and religious institutions would have to make the same choice, although, in their case, lapsed rights and claims on jurisdiction, debts, mortgages, endowments could not be disposed of by private treaty, but would revert to the state treasuries. Stanisław August's act of abdication was attached to the Convention, as a kind of Polish imprimatur to the partition proceedings. A secret and separate article insisted on 'the need to abolish everything which can recall the memory of the existence of the kingdom of Poland . . .'. A final indignity befell the royal insignia plundered by the Prussians from Kraków. In 1809 they were melted into coin.[48]

48. Convention of St Petersburg, 15/26 Jan. 1797, *CTS* LIII, pp. 411–27. W.H. Zawadzki, *A man of honour: Adam Czartoryski as a statesman of Russia and Poland 1795–1831* (Oxford, 1993), p. 33.

Epilogue

In July 1797, in the episcopal palace of the town of Reggio nell' Emilia in northern Italy, Józef Wybicki composed a patriotic march. He urged his friend, general Jan Henryk Dąbrowski, to lead the Polish soldiers under his command to liberate his non-existent country from its invaders. By 1800, the Polish legions formed under the aegis of revolutionary France, mainly from deserters and prisoners-of-war from the Austrian armies, numbered some 15,000 men. They were very useful to France against its enemies, but far too few to rescue and resuscitate Poland. The treaties of Campo Formio and Lunéville came as a bitter disappointment. Once peace was made, the Danubian and Italian legions' yearnings for a real country became an embarrassment. The Franco-Russian treaty of Paris of October 1801 not only restored peace, but banned from French territory any elements capable 'of fomenting troubles' on Russian territories. The Polish troops were recycled among France's Italian satellites, or incorporated into the French army. During 1802–3, some six thousand were sent with French troops to suppress Toussaint l'Ouverture's rising on Haiti. Three hundred and thirty returned.[1]

Wybicki's march, or Dąbrowski's *Mazurek*, was as resilient as those for whom it was written. By 1830, it had, to all intents and purposes, become the national anthem, even if it had to wait until 1927 for official sanction. Yet within five years of its composition, its opening words, 'Poland is not yet dead', must have seemed hollow to all but the most hardened optimists. Dąbrowski was among them. He had spent most of his early career in the Saxon army, he was married to a Saxon noblewoman and, to the end of his life, spoke with a heavy German accent. But Poniatowski's reign, the Four Years Sejm, its new army and the Kościuszko Insurrection had done their work. For a critical mass of men, a new idea of Poland and its right to

---

1. For the above and much of what follows, see J. Pachoński, *Generał Jan Henryk Dąbrowski* (Warsaw, 1981); J. Czubaty, *Wodzowie i politycy* (Warsaw, 1993); P. Wandycz, *The lands of partitioned Poland* (Seattle, 1984 edn). See also A. Nieuwazny, 'Napoleon and Polish identity', *History Today* 48, no. 4 (May 1998), pp. 50–5.

existence had been formed, proof against its diplomatic elimination. A generation earlier, Dąbrowski would almost certainly have become fully Germanised and assimilated into Saxon society.

In the first years of the new century, France was a fourth partitioning power at one remove, siphoning the resources and manpower of the old Commonwealth for its own ends. To many Poles revolutionary France and the beast Bonaparte were as bad as, or worse than, Prussia, Russia and Austria. Yet France offered hope as well as disappointment. With the collapse of Prussia at Jena and Auerstädt in 1806 and Frederick William III's undignified flight to Memel (what would his great-uncle have thought?) the way seemed open for Napoleon to restore Poland.

In fact, Napoleon used the hope that he might do so as the instrument to create a new eastern outpost and dependency. For all his victories, he could not afford to alienate the partitioning powers to such an extent that they would form a united hostile bloc. The full restoration of Poland would certainly have ensured this. In 1807, he settled for creating the 'duchy of Warsaw' out of Prussia's share of the Partitions. Two years later, it was extended to the south and east by territories from the Austrians after their disastrous war of 1809. Both the treaties of Tilsit (7 July 1807) and Schönbrunn (14 October 1809) stressed the duchy of Warsaw's status as the possession of Friedrich August I, king of Saxony – prior to 1806, elector Friedrich August III, the very man to whom the Poles had offered the crown in 1791. Then, he had turned it down, because Catherine the Great would not suffer it. In 1807, Napoleon allowed him a consolation prize. The emperor told Dąbrowski and Wybicki he was waiting to see 'if the Poles are worthy to be a nation'.

To do so, the tiny state virtually bankrupted itself. Less than 60,000 square miles in extent, it was smaller than the rump Commonwealth left by the Second Partition. In 1812 its 4,330,000 people were shouldering a per capita tax burden twelve times higher than that of Poland in 1768; the duchy put up an army of some 115,000 men – an exertion unprecedented in Polish military annals. It was a heavy price to pay for Napoleon's policies and for the recognition of Polish nationhood at the Congress of Vienna. But recognition did not extend to the restoration of an independent state. The frontiers were redrawn again, to carve the so-called 'Congress Kingdom' out of the Duchy. Its economically most valuable western lands were returned to Prussia as the Grand Duchy of Posen. Prussia was more than compensated for its other losses with lands in Westphalia. Austria kept the Galician border of 1772 and balanced the loss of 'New Galicia' by retaining territories in Venetia and Lombardy.

The defeat of Napoleon was, of course, a disaster for Poland – on 27 June 1813, at Reichenbach, Russia, Prussia and Austria renewed their alliances and agreed in principle to partition the duchy of Warsaw.[2] Russia emerged far stronger from the conflict than either of its partners. Tsar Alexander was able to use his dominant position and the failure of the Reichenbach agreement to prescribe the new borders to push Russia's frontier further west than at any time in its history. The duchy of Warsaw was indeed 'partitioned', but the bulk of it was attached to Russia.

The 'Congress Kingdom', known to its inhabitants half affectionately, half contemptuously by the diminutive, *Kongresówka*, was a tiny, constitutional monarchy tacked onto an autocracy which spanned two continents. Its 49,423 square miles and 3,300,000 people were 'irrevocably' joined to Russia. The tsar would be king of this 'Poland'. The Sejm restored, a property-based franchise was introduced, *habeas corpus* was reaffirmed, a separate Polish army was preserved. But the 'Czar, king of Poland' exercised full executive powers, he had the power of veto over any Sejm legislation and enjoyed the sole right of legislative initiative. Alexander chose to rule through a viceroy – his younger brother, the Grand Duke Constantine, that one of Catherine's grandsons to whom the reformers had tried to offer the Polish throne in 1792 in a desperate attempt to save the Third of May Constitution. The *Kongresówka* was closer to the rump state the Prussians had suggested creating for Platon Zubov in 1793 than to one with a genuine political existence of its own. Its presence horrified the Prussians and the Austrians, who feared it would be a perpetual source of revolution in their own lands and a cause for instability across international borders. Even more, it was a fig-leaf for the projection of Russian power into the very centre of Europe. Alexander insisted and got his way – in 1814 and 1815, Prussia and Austria were even less well placed to resist Russian expansion than in 1794 and 1795.[3]

The total destruction of old Poland and, hence, of a buffer state between the three great powers of eastern Europe, had created precisely the sorts of tensions between them which Kaunitz had foreseen. The only way to avoid them lay in the unthinkable – the resurrection of the *Rzeczpospolita* – and no one who mattered seriously contemplated the possibility. The Napoleonic adventure had shown just how difficult it was to implement the 1797 commitment

2. *CTS* LXII, p. 308. The agreement was renewed, in diluted form, by the treaties of Toeplitz of 9 Sept. 1813, ibid., pp. 368, 381.
3. P.W. Schroeder, *The transformation of European politics 1763–1848* (Oxford, 1996 edn), pp. 478, 523–38.

to efface the memory of the old Polish realm. The Congress of
Vienna created – on paper – a kind of virtual substitute. It agreed
to put in place 'liberal arrangements' to allow the inhabitants 'of
the full extent of the old kingdom of Poland, such as it existed
before the year 1772' freedom of movement and commerce. Even
the 'sujets mixtes', abolished in 1797, were restored 'in respect of
landed property'. This was not the same as independence. The
Partition agreements of 1772, 1793 and 1795, though amended by
subsequent territorial rearrangements, were not abrogated. Throughout the former Polish lands, each ruling government was to accord
its subjects such 'representation and national institutions' as it
thought fit. This meant anything and nothing. The Vienna stipulations on commerce and mobility remained a dead letter. Within a
decade, tariff warfare had erupted, to continue intermittently for
the rest of the century.[4]

Heinrich von Stein had warned Alexander in 1814 that the creation of a constitutional Poland would only 'complicate' Russian rule
and encourage Polish hopes of full independence. Foreign rule
was neither novel nor unusual in the eighteenth and nineteenth
centuries (the dynasty that ruled in Britain after 1714 was not only
German but also considerably less illustrious than any of those that
ruled in Poland after 1795). Poland was different in that its old
territories, as well as its Polish-speaking elements, were subject to a
three-way split. The alternative to the mirage of full independence
might have been the re-creation of the old Polish state under just
one of the partitioning rulers. At various times, all three dynasties
appeared as possible contenders. The highest hopes (if that is the
right word) stemmed from Adam Jerzy Czartoryski's links to tsar
Alexander prior to Tilsit. His *Mordplan gegen Preussen*, 'murder plan
against Prussia', as the historian Hermann Oncken indignantly
dubbed it in the 1880s (a sense of irony does not seem to have
been one of his stronger points), would indeed have destroyed
Prussia by placing its Polish territories under tsarist rule, but, as
Czartoryski was to discover, a Russo-Polish binary state was hardly
an alternative.[5]

The Poles' desire for independence was bound to bring them
into collision with the partitioning powers' determination to keep
it from them. The tensions were strongest in the Polish heartland

4. Texts of the treaties of Vienna of 3 May 1815, between Russia and Austria and
Russia and Prussia in *CTS* LXIV, pp. 135–44, 147–57.
5. W.H. Zawadzki, *A man of honour: Adam Czartoryski as a statesman of Russia and
Poland 1795–1831* (Oxford, 1993), pp. 79–87, 108–9, 125–36, 168–82.

of the *Kongresówka*. It is easy and tempting to view the disastrous uprisings of 1830–31 and 1863–64 as pointless. The first was accidental, the second was ill-considered, both were doomed, but both were also inevitable. The attempt to match Poland's libertarian, pluralistic traditions with Russia's centralising bureaucratism could not work. One or the other had to give way. When, back in the 1770s, the Russians viewed as 'well-intentioned', 'deserving well of their country', 'patriots' men of the ilk of Adam Poniński, they meant stooges who would do whatever Russia demanded of them.[6] Or, as Stanisław August put it in 1792:

> it is the empress's well-considered intention to debase, enfeeble and stultify us, to cut us off from other nations, to destroy our army, currency and education, to restore old Sarmatian prejudices.[7]

In October 1820, Alexander told his brother he had 'carte blanche' to use the constitution as he wished. He was asserting the Russian over the Polish political tradition: the two were utterly irreconcilable.[8]

Russia looked on its treaties with Poland not so much as agreements between equals or near-equals – *traktaty* – but as pledges of allegiance – *sherti* – of the sort it had routinely imposed on the Tatars, Bashkirs, Kazakhs and other non-Orthodox peoples of its periphery, preparatory to swallowing them up in its political system.[9] The other partitioning powers had to follow much the same policies. This was particularly true in Prussia, where, after 1795, about a third of the population were Polish, an ethnic succubus which doomed Prussia first to paralysis, then disaster against Napoleonic France.[10]

Austria, long accustomed to the problems of multiple nationalities, arrived at the best *modus vivendi* with its Polish subjects, at least after 1867. After the 1863 uprising, Russia deliberately set out to destroy all sense of Polish identity and separation, with far-reaching bans on language, restrictions on education and employment. The 'Kingdom of Poland' even lost its name, to become a province of

6. Catherine II's instruction to Caspar von Saldern, 5/16 Mar. 1771, *SIRIO* LXXXXVII, pp. 219, 221, 224; Panin to the bishop of Brześć Kujawski, 23 Feb./6 Mar. 1773, *SIRIO* CXVIII, pp. 335–6.

7. Quoted in E. Rostworowski, *Ostatni król Rzeczypospolitej* (Warsaw, 1965), p. 304.

8. W. Zajewski 'Powstanie listopadowe 1830–1831', in W. Zajewski, ed., *Trzy powstania narodowe* (Warsaw, 1997), pp. 151–61.

9. M. Khodarkovsky, 'From frontier to empire: the concept of the frontier in Russia, sixteenth–eighteenth centuries', *Russian History* 19 (1992), pp. 115–28.

10. B. Simms, *The impact of Napoleon* (Cambridge, 1997), chs 3–4.

the Russian empire supposedly no different to any other. Bismarck's anti-Polish policies, especially through land expropriation, were among the most damaging. It was nothing personal, just business: Bismarck appreciated that unless the Poles were finally assimilated, Prussia would not survive.[11]

That this did not happen had much to do with Stanisław August. His patronage of writers, painters, architects and, above all, the new schools laid the foundation of the paradoxical efflorescence of Polish cultural life during the nineteenth century. Adam Mickiewicz (1798–1855), Fryderyk Chopin (1810–49), Juliusz Słowacki (1809–49), Cyprian Norwid (1821–83), Jan Matejko (1838–93), Eliza Orzeszkowa (1841–1910), Bolesław Prus (1847–1912), Henryk Sienkiewicz (1846–1916), to name but a few – among the greatest literary and artistic talents Poland has ever produced – flourished when it did not exist. Although the papacy condemned the rising of 1830–31 and was guarded towards that of 1863–64, the *szlachta*'s old identification with Catholicism spread throughout Polish-speaking society. Hundreds of parish clergy were exiled to Siberia after 1864, sealing the bond between Poland and the Catholic religion which has proved so enduring in the face of oppression. A combination of high and low culture, failure and suffering, religion and resentment, and just getting on with life defied all the attempts to Russify, Germanise and destroy. The pressure was not unremitting, but at all times the Polish population remained at the political whim of their alien rulers. Only amid the debris of the First World War did the situation change. In 1815, Poland could not be resurrected because the partitioning powers were victorious. In 1918 the Poles could claw their way back to independence because those powers had collapsed under the combination of military catastrophe and internal disintegration.

Of course, it was, as it had to be, a very different Poland. The old unifying force of *szlachectwo* had to retreat in the face of new national and ethnic feeling within and beyond the lands comprehended by the borders of 1772. Choices which would have appeared ludicrously incomprehensible to eighteenth-century society had to be made. Oskar Miłosz (1877–1939), disgusted by the provincialism and anti-Semitism (his mother was Jewish) of the local Polish gentry, broke with them, settled in Paris, and opted to become a Lithuanian (learning the language from scratch) during the Paris peace conferences. He remained in France and wrote his mystical poetry

11. Apart from Wandycz, *Lands of partitioned Poland*, esp. chs 10–11, see the perceptive comments in M. Müller, *Die Teilungen Polens* (Munich, 1984), ch. 5.

in French, as Oscar Venceslas de Lubicz-Milosz. His gravestone at Fontainebleau gives the Lithuanised form – Milius. His nephew, Czesław, the Nobel laureate, born in 1911, opted to 'be' 'Polish', though it was a decision which, in a softer world, he would have preferred not to have had to face.[12]

Many such choices were made, dividing families and communities between 'Poles', 'Lithuanians', 'Ukrainians', 'Byelorussians', even 'Germans' – mournful testimony to the passing of that failed experiment, the *Rzeczpospolita szlachecka*. But Poland survived, even if in very different form. Between 1939 and 1945 came a fresh attempt to finish it off, utilising hitherto undreamed of industrial processes. The extermination policies, in all their variations, practised by Hitler's Germany and Stalin's Soviet Union were a logical response to earlier failures. The result was modern Poland: a state within narrowed and drastically recast frontiers and largely purged of 'non-Polish' ethnic groups.

Its many pasts haunt today's Republic. With such vicissitudes behind them, Poles, even after escaping the maw of the Soviet Union, are far from harmonious in their attitudes to wider European integration or to their neighbours, east and west. If much of this is a legacy of the twentieth century, much, too, has been handed down from the eighteenth. 'Targowica' remains the most sensitive epithet in a rich vocabulary of political venom. Poland is not alone in its fears for, and in debates about the meaning of, sovereignty and independence, but its history envelops them with a rare poignancy. Poland escaped from the Soviet orbit not merely by its own efforts, but because the Soviet Union fell apart under its internal pressures, just as the partitioning powers broke up in 1917 and 1919. Today's *Rzeczpospolita* might feel more secure within a wider, systemic European framework to which it freely accedes, but how comfortable it will be at the inevitable dilution of a sovereignty it has only fitfully enjoyed over the past three centuries is another matter.

12. My thanks to Dr Margaret Callender of Birmingham University's French Department for information about Oskar. Czesław Miłosz's works, especially *Dolina Issy* and *Rodzinna Europa*, remain unrivalled guides to the 'Polish–Lithuanian' Europe of the twentieth century. They are available in English translations as *The Issa Valley*, trans. L. Iribarne (London, 1981) and *Native Realm: a search for self-definition*, trans. C.L. Leach (London, 1981).

Appendix: Manuscript sources of sejmiki instructions, 1773–88
(see Chapter 5)

CONSTITUENCY (palatinates in upper case; counties in lower case)	1773	1776	1778	1780	1782	1784	1786	1788
BRACŁAW			AGAD/ZP 129, ff. 143–8					
BRZEŚĆ KUJAWSKI†	Pawiński, pp. 269–72	Pawiński, pp. 288–96	Pawiński, pp. 305–9		Pawiński, pp. 323–6, AGAD/ZP 126, ff. 166–7	Pawiński, pp. 331–5	Pawiński, pp. 342–6	Pawiński, pp. 355–8
CZERNICHÓW††								
Dobrzyń	Kluczycki, pp. 377–8	Kluczycki, pp. 380–2	Kluczycki, pp. 383–5			Kluczycki, pp. 391–2		Kluczycki, pp. 394–6
KIEV		AGAD/ZP 129, ff. 197–200						
KRAKÓW	AGAD/ZP 123, ff. 37–40	AGAD/ZP 125, ff. 36–47	AGAD/ZP 125, ff. 231–4					
LUBLIN				BPAN 8326, ff. 411–21		BPAN 8326, ff. 433–8	BPAN 8326, ff. 451–2	BPAN 8326, ff. 461–7
ŁĘCZYCA	AGAD/ZP 123, ff. 41–4	BPAN 8330, pp. 543–50	BPAN 8330, pp. 583–600	BPAN 8330, pp. 625–40	BPAN 8330, pp. 653–67	BPAN 8330, pp. 689–700		BPAN 8330, pp. 749–57
MAZOWSZE: Ciechanów	BPAN 8318, f. 320	BPAN 8318, ff. 323–4/327–9	BPAN 8318, ff. 339–40	BPAN 8318, ff. 343–4	BPAN 8318, ff. 347–8	BPAN 8318, ff. 351–2		BPAN 8318, ff. 359–60

MAZOWSZE: Czersk	BPAN 8320, f. 418	BPAN 8320, ff. 442-7	BPAN 8320, ff. 452-5	BPAN 8320, ff. 458-60	BPAN 8320, ff. 467-70	BPAN 8320, ff. 472-3	BPAN 8320, ff. 480/482-4	
MAZOWSZE: Liw	BPAN 8322, ff. 558-60	BPAN 8322, ff. 572-5	AGAD/ZP 125, ff. 223-5	BPAN 8322, ff. 584-7	BPAN 8322, ff. 591-4	BPAN 8322, ff. 598-9	BPAN 8322, ff. 600-1	
MAZOWSZE: Łomża	BPAN 8332, ff. 400-2	BPAN 8332, ff. 410-13	BPAN 8332, ff. 418-20					
MAZOWSZE: Nur	BPAN 8335, ff. 314-20	BPAN 8335, ff. 321-4	BPAN 8335, ff. 324-8	BPAN 8335, ff. 333-6	BPAN 8335, ff. 337-9	BPAN 8335, ff. 358-72/373-5		
MAZOWSZE: Różan	BPAN 8337, ff. 584-7	BPAN 8337, ff. 593-4	BPAN 8337, ff. 597-600	BPAN 8337, ff. 602-5	BPAN 8337, ff. 618-21	BPAN 8337, ff. 626-7	BPAN 8337, ff. 630-1	
MAZOWSZE: Wizna	BPAN 8351, ff. 286-7	BPAN 8351, ff. 311-13/316-17	BPAN 8351, ff. 341-3/346-7	BPAN 8351, ff. 373-5	BPAN 8351, ff. 380-3	BPAN 8351, ff. 388-9	BPAN 8351, ff. 392-3	BPAN 8351, ff. 396-8
MAZOWSZE: Wyszogród	BPAN 8352, ff. 267-9	BPAN 8352, ff. 287-8	BPAN 8352, ff. 293-4	BPAN 8352, ff. 304-5	BPAN 8352, ff. 310-11	BPAN 8352, f. 314	BPAN 8352, ff. 318-19	
MAZOWSZE: Zakroczym	BPAN 8354, ff. 273-4	BPAN 8354, ff. 281-7	BPAN 8354, ff. 293-5	BPAN 8354, ff. 302-4	BPAN 8354, ff. 307-9	BPAN 8354, ff. 313-18		
PODLASIE: Mielnik	AGAD/ZP 129, ff. 167-8							
PODOLE	AGAD/ZP 129, ff. 239-43	AGAD/ZP 125, ff. 219-22	AGAD/ZP 125, ff. 314-28					
RAWA: Sochaczew	BPAN 8347, ff. 439-44	BPAN 8347, ff. 448-50	BPAN 8347, ff. 453-5	BPAN 8347, ff. 458-60	BPAN 8347, ff. 463-5	BPAN 8347, ff. 468-9	BPAN 8347, ff. 472-6	
SANDOMIERZ	BPAN 8341, ff. 873-916	BPAN 8341, ff. 953-92	BPAN 8341, ff. 1017-36	BPAN 8341, ff. 1069-92	BPAN 8341, ff. 1161-80			
SIERADZ	BPAN 8345, ff. 721-8	BPAN 8345, ff. 769-78						
WIELKOPOLSKA: palatinates of KALISZ, POZNAŃ and GNIEZNO[†††]	AGAD/ZP 123, ff. 46-9	AGAD/ZP 125, ff. 198-203						
WOŁYŃ	AGAD/ZP 129, ff. 229-33	AGAD/ZP 125, ff. 213-17						

CONSTITUENCY (palatinates in upper case; counties in lower case)	1773	1776	1778	1780	1782	1784	1786	1788
			LITHUANIAN constituencies					
BRZEŚĆ LITEWSKI:								
Brześć Litewski	AGAD/ZP 123, ff. 55–6							
NOWOGRÓDEK:								
Nowogródek	BPAN 1155, pp. 58–62							
NOWOGRÓDEK:								
Wołkowysk	AGAD/ZP 123, ff. 57–8							
POŁOCK			AGAD/ZP 125, ff. 243–4					
TROKI: Kowno		AGAD/ZP 125, ff. 73–6						
WILNO: Brasław		AGAD/ZP 129, ff. 159–66						Akty izd. Arkh. Komm. II, pp. 189–94
principality of ZMUDŹ		AGAD/ZP 129, ff. 261–73	AGAD/ZP 125, ff. 205–12					

†Met jointly with the palatinate of Inowrocław at Radziejów. ††Sejmik-in-exile, meeting at Włodzimierz in the palatinate of Wołyń. †††Met jointly at Środa.

Akty izd. Arkh. Komm.: Akty izdavaemie Arkheograficheskoiu Kommissieiu, II (Vilnius, 1867)
Kluczycki: F. Kluczycki, ed., Lauda sejmikow ziemi dobrzyńskiej (Kraków, 1887)
Pawiński: A. Pawiński, Dzieje ziemi kujawskiej, V (Warsaw, 1888)

Bibliography

Unpublished sources

Archiwum Główne Akt Dawnych, Warsaw:
Zbiór Popielów, MSS 123, 125, 126, 129, 130, 421.
Biblioteka Czartoryskich, Kraków, MSS 320, 825, 3868.
Biblioteka Jagiellońska, Kraków, MS 6646II, t. 15.
Biblioteka Polskiej Akademii Nauk, Kraków, MSS 1115, 8318, 8320, 8322, 8326, 8330, 8332, 8335, 8337, 8341, 8345, 8347, 8351, 8352, 8354.
Public Record Office, London. State Papers 91/77. Foreign Office 62/4.

Published sources

Akty izdavaemyie Arkheograficheskoiu Kommissiieiu, II (Vilnius, 1867).
Arkhiv Gosudarstvennogo Soveta, I (St Petersburg, 1869).
The Annual Register (1791).
Burke, E., *The correspondence of Edmund Burke*, II, ed. L.S. Sutherland (Cambridge, 1960).
Chodźko, L.J.B. (pseud., comte D'Angeberg), ed., *Recueil des traités, conventions et actes diplomatiques concernant la Pologne 1762–1861*, I (Paris, 1862).
Consolidated Treaty Series, 231 vols, ed. C. Parry (Dobbs Ferry, New York, 1969–86).
Courier de Londres (1791).
Frederick II, king of Prussia, *Politische Correspondenz Friedrich's des Grossen*, 46 vols (Berlin 1879–1939).
Frederick II, king of Prussia, *Politische Correspondenz Friedrich's des Grossen. Ergänzungsband. Die Politischen Testamente Friedrichs des Grossen*, ed. G.B. Volz (Berlin, 1920).
Grześkowiak-Krwawicz, A., ed., *Za i Przeciw Ustawie Rządowej* (Warsaw, 1992).

KLUCZYCKI, F., ed., *Lauda sejmików ziemi dobrzyńskiej* (Kraków, 1887).

KOŁŁĄTAJ, H., 'Uwagi nad wpływaniem do interesów Rzeczypospolitej dwóch mocarstw . . .', in *Kołłątaj i orientacja pruska u progu Sejmu Czteroletniego*, ed. Z. Zielińska (Warsaw, 1991).

KONARSKI, S., *O Skutecznym Rad Sposobie*, 4 vols (Warsaw, 1760–63).

KONARSKI, S., *Pisma Wybrane*, 2 vols, ed. J. Nowak-Dłużewski (Warsaw, 1955).

KONOPCZYŃSKI, W., ed., *Konfederacja barska: wybór tekstów* (Kraków, 1928).

KONOPKA, T., *Historia domu naszego: raptularz z czasów Stanisława Augusta*, ed. M. Konopka (Warsaw, 1993).

[LIND, J.], *Letters concerning the present state of Poland* (London, 1774 edn).

[ŁOYKO, F.], *Les droits des trois puissances sur plusieurs provinces de la République de Pologne . . .*, 2 vols (London, 1774).

LUTOSTAŃSKI, K., ed., *Les partages de la Pologne et la lutte pour l'indépendance. Recueil des actes diplomatiques, traités et documents* (Lausanne, 1918).

MAJCHROWICZ, S., SJ, *Trwałość szczęśliwa królestw albo ich smutny upadek . . .* (Lwów, 1764).

MARTENS, F., ed., *Recueil des traités et conventions conclus par la Russie avec les puissances étrangères*, VI (St Petersburg, 1883).

MOTTAZ, E., ed., *Stanislas Poniatowski et Maurice Glayre. Correspondence relative aux partages de la Pologne* (Paris, 1897).

OZANAM, D., and ANTOINE, M., eds, *Correspondence secrète du comte de Broglie avec Louis XV (1756–1774)*, 2 vols (Paris, 1956).

PAWIŃSKI, A., *Dzieje ziemi kujawskiej*, V (Warsaw, 1888).

[PAWLIKOWSKI, J.], *Czy Polacy wybić się moga na niepodległość* (E. Halicz, ed., Warsaw, 1967 edn).

POPŁAWSKI, A., *Zbiór niektórych materyi politycznych* (Warsaw, 1774).

[RZEWUSKI, W.], *Myśli o niezawodnym utrzymaniu Sejmów y Liberi Veto . . . 1764* [n. pl.].

Sbornik Russkogo Imperatorskogo Istoricheskogo Obshchestva (St Petersburg, 148 vols in 141, 1867–1916).

SIENICKI, SZ., *Sposób nowo-obmyślony konkludowania obrad publicznych, dla utwierdzenia praw kardynalnych wolności, libertatis sentiendi & juris vetandi . . .*, 3 vols (Łowicz, 1764).

SIEVERS, J.J., *Jak doprowadziłem do drugiego rozbioru Polski* (reprint of *Drugi rozbiór Polski z pamiętników Sieversa*, Poznań, 1865), ed. B. Grochulska and P. Ugniewski (Warsaw, 1992).

SIRISA [i.e. August Sadebeck], *Polens Ende: historisch, statistisch und geographisch beschrieben* (Warsaw, 1797).

Stanisław August Poniatowski, *Mémoires du roi Stanislas-Auguste Poniatowski*, 2 vols (St Petersburg–Leningrad, 1914–24).

Staszic, S., *Uwagi nad Życiem Jana Zamoyskiego*, ed. S. Czarnowski (Wrocław, 1951 edn).

Theiner, A., ed., *Vetera Monumenta Poloniae et Lithuaniae gentiumque finitimarum historiam illustrantia*, IV (Rome, 1864).

Trębicki, A., *Opisanie Sejmu Ekstraordynaryjnego podziałowego roku 1793 w Grodnie* [and] *O Rewolucji roku 1794*, ed. J. Kowecki (Warsaw, 1967).

Voltaire, *The Complete Works of Voltaire*, CXXIII (= *Correspondence*, XXXIX), ed. T. Bestermann (Oxford, 1975).

Volumina Legum, 9 vols (St Petersburg–Kraków, 1859–89).

Wybicki, J., *Myśli polityczne o wolności cywilnej* (first published 1775–76), ed. E. Rostworowski (Wrocław, 1984).

Secondary Works

Adler, P.J., 'Habsburg school reform among the Orthodox minorities, 1770–1780', *Slavic Review* 33 (1974), pp. 23–45.

Alexander, J.T., *Catherine the Great: life and legend* (Oxford, 1989).

Aretin, K.O. von, 'Russia as a guarantor power of the Imperial Constitution under Catherine II', *Journal of Modern History* 78 (1986), pp. S141–S160.

Aretin, K.O. von, 'Tausch, Teilung und Länderschacher als Folgen des Gleichgewichtssystems der europäischen Grossmächte: die polnischen Teilungen als europäisches Schicksal', *Jahrbuch für die Geschichte Mittel- und Ostdeutschlands* 30 (1981), pp. 53–68.

Arneth, A. Ritter von, *Geschichte Maria Theresia's*, 10 vols (Vienna, 1863–79).

Askenazy, S., *Die letzte polnische Königswahl* (Göttingen, 1894).

Bär, M., *Westpreussen unter Friedrich dem Grossen*, 2 vols (Berlin, 1909).

Bardach, J., ed., *Historia Państwa i Prawa Polski*, II (Warsaw, 1971).

Bauer, K., *Blaski i cienie insurekcji kościuszkowskiej* (Warsaw, 1982).

Beales, D., *Joseph II* (Cambridge, 1987).

Beer, A., *Die Erste Theilung Polens*, 3 vols (Vienna, 1873).

Berkis, A.V., *The history of the duchy of Courland (1561–1795)* (Towson, Md., 1969).

Bieńkowski, L., 'Organizacja kościoła wschodniego w Polsce', in J. Kłoczowski, ed., *Kościół w Polsce*, II (Kraków, 1969), pp. 838–59.

Black, J., *British foreign policy in an age of revolutions 1783–1793* (Cambridge, 1994).

BLANNING, T.C.W., *The origins of the French revolutionary wars* (Harlow, 1986).

BÖMELBURG, H.-J., *Zwischen polnischer Ständegesellschaft und preussischem Obrigkeitsstaat. Vom Königlichen Preussen zu Westpreussen 1756–1806* (Munich, 1995).

BOREJSZA, J.W., 'The French Revolution in relation to Poland and East-Central Europe', in J. Klaits and M.H. Haltzel, eds, *The global ramifications of the French Revolution* (Cambridge, 1994), pp. 55–71.

BUCZEK, K., *The history of Polish cartography from the 15th to the 18th century* (Amsterdam, 1982).

BUTTERWICK, J., *Poland's last king and English culture* (Oxford, 1988).

BUTTERWICK, R., 'The visit to England in 1754 of Stanisław August Poniatowski', *Oxford Slavonic Papers*, NS 25 (1992), pp. 61–83.

CEGIELSKI, T., *Das alte Reich und die Erste Teilung Polens 1768–1774* (Wiesbaden, 1988).

CEGIELSKI, T., 'Poglądy na rozbiory Polski', *Kwartalnik Historyczny* 83 (1976), pp. 636–42.

CEGIELSKI, T., 'Preussische "Deutschland"- und Polenpolitik in dem Zeitraum 1740–1792', *Jahrbuch für die Geschichte Mittel- und Ostdeutschlands* 30 (1981), pp. 21–7.

CEGIELSKI, T., and KĄDZIELA, Ł., *Rozbiory Polski 1772–1793–1795* (Warsaw, 1990).

CHOJECKI, R., 'Patriotyczna opozycja na Sejmie 1773', *Kwartalnik Historyczny* 79 (1972), pp. 545–62.

CYNARSKI, S., 'The shape of Sarmatian ideology', *Acta Poloniae Historica* 19 (1968), pp. 5–17.

CZAJA, A., *Między tronem, buławą a dworem petersburskim: z dziejów Rady Nieustającej 1788–1789* (Warsaw, 1988).

CZAPLIŃSKI, W., 'Les territoires de l'ouest dans la politique de la Pologne de 1572 à 1764', *Acta Poloniae Historica* 9 (1964), pp. 26–7.

CZUBATY, J., *Wodzowie i politycy* (Warsaw, 1993).

DAVIES, N., *God's Playground: a history of Poland*, 2 vols (Oxford, 1981).

DAVIES, N., *Heart of Europe: a short history of Poland* (Oxford, 1984).

DE MADARIAGA, I., *Russia in the age of Catherine the Great* (London, 1981).

DE MADARIAGA, I., 'The secret Austro-Russian treaty of 1781', *Slavonic and East European Review* 38 (1959–60), pp. 114–45.

DROZDOWSKI, M.M., *Podstawy finansowe działalności państwowej w Polsce, 1763–1793* (Warsaw, 1975).

DROZDOWSKI, M.M., 'Przyjęcie traktatów rozbiorowych przez Delegację i sejm polski w 1773r.', *Roczniki Historyczne* 46 (1975), pp. 81–124.

DUFFY, C., *Russia's military way to the West: origins and nature of Russian military power 1700–1800* (London, 1981).

DUKES, P., *Catherine II and the Russian nobility* (Cambridge, 1967).

DUTKIEWICZ, J., 'Prusy a Polska w dobie Sejmu Czteroletniego w świetle korespondencji dyplomatycznej pruskiej', in H. Kocój, ed., *Cztery lata nadziei* (Katowice, 1980).

DYCK, H.L., 'Pondering the Russian fact: Kaunitz and the Catherinian Empire in the 1770s', *Canadian Slavonic Papers* 23 (1980–81), pp. 451–69.

EASUM, C.V., *Prince Henry of Prussia* (Westport, 1971 edn).

EVERSLEY, BARON (G.J. Shaw-Lefevre) *The Partitions of Poland* (London, 1915).

FABRE, J., *Stanislas-Auguste Poniatowski et l'Europe des Lumières* (Paris, 1952).

FELDMAN, J., *Stanisław Leszczyński* (Warsaw, 1984 edn).

FRIEDRICH, K., 'Facing both ways: new works on Prussia and Polish–Prussian relations', *German History* 15, no. 2 (1997), pp. 256–67.

FROST, R., 'The nobility of Poland-Lithuania, 1569–1795', in H.M. Scott, ed., *The European nobilities in the seventeenth and eighteenth centuries* (London, 1995), II, pp. 183–222.

GASTPARY, W., *Historia protestantyzmu w Polsce od połowy XVIIIw. do I wojny światowej* (Warsaw, 1977).

GLASSL, H., *Das österreichische Einrichtungswerk in Galizien (1772–1790)* (Wiesbaden, 1975).

GLASSL, H., 'Der Rechtsstreit um die Zips vor ihrer Rückgliederung an Ungarn', *Ungarn-Jahrbuch* 1 (1969), pp. 23–50.

GODECHOT, J., 'Robespierre et la Pologne', in A. Zahorski, ed., *Wiek XVIII: Polska i Świat* (Warsaw, 1974), pp. 369–74.

GÓRALSKI, Z., *Austria a trzeci rozbiór Polski* (Warsaw, 1979).

GÓRALSKI, Z., 'Die Grenzdemarkationen in Polen nach der dritten Teilung (1795–1797)', *Jahrbücher für Geschichte Osteuropas* 19 (1971), pp. 212–38.

GÓRALSKI, Z., *Stanisław August w insurekcji kościuszkowskiej* (Warsaw, 1988).

GRIFFITHS, D.M., 'The rise and fall of the Northern System', *Canadian Slavic Studies* 4 (1970), pp. 547–69.

GROCHULSKA, B., 'Échos de la faillite des banques de Varsovie, 1793', *Annales Historiques de la Révolution Française* 53 (246) (1981), pp. 529–40.

GROCHULSKA, B., 'The place of the Enlightenment in Polish social history', in J.K. Fedorowicz, ed., *A republic of nobles* (Cambridge, 1982), pp. 239–57.

GULDON, Z., *Związki handlowe dóbr magnackich na prawobrzeżnej Ukrainie z Gdańskiem w XVIII wieku* (Toruń, 1966).

HAGEN, W.W., 'The Partitions of Poland and the crisis of the Old Regime in Prussia, 1772–1806', *Central European History* 9 (1976), pp. 115–28.

HALECKI, O., 'Why was Poland partitioned', *Slavic Review* 22 (1963).

HASSINGER, E., *Brandenburg-Preussen, Schweden und Russland 1700–1713* (Munich, 1953).

HAUMANN, H., and SKOWRONEK, J., eds, *Der letzte Ritter und erste Bürger im Osten Europas': Kościuszko, das aufständische Reformpolen und die Verbundenheit zwischen Polen und der Schweiz* (Basel, 1996).

HERBST, S., *Z dziejów wojskowych powstania kościuszkowskiego 1794 roku* (Warsaw, 1983).

HOENSCH, J.K., 'Friedrichs II: Wahrungsmanipulationen im siebenjährigen Krieg und ihre Aufwirkung auf die polnische Münzreform von 1756/66', *Jahrbuch für die Geschichte Mittel- und Ost-Deutschlands* 22 (1973), pp. 110–34.

HOENSCH, J.K., *Sozialverfassung und politische Reform: Polen im vorrevolutionären Zeitalter* (Cologne, 1973).

HOENSCH, J.K., 'Der Streit um den polnischen Generalzoll 1764–1766', *Jahrbücher für Geschichte Osteuropas* NF 18 (1970), pp. 356–88.

HORN, D.B., *British public opinion and the First Partition of Poland* (Edinburgh, 1945).

HUBATSCH, W., *Frederick the Great of Prussia: absolutism and administration* (London, 1975).

JOBERT, A., *La Commission d'Éducation Nationale en Pologne (1773–1794)* (Paris, 1941).

JONES, R.E., 'Opposition to war and expansion in late eighteenth century Russia', *Jahrbücher für Geschichte Osteuropas* 32 (1984), pp. 34–51.

JONES, R.E., *Provincial development in Russia: Catherine II and Jakob Sievers* (New Brunswick, 1984).

JONES, R.E., 'Runaway peasants and Russian motives for the Partitions of Poland', in H. Ragsdale, ed., *Imperial Russian foreign policy* (Cambridge, 1993), pp. 103–16.

KALINKA, W., *Sejm Czteroletni*, 2 vols (Warsaw, 1991 edn).

KAMIŃSKI, A.S., *Republic vs. Autocracy: Poland-Lithuania and Russia, 1686–1697* (Cambridge, Mass., 1993).

KAPLAN, H.H., *The First Partition of Poland* (New York, 1962).

KASPEREK, J., *Gospodarka folwarczna ordynacji zamojskiej w drugiej połowie XVIII wieku* (Warsaw, 1972).

KĄDZIELA, Ł., 'Efemeryczna Rada Nieutająca z wiosny 1793 roku', *Wiek Oświecenia* 9 (1993), pp. 175–86.

KĄDZIELA, Ł., *Między zdradą a służbą Rzeczypospolitej* (Warsaw, 1993).

KĄDZIELA, Ł., 'O potrzebie badań nad dziejami Targowicy', *Przegląd Historyczny* 80 (1989), pp. 367–76.

KĄDZIELA, Ł., 'Polityczne znaczenie pruskich uzurpacji granicznych w 1793r.', in Ł. Kądziela [and others], eds, *Trudne stulecia: studia z dziejów XVII i XVIII wieku ofiarowane Profesorowi Jerzemu Michalskiemu w siedemdziesiątą rocznicę urodzin* (Warsaw, 1994), pp. 95–106.

KĄDZIELA, Ł., 'Polsko-pruskie negocjacje w sprawie traktatu handlowego za rządów Rady Nieustającej w latach 1793–1794', *Przegląd Historyczny* 80 (1989), pp. 456–73.

KĄDZIELA, Ł., 'Polsko-pruski traktat handlowy z 9 kwietnia 1794r.', *Przegląd Historyczny* 80 (1989), pp. 119–26.

KĄDZIELA, Ł., 'Rokowania o traktat handlowy z Prusami podczas sejmu grodzieńskiego 1793 roku', *Przegląd Historyczny*, 80 (1989), pp. 273–99.

KHODARKOVSKY, M., 'From frontier to empire: the concept of the frontier in Russia, sixteenth–eighteenth centuries', *Russian History* 19 (1992), pp. 115–28.

KLESIŃSKA, W., 'Okupacja Elbląga przez Brandenburgię w latach 1698–1700', *Rocznik Elbląski* 4 (1969), pp. 85–121.

KŁOCZOWSKI, J., 'The Polish church', in W.J. Callahan and D. Higgs, eds, *Church and society in Catholic Europe of the eighteenth century* (Cambridge, 1979).

KONOPCZYŃSKI, W., *Dzieje Polski Nowożytnej* 2 vols (Warsaw, 1986 edn).

KONOPCZYŃSKI, W., *Geneza i ustanowienie Rady Nieustającej* (Kraków, 1917).

KONOPCZYŃSKI, W., *Kazimierz Pułaski* (Kraków, 1931).

KONOPCZYŃSKI, W., *Konfederacja barska*, 2 vols (Warsaw, 1991 edn).

KONOPCZYŃSKI, W., 'Precedens wywłaszczenia w Wielkopolsce', *Mrok i Świt* (Warsaw, 1911), pp. 233–72.

KONOPCZYŃSKI, W., 'Sejm grodzieński 1752 roku', *Mrok i Świt* (Warsaw, 1911), pp. 37–135.

KORZON, T., *Wewnętrzne dzieje Polski za panowania Stanisława Augusta*, 6 vols (Kraków, 1897–98).

KOSER, R., *Geschichte Friedrichs des Grossen*, 4 vols (Darmstadt, 1974 edn).

KOSER, R., 'Die preussische Politik von 1786 bis 1806', *Deutsche Monatsschrift* 6 (1907), pp. 453–80, 612–37.

KOŚCIAŁKOWSKI, S., *Antoni Tyzenhauz*, 2 vols (London, 1970–71).

KOWECKI, J., *Pospolite ruszenie w insurekcji kościuszkowskiej* (Warsaw, 1969).

KOZŁOWSKI, W.H., 'Le dernier projet d'alliance franco-polonaise, 1792 et 1793', *Revue d'Histoire Diplomatique* 36 (1923), pp. 257–75, 464–99.

KRIEGSEISEN, W., *Ewangelicy polscy i litewscy w epoce saskiej* (Warsaw, 1996).

KULA, W., *An economic theory of the feudal system* (London, 1976).

KULA, W., *Szkice o manufakturach*, 2 vols (Warsaw, 1956).

KURDYBACHA, Ł., and DOBROWOLSKA, M., *Komisja Edukacji Narodowej* (Warsaw, 1973).

LABUDA, G., ed., *Historia Pomorza*, II (Poznań, 1984).

LEDONNE, J.P., *The Russian empire and the world, 1700–1917. The geopolitics of expansion and containment* (New York, 1997).

LEHTONEN, U.L., *Die polnischen Provinzen Russlands unter Katharina II. in den Jahren 1772–1782* (Berlin, 1907).

LEONARD, C.S., *Reform and regicide: the reign of Peter III of Russia* (Bloomington, 1993).

LEŚNODORSKI, B., 'La pensée politique de Rousseau en Pologne', *Annales Historiques de la Révolution Française*, 34 (1964), pp. 497–514.

LEŚNODORSKI, B., *Polscy Jakobini* (Warsaw, 1969).

LEWITTER, L.R., 'The Russo-Polish treaty of 1686 and its antecedents', *Polish Review* 9, nos. 3, 4 (1964), pp. 5–29, 21–37.

LEWITTER, L.R., 'Zur Vorgeschichte der Teilungen Polens (1697–1721)', *Österreichische Osthefte* Jahrgang 32 (1990), pp. 333–57.

LIBISZOWSKA, Z., 'Edmund Burke a Polska', *Kwartalnik Historyczny* 77 (1970), pp. 63–76.

LIBISZOWSKA, Z., 'Polska reforma w opinii angielskiej', in J. Kowecki, ed., *Sejm Czteroletni i jego tradycje* (Warsaw, 1991), pp. 63–74.

LIBISZOWSKA, Z., *Życie polskie w Londynie w XVIII wieku* (Warsaw, 1972).

LORD, R.H., *The Second Partition of Poland: a study in diplomatic history* (Cambridge, Mass., 1915).

LORD, R.H., 'The Third Partition of Poland', *Slavonic and East European Review* 3 (1924–25), pp. 481–98.

LORET, M., *Kościół katolicki a Katarzyna druga (1772–1784)* (Kraków, 1910).

LORET, M., 'Watykan a Polska w dobie rozbiorów', *Przegląd Współczesny* 13 (1934), pp. 337–60.

LUKOWSKI, J.T., 'Guarantee or annexation: a note on Russian plans to acquire Polish territory prior to the First Partition of Poland', *Bulletin of the Institute of Historical Research* 56, no. 133 (1983), pp. 60–5.

LUKOWSKI, J.T., *Liberty's Folly: the Polish–Lithuanian Commonwealth in the eighteenth century, 1697–1795* (London, 1991).

LUKOWSKI, J.T., 'The Papacy, Poland, Russia and religious reform, 1764–8', *Journal of Ecclesiastical History* 39 (1988), pp. 66–94.

LUKOWSKI, J.T., 'Recasting Utopia: Montesquieu, Rousseau and the Polish Constitution of 3 May 1791', *Historical Journal* 37 (1994), pp. 65–87.

LUKOWSKI, G.[J.]T., *The szlachta and the Confederacy of Radom, 1764–1767/68: a study of the Polish nobility* (= *Antemurale*, 21) (Rome, 1977).

LUKOWSKI, J.T., 'Towards Partition: Polish magnates and Russian intervention in Poland during the early reign of Stanisław August Poniatowski', *Historical Journal* 28 (1985), pp. 557–74.

LUKOWSKI, J.T., 'Unhelpful and unnecessary: Voltaire's *Essai historique et critique sur les dissensions des Églises de Pologne* (1767)', in U. Kölving and C. Mervaud, eds, *Voltaire et ses combats*, 2 vols (Oxford, 1997), I, pp. 645–54.

ŁASZEWSKI, R., 'Delegacja sejmowa jako instrument ratyfikacji I i II rozbioru Polski', *Czasopismo prawno-historyczne* 23 (1971), pp. 87–102.

ŁASZEWSKI, R., *Sejm polski w latach 1764–1793* (Warsaw, 1973).

ŁOJEK, J., 'Series librorum prohibitorum z 1793 roku', *Przegląd Humanistyczny*, no. 3 (1965), pp. 125–32.

ŁUBIEŃSKA, M.C., *Sprawa dysydencka 1764–1766* (Kraków, 1911).

McGREW, R.E., *Paul I of Russia 1754–1801* (Oxford, 1992).

MANN, Z., *Stanisław August na Sejmie ostatnim* (Warsaw, 1938).

MĄCZAK, A., ed., *Encyklopedia Historii Gospodarczej Polski do 1945 roku*, 2 vols (Warsaw, 1981).

MEDIGER, W., 'Great Britain, Hanover and the rise of Prussia', in R. Hatton and M.S. Anderson, eds, *Studies in Diplomatic History* (London, 1970), pp. 206–10.

MICHALSKI, J., 'Dyplomacja polska w latach 1764–1795', in *Historia Dyplomacji Polskiej* (II, 1572–1795), ed. Z. Wójcik (Warsaw, 1982).

MICHALSKI, J., 'Fryderyk Wielki i Grzegorz Potemkin w latach kryzysu przymierza prusko-polskiego', in T. Chyczewska-Hennel [and others], eds, *Między Wschodem a zachodem: Rzeczpospolita XVI–XVIIIw. Studia ofiarowane Zbigniewowi Wójcikowi w siedemdziesiątą rocznicę urodzin* (Warsaw, 1993), pp. 215–30.

MICHALSKI, J., 'Opozycja magnacka i jej cele w początkach Sejmu Czteroletniego', in J. Kowecki, ed., *Sejm Czteroletni i jego tradycje* (Warsaw, 1991), pp. 50–62.

MICHALSKI, J., 'Polen und Preussen in der Epoche der Teilungen', *Jahrbuch für die Geschichte Mittel- und Ostdeutschlands* 30 (1981), pp. 35–52.

MICHALSKI, J., *Polska wobec wojny o sukcesję bawarską* (Wrocław, 1964).

MICHALSKI, J., 'Problematyka aliansu polsko-rosyjskiego w czasach Stanisława Augusta. Lata 1764–1766', *Przegląd Historyczny* 75 (1984), pp. 695–721.

MICHALSKI, J., 'Rejtan i dylematy Polaków w dobie pierwszego rozbioru', *Kwartalnik Historyczny* 93 (1987 for 1986), pp. 969–1013.

MICHALSKI, J., 'Sejmiki poselskie 1788 roku', *Przegląd Historyczny* 51 (1960), pp. 52–73, 331–67, 465–82.

MICHALSKI, J., 'Zmierzch prokonsulatu Stackelberga', in J. Kowecki, ed., *Sejm Czteroletni i jego tradycje* (Warsaw, 1991), pp. 18–49.

MICHALSKI, J., ed., *Historia Sejmu Polskiego*, vol. I (Warsaw, 1984).

MIELESZKO, W.I., 'Formy i struktura feudalnej własności ziemskiej we wschodniej Białorusi w drugiej połowie XVII i w XVIII wieku', *Roczniki Dziejów Społecznych i Gospodarczych* 33 (1972), pp. 33–59.

MIŁOSZ, C., *The Issa Valley* (London, 1981).

MIŁOSZ, C., *Native Realm: a search for self-definition* (London, 1981).

MORITZ, E., 'Die Plaene der preussischen Regierung zur Teilung Polens in der Zeit des Kościuszko-Aufstandes', in G. Labuda, ed., *Węzłowe problemy dziejów Prus* (Poznań, 1971), pp. 57–71.

MORITZ, E., *Preussen und der Kościuszko-Aufstand 1794* (Berlin, 1968).

MROZOWSKA, K., *Funkcjonowanie systemu szkolnego Komisji Edukacji Narodowej na terenie Korony w latach 1783–1793* (Wrocław, 1985).

MÜLLER, M., *Die Teilungen Polens* (Munich, 1984).

NAUDÉ, A., 'Der preussische Staatschatz unter König Friedrich Wilhelm II. und seine Erschöpfung', *Forschungen zur Brandenburgischen und Preussischen Geschichte* 5 (1892), pp. 203–56.

NIEUWAZNY, A., 'Napoleon and Polish identity', *History Today* 48, no. 4 (May 1998), pp. 50–5.

OCHMAŃSKI, J., *Historia Litwy* (Wrocław, 1990 edn).

OLSZEWSKI, H., *Sejm Rzeczypospolitej epoki oligarchii* (Poznań, 1966).

PACHOŃSKI, J., *Generał Jan Henryk Dąbrowski 1755–1818* (Warsaw, 1981).

Polski Słownik Biograficzny, ed. W. Konopczyński and others (Kraków, 1935–).

RAGSDALE, H., 'Russian projects of conquest in the eighteenth century', in H. Ragsdale, ed., *Imperial Russian foreign policy* (Cambridge, 1993), pp. 82–102.

REAL, W., *Von Potsdam nach Basel. Studien zur Geschichte der Beziehungen Preussens zu den europäischen Mächten vom Regierungsantritt Friedrich Wilhelm II. bis zum Abschluss des Friedens vom Basel 1786–1795* (Stuttgart, 1958).

REINHOLD, J., *Polen/Litauen auf den Leipziger Messen des 18. Jahrhunderts* (Weimar, 1971).

ROIDER, K.A., *Austria's Eastern Question 1700–1790* (New Jersey, 1982).

ROIDER, K.A., *Baron Thugut and Austria's response to the French Revolution* (Princeton, 1987).

ROSTWOROWSKI, E., 'Fryderyk II wobec rozkładu przymierza francusko-austriackiego w latach 1769–1772', *Roczniki Historyczne* 18 (1949), pp. 181–204.

ROSTWOROWSKI, E., 'Ilu było w Rzeczypospolitej szlachty', *Kwartalnik Historyczny* 94, no. 3 (1988), pp. 3–40.

ROSTWOROWSKI, E., 'Korespondencja Szczęsnego Potockiego z Sewerynem Rzewuskim z lat 1788–1796', *Przegląd Historyczny* 45 (1954), pp. 722–40.

ROSTWOROWSKI, E., 'Marzenie dobrego obywatela, czyli królewski projekt Konstytucji', *idem, Legendy i Fakty XVIIIw.* (Warsaw, 1963), pp. 265–464.

ROSTWOROWSKI, E., 'Miasta i mieszczanie w ustroju Trzeciego Maja', in J. Kowecki, ed., *Sejm Czteroletni i jego tradycje* (Warsaw, 1991), pp. 138–51.

ROSTWOROWSKI, E., '*Myśli polityczne* Józefa Wybickiego, czyli droga od konfederacji barskiej do obiadów czwartkowych', *Wiek Oświecenia* 1 (1978), pp. 31–52.

ROSTWOROWSKI, E., *Ostatni król Rzeczypospolitej* (Warsaw, 1966).

ROSTWOROWSKI, E., 'Podbój Śląska przez Prusy a pierwszy rozbiór Polski', *Przegląd Historyczny* 63 (1972), pp. 389–412.

ROSTWOROWSKI, E., *Popioły i korzenie* (Kraków, 1985).

ROSTWOROWSKI, E., 'Sprawa zaplecza przemysłowego dla armii na Sejmie Czteroletnim', *Kwartalnik Historyczny* 63, no. 4 (1956), pp. 44–63.

RUDNICKI, K., *Biskup Kajetan Sołtyk, 1715–1788* (Kraków, 1906).

RUTKOWSKI, J., 'Les bases économiques des partages de l'ancienne Pologne', *Revue d'Histoire Moderne* (1932), pp. 363–89.

RYBARSKI, R., *Skarbowość Polski w dobie rozbiorów* (Kraków, 1937).

RYMSZYNA, M., *Kabinet Stanisława Augusta* (Warsaw, 1962).

SCHROEDER, P.W., *The transformation of European politics 1763–1848* (Oxford, 1996 edn).

SCOTT, H.M., *British foreign policy in the age of the American Revolution* (Oxford, 1990).

SCOTT, H.M., 'France and the Polish throne', *Slavonic and East European Review* 53 (1975), pp. 370–88.

SCOTT, H.M., 'Great Britain, Poland, and the Russian alliance, 1763–1767', *Historical Journal* 19, no. 1 (1976), pp. 53–74.

SCOTT, H.M., ed., *The European nobilities in the seventeenth and eighteenth centuries*, 2 vols. (London, 1995).

SEREJSKI, M.H., *Europa a rozbiory Polski* (Warsaw, 1970).

SIMMS, B., *The impact of Napoleon: Prussian high politics, foreign policy and the crisis of the executive, 1797–1806* (Cambridge, 1997).

SIMSCH, A., *Die Wirtschaftspolitik des preussischen Staates in der Provinz Südpreussen, 1793–1806/7* (Berlin, 1983).

SMOLEŃSKI, W., *Konfederacya Targowicka* (Kraków, 1903).

SMOLEŃSKI, W., *Ostatni rok Sejmu Wielkiego* (Kraków, 1897).

SOLOV'EV, S.M., *Istoriia Padeniia Pol'shi*, in *Sochineniia*, Bk XVI (Moscow, 1995).

SOLOV'EV, S.M., *Istoriia Rossii s'drevnikh vremen'*, 29 vols, in *Sochineniia*. Bks I–XV (Moscow, 1988–95).

STASZEWSKI, J., 'Ostatni "Wielki Plan" Augusta Mocnego', *Rocznik Gdański* 46, no. 1 (1986), pp. 45–67.

STASZEWSKI, J., 'Die polnisch-sächsische Union und die Hohenzollernmonarchie (1697–1763)', *Jahrbuch für die Geschichte Mittel- und Ostdeutschlands* 30 (1981), pp. 28–34.

STRIBRNY, W., *Die Russlandpolitik Friedrichs des Grossen 1764–1786* (Würzburg, 1966).

STRODS, H., 'Der Kościuszko-Aufstand 1794 und Kurland', *Acta Baltica* 34 (1996), pp. 123–30.

SZAJ, W., 'Organizacja i działalność administracyjna wielkopolskich komisji porządkowych cywilno-wojskowych (1789–1792), *Studia i materiały do dziejów Wielkopolski i Pomorza* 23 (1976), pp. 85–102.

ŚLIWA, T., 'Kościół prawosławny w latach 1696–1764', in B. Kumor and Z. Obertyński, eds, *Historia Kościoła w Polsce*, I (Poznań, 1974), pp. 481–6.

TOKARZ, W., *Insurekcja warszawska* (Warsaw, 1950 edn).

TOPOLSKI, J., 'Moralizatorstwo czy wyjaśnienie. O głównym motywie polskiej historiografii poświęconej rozbiorom', *Przegląd Historyczny*, 63 (1973), pp. 615–23.

TOPOLSKI, J., 'The Partitions of Poland in German and Polish historiography', *Polish Western Affairs* 13 (1972), pp. 3–42.

TOPOLSKI, J., 'The Polish–Prussian frontier during the period of the First Partition (1772–1777)', *Polish Western Affairs* 10 (1969), pp. 81–110.

TOPOLSKI, J., 'Reflections on the First Partition of Poland', *Acta Poloniae Historica* 27 (1973), pp. 89–104.

TOPOLSKI, J., 'Rozwój absolutnego państwa pruskiego i rola Prus w rozbiorach Polski', *Węzłowe problemy dziejów Prus XVII–XX wieku*, G. Labuda, ed. (Poznań, 1971), pp. 39–55.

TOPOLSKI, J., ed., *Dzieje Wielkopolski* (Poznań, 1969), I.

VAHLE, H., 'Die polnische Verfassung vom 3. Mai 1791 im zeitgenössischen deutschen Urteil', *Jahrbücher für Geschichte Osteuropas*, NF 19 (1971), pp. 347–70.

VAN HORN MELTON, J., 'From Enlightenment to Revolution: Hertzberg, Schlözer and the problem of despotism in the late *Aufklärung*', *Central European History* 12 (1979), pp. 103–23.

VOLZ, G.B., 'Friedrich der Grosse und die erste Teilung Polens', *Forschungen zur Brandenburgischen und Preussischen Geschichte* 23 (1910), pp. 71–143, 225–6.

VOLZ, G.B., 'Die Massinschen Vorschläge: ein Beitrag zur Vorgeschichte der ersten Teilung Polens', *Historische Vierteljahrsschrift* 10 (1907), pp. 355–81.

VOLZ, G.B., 'Prinz Heinrich und die Vorgeschichte der Ersten Teilung Polens', *Forschungen zur Brandenburgischen und Preussischen Geschichte* 35 (1923), pp. 193–211.

VOLZ, G.B., 'Prinz Heinrich von Preussen und die polnische Krone', *Forschungen zur Brandenburgischen und Preussischen Geschichte* 18 (1905), pp. 188–201.

VOLZ, G.B., 'Prinz Heinrich von Preussen und die preussische Politik vor der ersten Teilung Polens', *Forschungen zur Brandenburgischen und Preussischen Geschichte* 18 (1905), pp. 150–88.

WACHOWIAK, B., 'Polityka Brandenburgii-Prus wobec Polski w latach 1618–1763', *Roczniki Historyczne* 49 (1983), pp. 49–89.

WANDYCZ, P., *The lands of partitioned Poland* (Seattle, 1984 edn).

WIDACKA, H., '*Kołacz Królewski*, czyli alegoria rozbioru Polski w grafice XVIII i XIX wieku', *Kronika Zamkowa* 1/33 (1996), pp. 8–22.

WILDER, J.A., *Traktat handlowy polsko-pruski z roku 1775* (Warsaw, 1937).

WOJAKOWSKI, J., *Straż Praw* (Warsaw, 1982).

WOLSKA, B., *Poezja polityczna czasów pierwszego rozbioru i sejmu delegacyjnego 1772–1775* (Wrocław, 1982).

WOLTANOWSKI, A., 'Tadeusz Kościuszko i pierwszy etap reform włościańskich', *Przegląd Historyczny*, 78 (1987), pp. 19–44.

WÓJCIK, Z., 'Rokowania polsko-rosyjskie o "Pokój Wieczysty" w Moskwie w roku 1686', in *Z dziejów polityki i dyplomacji polskiej* (Warsaw, 1994), pp. 38–55.

ZACZEK, A., 'Gdańsk w walce z agresją pruską 1772–1793', *Gdańskie Zeszyty Humanistyczne* 2 (1959), pp. 49–86.

ZAHORSKI, A., *Warszawa w powstaniu kościuszkowskim* (Warsaw, 1967).

ZAJEWSKI, W., ed., *Trzy powstania narodowe* (Warsaw, 1997).

ZAMOYSKI, A., *The last king of Poland* (London, 1992).

ZAWADZKI, W.H., *A man of honour: Adam Czartoryski as a statesman of Russia and Poland 1795–1831* (Oxford, 1993).

ZERNACK, K., 'Negative Polenpolitik als Grundlage deutsch-russischer Diplomatie in der Mächtepolitik des 18. Jahrhunderts', *Kieler Historischer Studien*, 22 (1974), pp. 144–59.

ZERNACK, K., 'Das preussische Königtum und die polnische Republik im europäischen Mächtesystem des 18. Jahrhunderts', *Jahrbuch für die Geschichte Mittel- und Ostdeutschlands* 30 (1981), pp. 4–20.

ZERNACK, K., '1795 – *Finis Poloniae*: le dilemme des grandes puissances', *Studies on Voltaire and the Eighteenth Century* 346, no. 1 (1996), pp. 137–47.

ZIELIŃSKA, Z., *'O sukcesyi tronu w Polszcze' 1787–1790* (Warsaw, 1991).

ZIELIŃSKA, Z., *Walka 'Familii' o reformę Rzeczypospolitej 1743–1752* (Warsaw, 1983).

ŻYWIRSKA, M., *Ostatnie lata Stanisława Augusta* (Warsaw, 1975).

Maps

Map 1   Europe c.1772

The Partitions of Poland

Map 2   The Polish–Lithuanian Commonwealth

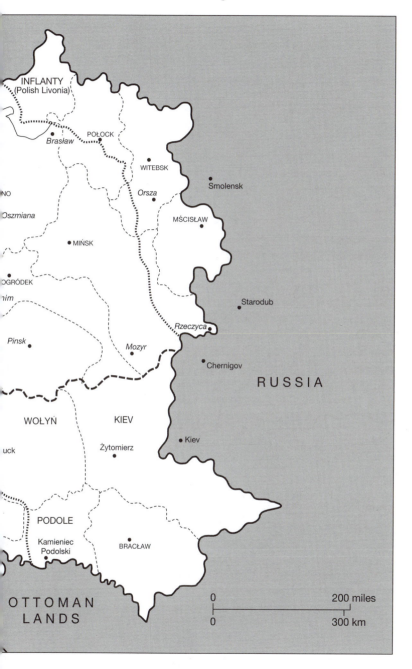

Map 3   The First Partition of the Polish–Lithuanian Commonwealth (177

0   200 miles

0   300 km

R. Dźwina

Połock

Witebsk

Smolensk

R. Dnieper

Szkłów

Mścisław

Minsk

Mohylew

Nowogródek

Słuck

THUANIA

RUSSIA

Pinsk

Chernigov

Kiev

Biała Cerkiew

R. Dnieper

Bar

Targowica

Bracław

R. Zbrucz

Kamieniec Podolski

Khotin

R. Dniester

Balta

OVINA

MOLDAVIA

Jassy

OTTOMAN LANDS

CRIMEAN KHANATE

Map 4   The Second Partition of the Polish–Lithuanian
Commonwealth (1793)

GUBERNIA of POLOTSK

R. Dvina

Polotsk

Vitebsk

Smolensk

Minsk

Mogilev

GUBERNIA of MOGILEV

emen

vogródek

R U S S I A

Pinsk

Chernigov

Kiev

Biała Cerkiew

Kaniów

R. Dnieper

Targowica

Ekaterinoslav

Bracław

GUBERNIA of NOVOROSSIIA

Kamieniec Podolski

KOVINA

R. Dniester

OTTOMAN
LANDS

Balta

Jassy

to Russia, 1774

CRIMEA
(independent 1774 –
83, to Russia, 1783)

0   200 miles

0   300 km

Map 5   The Third Partition of the Polish–Lithuanian
Commonwealth (1795)

R. Dvina

Smolensk

RUSSIA

Minsk

emen

Kiev

R. Dnieper

0   200 miles

0   300 km

OTTOMAN
LANDS

Map 6   The Duchy of Warsaw and the Congress Kingdom

Wilno

Smolensk

Minsk

RUSSIAN EMPIRE

Kiev

| 0 | 200 miles |
| 0 | 300 km |

OTTOMAN
LANDS

Index

Regnal dates of rulers are separated from birth date by /; alternative place-names are shown in brackets. Following the Polish convention, accented letters are treated as wholly separate from their unaccented forms, and appear after them in the index.

Radziejów 108, 192
Radziwiłł, Michał (1744–1831) 90
Rautenfeld, Russian general 158
Rawa 153
Razumovskii, Andrei Kirillovich
(1752–1836) 152
Reggio nell'Emilia 183
Rejtan, Tadeusz (1742–80) 87, 107,
165
Repnin, Nikolai (1734–1801) 33, 35,
37, 38, 39, 40, 41, 42, 43, 44, 46,
64, 71, 86, 88, 99, 111, 163, 180
Reviczky, Carl von (1739–93) 134, 141,
142–3, 151, 155, 162
Richelieu, cardinal, Armand-Jean du
Plessis (1585–1642) 17
Riga 13, 111
Rohd, Jakob Friedrich von (Prussian
ambassador to Austria) 91, 58, 65,
76
Rousseau, Jean-Jacques (1712–78) 113,
126
Różan 107
Rumiantsev, Petr (1725–96) 55, 101
Rumiantsev, Sergei (1755–1838) 121
Russia 29, 42, 161
army 10, 45, 82, 111, 117, 130, 148,
159–60, 162
relations with Poland prior to 1762
11, 12–16, 19–20, 25, 26, 27, 31,
44
1726 alliance with Austria 15–16
alliance with Frederick the Great 16,
28, 33–4, 48, 59–60, 61, 67, 94,
119, 121
French hostility 18, 45, 48, 49–50
policy in Poland, 1763–68 28–9,
31–8, 42–4
and Orthodoxy in Poland 21–2, 24,
32, 34–7, 38, 39, 40, 49, 55, 60, 62,
99, 103
and Polish Protestants 33–4, 35–8,
39, 40, 42, 43, 49, 55, 60, 62, 99,
103
surveys of Polish territory, 1767 43
Polish constitutional settlement of
1767–68 and Russian guarantee
39–43, 46–7, 71, 73
and Confederacy of Bar 44–9, 69–70,
72, 75

1768–74 war with Turkey 45–8,
50–1, 55, 58–63, 66, 67–9, 73,
74–6, 77, 119
and 'Lynar Plan' 53
and Austrian takeover of Zips 58, 69
Prince Henry's mission 61–5
and First Partition 64, 65, 69–92,
94–6, 97, 99, 105
and commercial relations with
Poland 93, 94, 111, 116, 125
gains under the First Partition 100
and Austrian acquisition of the
Bukovina 101
Russo-Polish relations, 1775–88
102–4, 115–17, 118, 121–3, 124,
125–6
and War of the Bavarian Succession
118–19
rapprochement and alliance with
Austria 119–21, 128–9, 177
the 'Greek Project' 120
Russo-Turkish war, 1787–92 122–3,
128, 131, 137–8
Russo-Swedish war, 1788–91 122,
128, 131, 134, 138
Russo-Polish relations during the
Four Years Sejm 128–9, 130, 131,
135, 136, 141–3
invasion of Poland, 1792 144–7,
148–50, 169
and Second Partition 144–5, 147–8,
151–7, 162
gains under the Second Partition
157
alliance with Prussia, 1792 151, 152
relationship with post-1793 Polish
state 159–63
and 1794 Insurrection 163–6, 168–9,
171, 172, 173–5
and Third Partition 163, 171–3,
175–82
gains under the Third Partition 177
incorporation of Courland 176
Russia and Polish affairs during the
Napoleonic era 183–5
Russia and the Congress Kingdom
184, 185–8
USSR 189
Rzeszów 136
Rzewuski, family of 103, 117